THE STATE OF SCHOLARLY PUBLISHING

THE STATE OF SCHOLARLY PUBLISHING

Challenges and Opportunities

Albert N. Greco, editor

Transaction Publishers
New Brunswick (U.S.A.) and London (U.K.)

Copyright © 2009 by Transaction Publishers, New Brunswick, New Jersey.

All rights reserved under International and Pan-American Copyright Conventions. No part of this book may be reproduced or transmitted in any form or by any means, electronic or mechanical, including photocopy, recording, or any information storage and retrieval system, without prior permission in writing from the publisher. All inquiries should be addressed to Transaction Publishers, Rutgers—The State University of New Jersey, 35 Berrue Circle, Piscataway, New Jersey 08854-8042. www.transactionpub.com

This book is printed on acid-free paper that meets the American National Standard for Permanence of Paper for Printed Library Materials.

Library of Congress Catalog Number: 2009015507
ISBN: 978-1-4128-1058-6
Printed in the United States of America

Library of Congress Cataloging-in-Publication Data

The state of scholarly publishing : challenges and opportunities / [edited by] Albert N. Greco.
      p. cm.
Includes bibliographical references and index.
ISBN 978-1-4128-1058-6
  1. Scholarly publishing. 2. Scholarly publishing--United States. 3. University presses. 4. Scholarly electronic publishing. 5. Communication in learning and scholarship--Technological innovations. I. Greco, Albert N., 1945-
Z286.S37S73 2009
070.5--dc22

2009015507

Contents

Introduction — vii
Albert N. Greco

The State of Scholarly Publishing

Scribble, Scribble Toil and Trouble: Forced Productivity in the Modern University — 1
William W. Savage, Jr.

Conflicting Agendas for Scholars, Publishers, and Institutions — 9
Cass T. Miller and Julianna C. Harris

Scholarship and Silence — 27
Lindsay Waters

The Futures of Scholarly Publishing — 35
Cathy N. Davidson

The Changing Market for University Press Books in the United States: 1997-2002 — 49
Albert N. Greco, Robert M. Wharton, and Hooman Estelami

Scholarly Publishing in Developing Nations

A University Press Publishing Consortium for Africa: Lessons from Academic Libraries — 83
Kwasi Darko-Ampem

Scholarly Publishing Trends in the Academic Disciplines

The Publishing Experiences of Historians — 107
Margaret Stieg Dalton

Electronic Publishing in Archaeology   147
   Jingfeng Xia

The Value of Knowledge Created by Individual   163
Scientists and Research Groups
   Chen-Chi Chang

Open Access, Intellectual Property and Sustainability Issues

Exploring the Willingness of Scholars to Accept   181
Open Access: A Grounded Theory Approach
   Ji-Hong Park and Jian Qin

Fair Use in Theory and Practice: Reflections on   207
Its History and the Google Case
   Sanford G. Thatcher

A Cooperative Publishing Model for Sustainable   219
Scholarship
   Robert Schroeder and Gretta E. Siegel

Selected Bibliography   231

Index   249

Introduction:

"The Changing Market for Scholarly Books and Scholarly Journals"

In the United States, trade books are "glamorous;" religious titles are inspirational; and educational titles (i.e., elementary and high school texts and college texts) are critically important in our society since they provide a platform necessary in the education of our children. However, scholarly and professional books are "defensive," at least to those "Wall Street" financial service companies that invest heavily in the public stocks of these companies.* What makes them "defensive?"

A review of this sector is needed in order to understand the "defensive" nature of scholarly and professional publishing. This sector contains two distinct types of publishing companies.

University Presses

The first one is the important cluster of approximately 96 U.S.-based university presses (including two European universities with editorial, sales, and marketing operating units located in New York City). In 2008 university presses generated $451 million in net publishers' revenues (i.e., gross sales minus returns equals net sales) for their scholarly and professional book titles; and by 2013, revenues fell to $434 (-3.77 percent). Hardcover books, during those same years, declined 6.62 percent; and paperbacks were off a more modest 1.08 percent. Net units, on the other hand, were rather unsettling. Total units (again for 2008-2013) fell 13.13 percent, with -19.32 percent and paperbacks -9.94 percent. Tables 1 and 2 outline these trends.

University presses also have other revenue streams. A number of presses have active journal publications, most of which are highly regarded and essentially "profitable" (i.e., they generate a "surplus"). While

---

* The phrase "Wall Street firms" refers to financial service companies located on Wall Street, in New York City, Greenwich, CT, Boston, San Francisco, London, Paris, Asia, etc.

Table 1
University Press Books: Net Publishers' Revenues ($ Millions): 2008-2013

	University Press Books Total	Hardcover Books	Paperbound Books
2008	451.9	219.0	232.0
2009	424.5	205.3	219.2
2010	407.4	195.2	212.2
2011	415.5	199.2	216.3
2012	424.8	202.6	222.2
2013	434.0	204.5	229.5

Source: Greco.

Table 2
University Press Books: Net Publishers' Units (Millions): 2008-2013

	Total	Hardcover Books	Paperbound Books
2008	25.9	8.8	17.1
2009	23.9	8.0	15.9
2010	22.7	7.4	15.3
2011	22.7	7.4	15.3
2012	22.7	7.3	15.3
2013	22.5	7.1	15.4

Source: Greco.

some of these journals are "contract journals" (i.e., journals that are not owned by the press, which handles editorial, publishing, and fulfillment functions), many presses own their own journals, which tend to provide a steady cash flow (and a surplus) for these presses.

A small number of presses have third party distribution functions (i.e., a press warehouses, sells, and handles fulfillment tasks, including returns) for a press unable or unwilling to perform these responsibilities. These operations tend to be highly "profitable" for the presses handling these third party functions.

Regrettably, the vast majority of all university presses require subsidies from their home university, and, even with subsidies, very few presses end up in the "black" at the end of their fiscal year. Additional areas of concern confronting these university presses include: the migration from print to the digital transmission of content, and few presses have the financial resources to address effectively this challenge; the "Open Access" movement (i.e., academics placing a book online and allowing the free downloading of this content); concern on many college campuses that continued financial support of a university press is becoming a luxury and not a necessity since commercial academic presses have increased their title output of important research studies; and declining unit sales.

While important in the transmission of ideas in our society, university presses are not "defensive" publishing operations.

Commercial Scholarly and Professional Presses

Commercial scholarly and professional publishing presses comprise the "defensive" sector. Dominated by a cluster of global firms, this sector has grown dramatically since 2002. The companies that have a leadership position in this sector include (this list is ranked based on revenues):

- Reed Elsevier
- Thomson Reuters
- Wolters Kluwer
- Informa
- Springer
- Pearson
- John Wiley-Blackwell
- McGraw-Hill

A partial list of the "Wall Street" firms holding a position in some of the companies listed above include (this list is in alphabetical order):

- Allianz Global Investors of America L.P.
- Bank of America Corporation
- Bank of New York Mellon
- Barclays Global Investors UK Holdings Ltd.
- Cantillon Capital Management LLC
- College Retirement Equities Fund- Stock Account
- Deutsche Bank
- First Manhattan Company
- Goldman Sachs Group Inc.
- Invesco Ltd.
- JP Morgan Chase & Company
- Nuveen Tax-Advantaged Dividend Growth Fund
- Pioneer Investment Management Inc.
- T. Rowe Price Associates Inc.
- State Street Corporation
- Vanguard Group, Inc.

Between 2008 and 2013, these commercial scholarly and professional publishers posted a 127.3 percent increase in their digital book revenue operations (i.e., non-textbooks; their book categories included legal; business; medical; mathematics, the sciences, and technical areas;

Table 3
Professional and Scholarly Books: Net Publishers'
Revenues Printed Books ($ Millions): 2008-2013

	Total	Hardcover Books	Paperbound Books
2008	5,291.7	3,802.7	1,488.9
2009	5,515.7	3,978.4	1,537.3
2010	5,773.3	4,177.6	1,595.7
2011	6,033.1	4,374.0	1,659.1
2012	6,281.6	4,563.0	1,718.6
2013	6,520.3	4,743.2	1,777.1

Source: Greco.

Table 4
Professional and Scholarly Books: Net Publishers'
Units Printed Books (Millions): 2008-2013

	Total	Hardcover Books	Paperbound Books
2008	85.7	53.9	31.75
2009	86.7	54.8	31.8
2010	88.2	56.1	32.1
2011	89.7	57.3	32.4
2012	90.5	57.9	32.6
2013	91.0	58.5	32.6

Source: Greco.

humanities; and the social sciences). Printed books generated a 23.22 percent growth rate, with hardbound books +24.73 percent and paperbacks +19.35 percent. Printed book units posted a 6.21 percent increase between 2008-2013, with hardcovers +8.38 percent and paperbacks +2.52 percent. Tables 3 and 4 address these trends.

Why is this sector of interest to these global "Wall Street" financial service companies? In spite of a plethora of recent economic and business events, indicating that far too many financial service firms "abandoned" or "minimized" generally accepted financial diversification strategies and procedures, the firms listed above sought to craft a portfolio of companies in the spirit of Benjamin Graham's famous "margin of safety" value investing strategy. These "Wall Street" companies realized that the economics of publishing were harsh and unforgiving; but they were understandable and quantifiable. This meant realistic financial models (and not the "black box" theories espoused by certain "quants" at Wall Street hedge funds) could be created to predict with certain levels of accuracy future earnings. While these returns might not rival the performance of certain "hot stocks," these publishing companies provided steady and predicable revenue streams, especially once these publishing houses moved toward the sale or "rental" of digital content.

Key Market Drivers

The market drivers of this sector are as follows.

First, their printed books and journals (and their digital versions) are "must have, need to know information." There has been a steady increase in the number of people in the world who require this information, especially scientists. The people who must have access to this information work in industries that will pay to buy this information, a situation of price elasticity (especially in the library market; see Table 5).

Second, their journals and books are subject to rigorous blind review, and many authors submit manuscripts because they are caught up in the "publish or perish" world of the academy.

Third, there has been a steady increase in the amount of information and the complexity of this information, making clear, realistic evaluations of this information a valuable commodity.

Fourth, these commercial scholarly and professional companies posted strong annual growth rates in revenues and profits. These publishing companies expanded their operations through a series of successful mergers and acquisitions (they made "synergy" really work).

Table 5
Purchase of Scholarly Monographs and Scholarly Journals
by Academic Libraries: 2002-2006

Year	Unit Serial Cost	Serial Expenditures	Monograph Unit Cost	Monograph Expenditures	Serials Purchased	Monographs Purchased
2002	$289.84	$4,939,225	$50.61	$1,812,826	17,594	31,578
2003	282.20	5,392,007	52.83	1,873,157	18,115	33,208
2004	256.01	5,580,157	51.36	1,839,412	22,311	30,155
2005	239.58	5,962,446	53.57	1,784,841	22,404	30,546
2006	251.38	6,307,292	52.04	2,044,272	23,849	33,145

Source: Association of Research Libraries.

Table 6
Average Price of Scholarly Journals: 2002-2008

	2002	2003	2004	2005	2006	2007	2008
Agriculture	$ 631	647	773	833	889	964	1,034
Anthropology	300	415	385	415	432	474	530
Art & Architecture	154	144	176	188	210	222	243
Astronomy	1,256	1,123	1,289	1,340	1,488	1,551	1,671
Biology	1,089	1,207	1,292	1,406	1,536	1,674	1,810
Botany	880	830	1,059	1,165	1,256	1,364	1,491
Business & Economics	527	618	677	733	781	830	897
Chemistry	2,432	2,635	2,582	2,748	2,965	3,187	3,490
Education	300	309	379	419	460	509	545
Engineering	1,305	1,561	1,452	1,561	1,652	1,767	1,919
Food Science	897	978	1,133	1,239	1,337	1,409	1,554
General Science	810	865	910	975	1,040	1,142	1,213
General Works	181	186	121	132	137	147	158
Geography	746	808	812	855	909	989	1,086
Geology	1,012	1,079	1,147	1,245	1,312	1,413	1,521
Health Sciences	808	846	932	1,010	1,105	1,207	1,330
History	132	143	171	184	197	215	238
Language & Literature	120	129	159	173	185	200	221
Law	159	176	198	206	231	257	275
Library & Information Science	286	319	360	403	424	453	487
Math & Computer Science	981	1,039	1,109	1,181	1,235	1,323	1,411
Military & Naval Science	346	472	454	512	598	623	634
Music	96	98	101	125	129	141	161
Philosophy & Religion	156	146	210	452	483	529	584
Physics	2,178	2,262	2,380	2,526	2,687	2,918	3,103
Political Science	288	292	386	400	440	486	541
Psychology	358	389	437	467	509	551	598
Recreation	146	116	200	227	247	277	322
Sociology	332	361	411	450	487	533	586
Technology	1,151	1,232	1,330	1,432	1,535	1,640	1,776
Zoology	973	977	958	1,032	1,115	1,206	1,311

Source: Library Journal.

Fifth, these publishing corporations figured out how to monetize print books and print journals, and they expanded into digital content distribution (e.g., Springer has more than 25,000 books available for digital downloads). While journals have an advertising revenue stream, these publishers rely extensively on paid subscriptions of journals (e.g., Elsevier's journal *Brain Research* has an annual subscription of $23,000;

see Table 6) and books. All of these publishing firms aggregate and own their content, are global in focus, and financially successful. Their mastery of fulfillment and the intricate channels of distribution provided them with a unique competitive advantage.

The ability of these publishing firms to develop, monetize, and distribute great content in the U.S. and in global markets is why this is the "defensive" sector in the entire book industry in the U.S.

Clearly, this sector has confronted a series of opportunities and challenges in the past, and they were able to take advantage of shifts in the marketplace and overcome many market threats (an extensive review of the balance sheets of the firms listed above confirms their successes).

However, as Newton pointed out, an object at rest remains at rest; and an object in motion remains in motion in a straight line and at a constant speed unless acted upon by an unbalancing force. While publishers rarely confront Newtonian friction or gravity, they do have the daily chore of remaining competitive in the marketplace of ideas.

In the chapters that follow, we selected some (but clearly not all) of the best papers that originally appeared in the University of Toronto Press' preeminent *Journal of Scholarly Publishing*. The goal was simple. To present readers with insightful papers about copyrights, pivotal print and digital issues, Open Access, scholarly publishing in emerging nations, and how certain academic disciplines were trying to cope with an industry in transition.

I have to thank Tom Radko (editor of the *Journal of Scholarly Publishing*) for his superb guidance; the wonderful editorial staff at the University of Toronto Press who provided us with access to these papers; Irving Louis Horowitz and Mary Curtis (two of the leaders in the scholarly publishing industry) for their continued support of this book; and the excellent supportive editorial and sales staff at Transaction for helping produce what we hope will be a useful, stimulating collection of papers.

—Albert N. Greco

Scribble, Scribble Toil and Trouble: Forced Productivity in the Modern University

William W. Savage, Jr.

The book has become the standard measure of research in performance-based evaluations of faculty in the modern university. Emphasis on book publication as the sole evidence of faculty productivity has led to a variety of unhappy consequences for those pressured to write books and for scholarly presses expected to issue them, principally panic and pandemonium.

The professor's book, a biography of a second-rate diplomat, had been nominated by its publisher for a Pulitzer Prize, and the event occasioned a newspaper interview wherein a reporter asked the scholar why he had written the book and how he had selected his subject. The professor replied that he knew he "had to write another book," and the subject's personal papers were located conveniently in a nearby library. *Voila,* one supposes. It was, I later learned, "another book" beyond the one that had gotten him tenure, and he "had to write it" in order to be promoted to full professor. The biography, by its author's own admission, was not a labor of love, and it did not proceed from a burning desire to serve scholarship. Rather, its publication was a requirement of his academic department; and his effort was a career move, about which even he was cynical.

This sort of thing, which I shall call forced productivity, is nothing new in North American colleges and universities, but it has grown to the point that young instructors either learn the hard lessons of Ecclesiastes 12:12 or move in short order to other occupations.[1] During the annual faculty evaluations held nowadays in the name of "accountability," two frequently asked questions are, "How is your next book coming along, and when can we expect to see it?" They are interesting questions because of what they suggest about the institutional context. The idea of a "next" book is predicated on the existence of one or more previous volumes; and the inquiry about its status assumes that work is in progress or implies that it should be. The request for a peek at the opus indicates a certain impatience on the part of administrators awaiting tangible results. The fact that questions are asked annually conveys to their recipient the importance of the enterprise. That the answers may have direct bearing on raises and promotions bespeaks the carrot-and-stick philosophy of the modern academy.[2]

The Ph.D. is a research degree, and employers might reasonably expect that persons in possession of it would be chomping at the figurative bit to pursue the interests that led them to earn the degree in the first place. Beginners have a few years of grace for the birthing of their first book and obtaining tenure. Once those goals are reached, the beginners, who are perhaps starting to think of themselves as seasoned veterans, come to understand that the clock is still ticking. Junior faculty who publish nothing else in the next three or four years may win such behind-the-back honorifics as "One-Book Wonder" or "World's Oldest Associate Professor" or something equally painful.[3] They learn that they cannot rest long on their laurels. They will be asked incessantly about their "next" book, and they will have to deal with the institutional query implied therein: "What have you done for us lately?" Once, as Jacqueline Susann said in a somewhat different context, is not enough.

There are many in higher education who make a connection between research and effective teaching, arguing that the professor who does no research is denying students access to the latest information. That may indeed be a valid assertion, but it does not follow that failure to publish a book (whether it proceeds from inability or reluctance or any other root cause) indicates failure to engage in research. The problem is that the book has become the standard measure of research, and many institutions will accept no other. I know of an associate professor of literature who has published more than three dozen articles in scholarly journals, but his department considers them irrelevant and will not move toward promotion until such time as he produces a book.[4]

The irony of the current situation is inescapable. Nobody asks, "Do you have anything worth writing about, and, if you do, does it belong between hard covers?" On the contrary, the quality of the research will be judged only after the book is published. The important thing, the thing from which the prestige of department and university derives, is publication. Who cares if no one reads it? In fact, who cares if no one wants to read it? And for that matter, who cares if it is unreadable? In the academy, book publication is an end in itself, though only briefly. Questions about the "next" book will be asked almost at once.

The situation should be of concern to all scholarly publishers who one day hope to break even, if not show some small profit. Forced productivity results in manuscripts—lots and lots of manuscripts—that must go somewhere and occupy someone's time and energy. Most of them will be utterly worthless except as monuments to their authors' aspirations and thus their vanity. Many of them will be published anyway, for deplorable reasons that I have discussed elsewhere.[5] But only a few hundred copies of each book will be printed, and only a fraction of those will sell. The few people who can be relied upon actually to read the books will be reviewers for professional journals, and some of them will confine their ocular excursions to front matter, conclusions, and jacket copy. Published authors may benefit for the moment by having satisfied their universities' requirements, regardless of poor readership; but unpublished authors will have to continue flogging their manuscripts, hoping to find a sympathetic house with vacancies on its list.

Occasionally, in secondhand bookshops, I will locate the remnants of some elderly professor's library, and among the assorted volumes there will be the inevitable stack of professional journals, dating back to perhaps the early 1950s. Perusing these, I am always surprised by how slender they are, and how few book reviews they contain. In contrast, the modern journal is as thick as a medium-sized city's telephone directory, and it is largely devoted to book reviews and notices. I received two journals in the mail recently and beheld in their book review sections mention of enough titles relevant to my interests to keep me busy until Social Security kicks in. And there will be three more issues of these journals before year's end, presenting still other books I must read if I am to be current on the literature in my field. Sadly, I do not think I shall be able to keep up.

Nor, in point of fact, will anyone else; and honest scholars freely admit it. In my field, which is history, we are not so much the beneficiaries of an information explosion as we are the victims of information overload. One may keep abreast only by keeping awake and ignoring bodily functions that do not involve eye, brain, and printed page. But why, one might ask, would any rational, reasonable human being care to do that? There is no such thing as cutting-edge history—or, for that matter, cutting-edge philosophy, political science, or English literature, to tar but three other disciplines with the same brush—so where is the urgency? It is to be felt by the academic authors who must find publishers for their books, and certainly by the universities that employ those authors, but most assuredly by nobody else.

Forced productivity creates both panic and pandemonium. Scholarly publishers are besieged by the detritus pouring from word processors within the halls of ivy. Competition for space on publishers' lists is so intense these days that young Ph.Ds, feeling shut out of the process and badly in need of opportunity, clamor for electronic publication, arguing that the launch of one's opus into cyberspace should count just as much as its appearance in sewn signatures.[6] Critics reply that electronic publication may circumvent the vetting process and could not pass muster in universities where it is now *de rigueur* to differentiate between "refereed" publications and any other kind. Some scholars (older ones, with books) even equate electronic publication with vanity publication, a taboo practice that will lead to termination of employment at reputable institutions. Youngsters rant, geezers argue, publishers work overtime, and the printed matter keeps on coming, right along with exam papers, term papers, theses, and dissertations, gladdening the hearts of optometrists everywhere.

The forced productivity feeding this glut also contributes mightily to the frenetic life on the modern campus, where nothing—teaching, research, writing, thinking—is allowed to occur at a leisurely pace. The environment will not permit the varieties of contemplation essential to genuine scholarship. And apparently it is no secret. An editor, soliciting some freelance work, recently directed these remarks to historians:

> Good academic prose is a seamless complement of form and content, leaving the impression that the writer could not have conveyed the information in any other way. But that kind of writing takes time and concentration, and academics are too busy to do it.[7]

This fellow is onto something, and if he hires a staff of fifty or sixty other people who also have time and concentration, he should be one rich editor by next Christmas. The cat indeed would appear to be out of the bag.

Forced productivity has led faculty to develop defensive strategies based on the perception that quality is less important than quantity. I remember the assistant professor who was informed by his chairperson that he would not be promoted in the near future because what he had published to that point was considered "rubbish" by his colleagues.[8] "If you're going to be promoted for publishing rubbish," the chairperson said, "you're going to have to publish more of it than you've published so far."

The subjective evaluation of the junior person's work was relevant only because of the faculty's determination that, bad as the work may have been, it would become acceptable within the system if only there were more of it. The assistant professor increased his output of rubbish (in book form, of course) and received his promotion. Thus are the incompetent and witless encouraged by forced productivity.

Another strategy involves publishing the same book as many times as possible. Well, not *exactly* the same book, perhaps, but five or six or seven, which are enough alike in concept, content, and execution to suggest cloning. The uninitiated may think such practice intellectually bankrupt, or maybe only downright silly and a waste of paper and ink; but it is certainly accepted in the academy, and sometimes it is even encouraged for what are claimed to be professional reasons. "You have to write at least two books on the same topic," a historian (who was in the process of doing it) once told me, "or you can never be taken seriously as an authority."[9] I noted in his comment nothing to suggest that the books had to be any good. The point was, authority came with two books about the same thing. What came with producing five or six or seven could be nothing less than near-papal infallibility, I suppose. I am not sure why no one stands up and says that writing several books on almost identical subjects is surely an easier thing to do than writing several books on different subjects; but no one does.

So, one way or another, faculty must trot their stuff to meet the quantitative demands of Old Siwash,[10] where the message is no longer "publish or perish" but "publish or else." Whereas insufficiently productive junior faculty may be denied tenure and promotion, senior faculty may be threatened with loss of sabbatical leave or with a heavier teaching load to compensate the school for their failure to publish enough. Teaching-as-punishment is surely a remarkable concept, when you think about it. And when you think about it, you begin to understand just how seriously the academy takes the matter of productivity.

A quarter of a century ago, as odd as it now seems, one could find faculty who worried about publishing too much, thereby alienating colleagues and damaging their own careers. In 1973, an anonymous critic of higher education, a man who claimed to have been denied employment on at least one occasion because he had published more than the entire faculty he sought to join, offered this advice to novice professors:

> ... I would suggest as a safe goal an article a year and a book every five years. This is sufficient to satisfy the head of [your] department and [your] dean, but not so much as to threaten [your] colleagues unduly.[11]

Those are lines from a bygone time, a lost age of innocence. Forced productivity has ushered in a new era, one characterized by the appearance of increasing numbers of irrelevant, unwanted books. Catalogues from remainder houses, already the size of tabloid newspapers, may soon resemble the Sunday edition of *The New York Times,* should all of this continue. And until a few dozen major universities experience catastrophe—fiscal implosion, for example—it probably will.

Contributor

William W. Savage, Jr., is Professor of History at the University of Oklahoma. His next book will be his twelfth.

Notes

1. Ecclesiastes 12:12 says, "And further, by these, my son, be admonished: of making many books *there is* no end; and much study *is* a weariness of the flesh," according to persons in the employ of James I of England, an early seventeenth-century scholarly publisher. Consider also "An Honest Preface," in Walter Prescott Webb, *An Honest Preface and Other Essays* (Boston: Houghton Mifflin, 1959): 61–65. The entire collection may be read to advantage.
2. In theory, faculty are evaluated on the basis of teaching, research, and service, as if one's immediate future rested on a tripod of equally strong legs. In practice, research (represented by publication) will bear all the weight by itself, meaning that the well-published professor can be the worst teacher imaginable and get away with it. The service category has to do with sitting on committees, and the well-published are not compelled to participate.
3. The "one-book wonder" is the central figure in such cinematic treatments as *Wonder Boys* (2000), directed by Curtis Hanson, and *Finding Forrester* (2000), directed by Gus Van Sant. Both films concern aging writers who have trouble producing second books after publishing notable first ones. The professoriat is, to a greater or lesser extent, lampooned in each. Well, *cave ab homine unius libri,* I reckon.
4. I admit to prejudice on this point. Of the three professors who had the greatest influence on my choice of careers, only one had written any books; and his best-known work had been out of print for thirty years by the time I encountered him in the classroom. All three men were brilliant teachers, and all of them worked hard in their respective fields, which was evident in the content of their lectures and the condition of their office shelves and cabinets. I am thankful that they taught when they did. They would have had trouble finding and retaining employment today.
5. William W. Savage, Jr. "Times Ain't Now Nothin' Like They Used To Be," *Journal of Scholarly Publishing,* vol. 34, no. 3 (April 2003): 146–52.
6. For a survey of the issue, see MLA Ad Hoc Committee on the Future of Scholarly Publishing, "The Future of Scholarly Publishing," *Journal of Scholarly Publishing,* vol. 34, no. 2 (January 2003): 65-82, with its useful bibliography.
7. Advertisement, *Perspectives,* vol. 41, no. 5 (May 2003): 11.
8. The actual word was not "rubbish" but a vulgar synonym for excrement, a fact I mention here only to indicate more precisely the low esteem in which the young person's department held his work.

9. I do not believe he ever finished the second book. Instead, he went away to be taken seriously as an administrator.
10. Old Siwash was a fictitious institution of higher learning invented by a Midwestern journalist named George Fitch (1877–1915) for a series of short stories. The name has since become a generic for any remote educational backwater of small size. This is an example of just the sort of footnote to which forced productivity can lead.
11. Professor X, *This Beats Working for a Living: The Dark Secrets of a College Professor* (New Rochelle, NY: Arlington House, 1973): 64.

Conflicting Agendas for Scholars, Publishers, and Institutions

Cass T. Miller and Julianna C. Harris

There are four main parties involved in publishing scholarly scientific journals: scholars, who produce the work and are its ultimate consumers; editors, who manage the publication process; publishers, who publish the work; and subscribers, largely institutions, who purchase the work. Because of conflicting agendas, natural tensions exist among these four parties. At the same time, some recent and ongoing trends have exacerbated these tensions: the rate at which new information is being produced, the growth of electronic communication, and the strained budgets of many institutions. This article summarizes these aspects of the scholarly communication environment, assesses some of the reasons for the current situation, and provides a commentary on what the future might bring. The current situation in scholarly scientific journal publications cannot be sustained; therefore, it is necessary for all the parties to collaborate in creating an environment of mutual respect, sharing ownership of the problems, and encouraging efforts to move toward a sustainable system.

Introduction

The process of scholarly scientific journal publication is characterized by the tensions created by the conflicting agendas of the parties involved in the production, refereeing, distribution, and consumption of knowledge. These tensions, along with a rapid increase in the production of new knowledge, the rate of technological change, and the strained budgets of many libraries, have resulted in a system pushed to its limits and facing a crisis. For decades, librarians and publishers have recognized the dangers of spiralling print journal costs and have predicted the eventual transformation of the current system.[1] And for decades, libraries and publishers have nevertheless managed to sustain this system without drastic change by reducing the percentage of money spent on books and decreasing the number of journal titles retained.[2] Now, however, with the explosion of electronic resources—many of which are extremely expensive—the system may finally have reached its breaking point.[3] Simply put, the rate of increase in the cost of institutional subscriptions for scientific journals, coupled with the added cost of electronic publications that has occurred over the last decade, cannot be sustained; significant changes to the system are inevitable.

The overall goal of this article is to investigate the current status and likely future of scholarly publication. The specific objectives are: (1) to review the scientific publication process; (2) to examine the publication process from multiple perspectives; (3) to explore current trends in scientific publication; (4) to summarize the implications of the current publication system and trends; and (5) to identify some possible solutions to the problems inherent in the system.

The Publication Process

The scientific publication process is highly developed and a routine part of an academic career. While differences can exist from journal to journal, most aspects of the process are fairly standardized within the scientific publishing community. Although this process is familiar to those who publish scientific papers, it is not universally understood within the larger scholarly communications community, which includes many librarians and scientific information procurement and distribution specialists. Because this process forms a foundation for many of the comments that follow, a brief summary is appropriate.

Scientific journals, under the leadership of an editor and editorial board, position themselves within a given area of science by means of the title of the journal and its aims and scope. The aims and scope of the journal inform potential authors of the nature of the subject matter that is appropriate for submission to the journal. The editor and editorial board represent and promote the journal, encouraging submissions and guiding the peer review process. Since attracting high-quality papers is a competitive proposition, the leadership of successful journals seeks to establish as unique an identity as possible in the marketplace and to entice the leading scholars in the field to publish their work in the journal. The success and standing of the journal in the field depend upon the degree of success achieved in this endeavor.

Authors of scientific papers can usually choose among a few journals to which a given piece of work could make an appropriate contribution. They select this set based upon their impressions of a candidate set of journals, which are usually based upon the type of papers typically published in each journal, the journal's aims and scope, and the scientific reputation of the editorial board and the editor. Once a set of journals has been identified, the authors decide upon a single journal to which to submit a given manuscript based upon all factors, including their analysis of the relative qualities of the journal, the efficiency of the expected review process, and the estimated likelihood of acceptance by each journal.

Once a journal has been targeted, authors submit their manuscripts according to that journal's guidelines for authors, usually available in print and on the Web. Depending upon the journal, the manuscript might be submitted directly to an editor or to the publisher, who would in turn pass the manuscript on to the editor. Increasingly, journals use Web-based approaches to facilitate the submission and review of manuscripts. This trend is one that is expected to continue.

Once a manuscript has been submitted to a journal, the editor seeks active scientists in the field who are knowledgeable about the manuscript's subject matter. This set of potential reviewers may be small, in some cases, if the subject matter is especially technical and specialized. Ultimately, the editor selects a set of reviewers, who agree to provide a timely review of the manuscript. Usually this review process is "single blind," meaning that the reviewers know the authors' identities but the authors do not know the reviewers' identities. Occasionally, the review process may be "double blind" or transparent. The editor, or her designate, manages this aspect of the publication process to ensure that reviews are completed within a reasonable time frame. What is considered reasonable by a journal can vary from as little as a few days to as much as several months.

Based upon the peer reviewers' comments, the editor transmits the reports and her decision to the authors. The decision can be to accept the manuscript as is, which is very rare in scientific publishing; to decline the manuscript from further consideration, which can occur as frequently as 90 percent of the time with some journals; or to suggest revisions to improve the manuscript, with the promise of reviewing the revised work. For manuscripts to which revisions are suggested, the scope of these revisions can range from minor editing to extensive changes that require months of additional work. If a manuscript is declined, the authors are then free to make changes and submit the manuscript for peer review to another journal or, in some cases, after significant additional work, to resubmit the revised manuscript to the original journal.

Assuming that the editor requests revisions, the authors must decide whether they will pursue publication of the work in the original journal or withdraw the manuscript from further consideration. A decision to withdraw may result if the authors deem that the scope of the required revisions is too large or impossible. Once withdrawn, the manuscript can be submitted for peer review to another journal. If the authors decide to revise the manuscript, they are typically given a time frame in which to complete their revisions. They then prepare a revised manuscript within this time frame and provide the editor with a revised manuscript and a point-by-point response to all reviewers' comments. The editor then typically makes a decision as to whether to accept or decline the manuscript, often with the help of another round of peer review. Additional changes may be needed, and in this case the authors would be asked to prepare yet another revised manuscript.

Once a manuscript is accepted, the editor usually transmits the manuscript to the publisher, including with it all figures, tables, text, author information, and a record detailing the dates when the manuscript was first submitted, revised, and accepted. The publisher then corresponds directly with the author to ensure that the final published version of the manuscript is consistent with both the author's intended meaning and the style, grammar, and usage standards of the journal. To this end, the publisher usually sends the author typeset proofs to review. After the author's review of the galley proofs, the publisher may then either complete the preparation of the final version or outsource this task to a third party.

It is the publisher's responsibility to archive the completed work, promote the journal, manage subscriptions, and otherwise ensure the widest possible dissemination of the scholarly work published in the journal. It is also the publisher's responsibility to monitor the quality of the journal and author and reader satisfaction, as well as to ensure that the editorial and production aspects of the journal are being efficiently and carefully performed, since these aspects of the journal affect its quality.

Perspectives

The publication process is complex and involves several different stakeholder groups. Each of these groups has a different perspective on what is important in the publication process, and these varying perspectives lead to conflicting agendas, tensions in the process, and a lack of understanding of the perspectives and roles of the others. These groups can be broadly identified as representing the scholar, the editor, the publisher, and the institution.

Scholar

From the perspective of the scientific scholar, publication is usually the key credential for survival and advancement in a research university. The scholar's career is greatly affected by his rate of refereed journal publication and the quality of the work being published. The quality of this work is judged in a number of ways: using citation statistics for the journal, using citation rates of papers that scholar has published, and relying on the opinions of referees who are asked to comment on the scholarly record of an individual being considered for appointment, promotion, or tenure. The comments of referees often include an assessment of the quality of the journal in which the scholar has published, as well as of the specific works of the scholar. Citation rates are one measure of quality, but certainly not the sole, or even the best, measure, as many studies have asserted.[4] Thus, the opinions of scholars working in a field are often given more weight than simple citation statistics in such matters.

Given this situation, it is easy to understand what aspects of scholarly journal publication are most important to the scholar: the prestige of the journal, the efficiency and fairness of the review process, the timeliness of publication, and the cost to the author. The prestige of the journal is its standing within the scientific community, and, while this is a somewhat subjective characteristic, the consensus opinion or ranking by experts in the field is important, since these experts form the community evaluating the quality of work for promotion and tenure cases. Reappointment decisions in the tenure track are usually made by the end of the third year, necessitating that the review process start after about two and one-half years. This short period of time to secure funding, recruit students, produce publishable work, and make it through the peer review process emphasizes the importance that authors place on timeliness and efficiency in the publication process. Even the five and one-half years before a tenure review is a relatively short period of time for many fields of scientific research. Thus, most young researchers do not have the luxury of submitting their work to a journal that is not efficient in reviewing and publishing manuscripts.

Publication also affects scholars financially. Many societies (e.g., the American Geophysical Union, the Soil Science Society of America) have "page charges" for some of their journals.[5] Page charges are charges billed to the author, usually depending upon the length of the article. These charges can be substantial, up to a few thousand dollars for a single article in some cases; they are the responsibility of the author, although grant funds or institutional funds may be available to pay some portion of these costs in most cases. Most journals also charge extra for color figures, which have become commonplace in scientific publishing. Color charges can also be substantial and depend upon the number of color figures or the number of pages. Page and color charges are important to scholars and will often affect their choice of where to publish their work.

On the other hand, most scholars are relatively unaware of the institutional subscription costs for scientific journals in their field. They may be aware that funding for libraries is strained and that each year difficult choices about journal cancellations must be made, but most do not fully understand the rapid increases in serial costs and the magnitude of both current institutional subscription costs and the rate of increase in the cost of journals in their field.[6] Thus, rarely would a scholar give much consideration to the institutional cost of a journal when making a decision about where to publish her work.

The scholar is also the ultimate consumer of the information published in scientific journals. However, whether this information is used in making promotion and tenure decisions, to maintain knowledge in a specific area, or to conduct literature reviews to justify new research or refine research that has already been conducted, in many cases institutions provide the avenue through which scholars use the information that they have created and published. This disconnect between those who pay for information and those who consume it, along with the disconnect between those creating the information and those generating monetary profit from it, adds to the confusion and misunderstanding that is endemic to the current scholarly publishing system.

Editor

Editors are servants of the scientific community, who, generally for largely altruistic reasons, have agreed to make a significant commitment in time and energy to the advancement of their discipline. Editors are motivated to maintain and improve the quality of the journals they serve, since the health and prestige of the journal is a reflection of their leadership. Because editorial positions are very time and labor intensive, and are held in addition to a typically substantial set of professional commitments, several things are important to an editor. First, the subject area, prestige, and potential of a journal must be appealing to the editor; he must believe that they can make a contribution to a scientific community and can serve the portion of the community that they are committed to serving. Second, the editor must be comfortable with the circulation of the journal and the impact that it has on the scientific community. Third, the editor must have the support of the publisher—not only in financial terms but for editorial support, promotion of the journal, quality, and timeliness of publication, and willingness to be innovative to improve the quality of the journal. For many scientific journals, the financial support offered by the publisher to the editor pays only a small fraction of the actual costs of the duties performed. This arrangement means that institutions are subsidizing editorial efforts, although most institutions likely do not realize the extent to which this is true. Though figures are not widely available from publishers, it is probable that only 5 to 10 percent of the gross revenues from a scientific journal are budgeted for providing all editorial support.[7]

Publisher

From the publisher's perspective, scientific journals are published in order to make money, or at least to break even, in the case of a society publication. Most of the publisher's other values are driven by this consideration. Publishers are strongly motivated to maintain or improve the financial health of a scientific journal; this requires some combination of maintaining or increasing the number and/or price of subscriptions while holding the line on costs. Since most scientific journals have experienced a decrease in print subscriptions, publishers must resort to other options to continue to keep journals profitable. Writes Richard Poynder: "Derk Haank, CEO of Elsevier Science, agrees that publishers have got themselves in a difficult situation. 'In the good old days when you had an academic journal everybody had their own subscription. But journals became bigger and bigger, and every time they became bigger the price was increased. And every price increase lost us a few subscribers. It was a spiral with no winners.'"[8] As far back as 1983, Howard Sanders noted a decline in scientific journal subscriptions.[9] More recently, John Budd has observed this subscription decline in the social sciences literature.[10] Finally, Carol Tenopir and Donald King have noted a decline in the average number of personal subscriptions to scholarly journals by university and non-university scientists from 1977 to 1998 (see Table 1).[11]

As a result, publishers are eager to increase the number of pages in their journals to justify an increase in subscription costs above the consumer price index. Publishers are also actively involved in finding ways in which their journals can be packaged into larger units to ensure wider dissemination through, for example, electronic means. An increasingly common business model among scientific journal publishers is to tie

Table 1
Average Number of Personal Subscriptions to Scholarly Journals by University and Non-University Scientists

	Years of observation					
	1977	1978–1983	1984	1985–1989	1990–1993	1994–1998
University scientists	4.21	–	3.96	–	3.86	–
Non-university scientists	6.20	4.60	4.26	3.70	2.98	2.44

Source: Carol Tenopir and Donald W. King, *Towards Electronic Journals: Realities for Scientists, Librarians, and Publishers* (Washington, DC: SLA Publishing 2000).

their print subscriptions to electronic access. In this model, the publisher severely limits or entirely prohibits the cancellation of print subscriptions while offering caps on print price increases. The library then commits itself to maintaining its print subscriptions as well as paying the additional surcharge for electronic access. The result for publishers is a stable print base, a predictable annual increase, and an added surcharge above the price of print for access to the same content on the Web. For libraries, the result is a continuation of spiralling print journal costs coupled with the added, and sometimes enormous, expense for the duplicated content.[12]

Because commercial publishers must answer to shareholders, they are not inclined to be innovative unless innovation leads to increased revenues; innovation purely to improve the quality of a journal is not a high priority for most commercial publishers. Publishers are also constantly on the lookout for ways to maintain or decrease their costs. This cost-conscious mentality may manifest itself in providing the minimal possible support for editorial services and, increasingly, in outsourcing the production of printed material or electronic content.

The quality of the research published in a journal is also important to a publisher, because it will likely be reflected in revenues. However, most publishers are not able to evaluate directly the scholarly contribution of a journal that they publish, since they typically do not have world-class scientists on staff. Instead, publishers monitor quality through surveys of authors and readers, citation statistics, and trends in rates of submission, publication, and efficiency of the review process.

Institution

There are two aspects to an institution's perspective on scholarly scientific journal publications: the managing librarian's perspective and the administration's. From the librarian's perspective, the apparent runaway growth in the cost of scientific journals over the last decade is a major concern. Statistics gathered by the Association of Research Libraries (ARL) show that serial costs have increased 227 percent since 1986.[13] These continually increasing serial costs have strained many library budgets to the breaking point, resulting in yearly reviews to determine cancellations in order to control costs. Library managers try to make informed decisions, so they rely on serial usage statistics, faculty input, journal citation reports, and cost data to determine specific titles for cancellation. Library managers are generally not in a position to independently analyze the quality of a journal or its worth to the local scientific community that they serve. While value is important to the library manager, user satisfaction is paramount. With this priority in mind, libraries will frequently cancel many less expensive journals in order to retain a few more prestigious titles that may be more expensive. Increasingly, bundling of journals in electronic format is thought to provide increased value. The current reality, however, is that although benefits are gained with the increased access to and searchability of data, no reductions in library cost have yet been realized. The complexity of negotiations with publishers over electronic content in an industry devoid of any standards is a mounting concern as well.[14]

The administration of an institution has a broader perspective than the library manager's. Administrators are concerned about the cost of providing the reference materials necessary to support the missions of the university, but they have additional concerns as well: they want access to the best journals in the appropriate scientific fields; they want their faculty and students to publish in these journals; and they want their faculty to serve in editorial capacities for these journals. They increasingly rely on assessments of journal quality and citation statistics when making promotion and tenure decisions. Editorial positions held by faculty are also a measure of institutional quality. The administration typically does not track the cost at which such editorial positions come, which can be substantial.

Publishing Trends

Several trends in publishing are important and deserve consideration here. Knowledge is increasing rapidly. One measure of this increase in new knowledge is found in the number of published pages in scientific journals. Tenopir and King, building on journal cost studies conducted by the National Science Foundation in 1975, developed a cost model that reports inflation-adjusted averages in the publishing parameters listed in Table 2.[15] Specifically, they found increases in the average number of issues, average number of articles per title, and average total number of journal pages between 1975 and 1995.[16]

Albert Henderson, in summarizing research by Derek de Solla Price, found that, since the beginning of the twentieth century, the trend has been a rough doubling of knowledge every fifteen years. Price observed this phenomenon through the increasing number of citations in major discipline-oriented bibliographies such as Physics Abstracts, Engineering Index, and Chemical Abstracts Service.[17] Price noted that counting titles or articles is less indicative of the state of scientific communication than counting citations; nevertheless, an increase in the number of journals has also been noted. Michael Mabe and Mayur Amin found a fairly steady compound growth rate of 3.3 percent in active, refereed academic journals from 1940 through 1999. This rate reflects a similar increase in the number of scientists conducting research.[18]

The ARL reported in 2003 that the percentage change in serial unit cost since 1986 was +227 percent compared with a consumer price index (CPI) change of +64 percent. Serial unit costs have risen by more than 3.5 times the increase in the CPI. This figure is somewhat deceiving, since the average number of published pages per serial also increased 52.5 percent between 1975 and 1995.[19] Nonetheless, the net result of increased costs is clear: purchases of both serials and monographs have

Table 2
Scholarly Journal Publishing Parameters: 1975 and 1995

Cost model parameter	Year	
	1975	1995
Number of issues	6.5	8.3
Number of articles/title	85	123
Number of manuscripts submitted	90	205
Number of article pages	630	1439
Number of special graphics pages	114	260
Number of total pages	820	1728
Number of subscriptions (median)	2900	1900

Source: Carol Tenopir and Donald W. King, Towards Electronic Journals: Realities for Scientists, Librarians, and Publishers (Washington, DC: SLA Publishing 2000).

decreased, with monograph purchases bearing the brunt of the decreases, to allow sufficient funds for the remaining serials. This situation is not healthy for scholars, publishers, or institutions and clearly shows that the research university library system is under considerable stress.

Over the past several years, many journals have become accessible, in whole or in part, on the Web. The advent of electronic journals has led to a wide variety of pricing and packaging schemes and a lack of uniformity in the industry. Tenopir and King noted at least nine different pricing schemes for electronic journals.[20] While electronic storage and retrieval in lieu of paper would seem to offer marked economical advantages, these savings have generally not been realized or, at least, passed on to the consumer. Many commercial and professional publishers are struggling to provide electronic access without a loss in revenues. Thus the promise of more widespread access and cheaper serial publication subscriptions has yet to be fulfilled. Again, Tenopir and King found wide variations in estimated cost savings for exclusively electronic serials, ranging anywhere from 10 percent to 75 percent.[21]

A further complication of the advent of electronic serials is the question of maintaining an archive of the scholarly record. Institutions generally lease, not own, electronic content and are now dependent on the publisher to continue to maintain it. In the past, this archival role was not the publishers' but the libraries'; but libraries are now contractually constrained from fulfilling this function, and publishers have been relatively slow to accept it. One of the reasons libraries continue to subscribe to both print and online versions of journals, despite the fact that users tend to prefer Web access to print, is that libraries cannot otherwise ensure that electronic journal content will be accessible to users in the future. Another reason has to do with institutional rankings, which are dependent on the number of print titles held by an institution's libraries. In the first case, there is evidence to suggest that publishers now see a way to turn the archiving of their publications to a profit. In the second, there is evidence of some shift in definitions so that electronic-only subscriptions may in fact no longer threaten an institution's ranking. Ann Okerson raises pertinent issues in this regard: "In the world of print, research libraries have effectively contributed as a public good their services as aftermarket preservers and maintainers of archives. There are real and quite substantial costs associated with this service, costs that have traditionally not been accounted for in the overall economics of information distribution.... The fear is that information which has lost its commercial value may disappear if left in the hands of commercial ... owners only; but there is yet no model for transferring control and responsibility to any not-for-profit entity or group of entities."[22]

The electronic age has had a positive influence on certain critical aspects of the publishing business. An excellent example of this is the shorter time now required for review of a manuscript and the decreased time from acceptance to publication. Editorial management of the peer review process is much more efficient if this process is performed using electronic means because the time lag inherent in using the postal system disappears. Altogether, the savings can amount to a few weeks. The time from acceptance to publication has decreased, in many instances, because accepted papers are available electronically and the date of record is the electronic date the paper is posted, not when, or if, it appears in print.

Institutions of higher education are undergoing financial stress as a result of the nation's recent economic downturn—as endowments have shrunk, student enrolment has grown, and with it the pressure to provide additional building infrastructure. This scenario places the libraries' need for growing budgets to meet its acquisition goals in direct opposition to a wide variety of other needs at major research universities. It seems unlikely that the physical space and budget of libraries will be able to grow at the same rate at which new knowledge is being produced. Increasingly, library budgets are losing ground to the increasing costs for physical space and for the volume of new knowledge being produced. ARL statistics show that, on a per student basis, since 1986 university libraries have experienced decreases in the volumes added (-7%), serials purchased (-8%), total staff (-18%), and monographs purchased (-28%).[23]

Implications

The current situation and current trends in scholarly scientific journal publications are not sustainable. Institutional resources have been strained to the limit for years, and institutions have continually decreased the number of serial subscriptions over the last decade as unit costs have continually increased. In part, these costs can be explained by the rapid growth in production of new knowledge, which has led in turn to an increased number of pages being published per year. These increases are not the whole story, however. In the long term, library budgets cannot be expected to grow much faster than the CPI. In order for both journals and libraries to continue to function, dramatic changes in the production, delivery, and storage of the ever-increasing body of knowledge must occur.

Libraries are also running out of physical space to store the material being produced. The days when a university's entire research library holdings were readily accessible are fading. Many universities are finding it necessary to store significant amounts of archival material off-site to cut costs and to free up space for more current information.[24] Furthermore, libraries do not operate in isolation. As part of larger institutions, they are subject to the financial pressures faced by their parent institutions. These institutions generally cannot afford to expand library facilities to keep up with increased production of published journal pages because capital budgets for such projects compete with other worthy projects necessary to accommodate the vitality of our nation's research universities.

An understanding on the part of editors and their institutions of the extent to which they are subsidizing the scientific publishing enterprise is also growing. In many cases, the editor is responsible for recruiting the editorial board, soliciting papers, identifying and seeking qualified and conscientious reviewers, and, in short, producing a manuscript that is worthy of publication. As the tools have matured, the finished product submitted to the publisher is increasingly closer to the final typeset product. Yet publishers typically provide only token support for editorial services and rely upon institutional subsidies or personal, altruistic sacrifices to sustain the enterprise. This expectation is neither reasonable nor sustainable.

Scholars are also affected by the current trends. Scientists are refusing to submit their work to or to provide peer review for journals published by publishers that their institutions view as participating in predatory pricing. At the same time, scholars are pressured to publish in high-impact journals, which in many cases are those whose costs have increased most rapidly. Citation statistics for an individual's published work are now routinely part of the data collected when considering promotion and tenure decisions at major research universities. If such trends continue, increasing pressures will be brought to bear on publishers and low-impact, low-quality journals will rise to the top of the annual cancellation lists; the marketplace will speak.

Possible Solutions

Clearly, the current situation has evolved for good reasons: knowledge is being produced at an increasing rate, technology is requiring significant changes that are costly to implement, shareholders of commercial publishers are expecting increasing profits, and scholars at major research universities are publishing at increasing rates and in high-impact journals.

Putting aside these reasons for the current situation in scientific publishing, this situation has created adversarial relationships based on the conflicting agendas of the various stakeholders. What is needed to make real progress in resolving this critical situation is an atmosphere of mutual respect. Publishers must understand the untenable position of modern libraries, which are unable to purchase the materials necessary to sustain the research enterprise as a result of ever-increasing prices for serials. Publishers must also realize their obligation to support the producers of knowledge upon whom they depend for their profits. If a journal loses the general goodwill of the scientific community it is intended to serve, it will fail.

Institutions must understand that commercial publishers must make a profit to stay in business and that they are entitled to do so. Institutions must also learn the extent to which they are directly subsidizing the scientific publishing business through the editorial commitments of their faculty and make a reasoned decision regarding the value of these commitments. Furthermore, they must realize that significant changes may be needed and, in fact, are under way in the scientific publishing business. Today's high-impact journals may not be tomorrow's high-impact journals, and alternatives to commercial publishers may become increasingly popular outlets for scientific publication.[25] These non-traditional venues must be given full consideration when conducting faculty reviews. To fail to consider such publications is to hamstring the very changes that are needed to produce a sustainable system. Institutions must make greater strides in educating scholars about the nature of the economic problems they face and enlisting them in helping to effect change.

Scholars must become invested in the process as well. They must understand that the current situation is not sustainable and that runaway prices for scholarly publications are in direct competition with other needs of their institutions. They must be willing to forgo publications that are not fairly priced or that do not give appropriate access. They should be willing to let publisher–institution relationships affect where they submit their work and for whom they choose to do reviews. They must also be willing, when necessary, to assume collective ownership of the intellectual property of a scientific field and become leaders in a scientific community that bands together to produce its own journal outside the constraints of the dominant commercial publishers. Publishing tools and the Web have certainly evolved to the point where this can easily be done, provided that a rigorous peer review of manuscripts is still guaranteed.

The changes outlined above would affect the balance of power in the current situation and put the intellectual property of scholars back in their hands, providing a means for controlling the runaway prices. If this happens, commercial publishing may initially suffer, but this need not be the case. Commercial publishers already have the means to reduce costs drastically—by moving to electronic receipt, review, publishing, and archival systems. They can adopt straightforward and fair pricing policies for access to electronic materials. They can move to policies that do not require subscribers to purchase print materials in order to qualify for electronic access. In the not-too-distant future, paper scientific journal subscriptions may fall precipitously, and the chief form of access will be electronic. With proper systems in place, the production, distribution, storage, and retrieval of these electronic materials can be accomplished at substantial savings compared to the current system.[26] The gains from this increasing efficiency must be passed on to institutions, or they will be compelled to encourage their faculty to consider alternative publication venues and to discourage editorial roles for their faculty.

Conclusions

Several conclusions arise from this work. The average price of scientific journals has increased much faster than the consumer price index over the last several years, straining the budgets of research institution libraries and leading, on average, to decreasing numbers of subscriptions for each journal. Libraries are stretched to their limits, both financially and physically, and runaway price increases cannot be sustained. Conflicting agendas among scholars, editors, publishers, and institutions have led to an adversarial relationship and a lack of mutual understanding. However, several steps can be taken that will lead to a sustainable system for the publication, distribution, and archival storage of scientific knowledge:

1) An increasingly rapid transition to all-electronic, paperless systems for scientific publication, from review to archival storage, should be embraced; this could lead to substantial gains in efficiencies and dramatic reductions in costs per published page, which must then be passed on to subscribing institutions.
2) Institutions and scholars must advocate for landmark changes in our traditional way of publishing scientific information.
3) Alternatives to traditional publishing exist and need to be pursued in order to control prices and return the balance of power to the producers of the intellectual property in a given scientific field.

Because society is best served when research scientists focus on producing new knowledge and not on operating publishing endeavors, all would be best served if the existing publishing system would embrace the needed changes, become more efficient, universally offer electronic access and archival services, and hold the line on price increases. Substantial changes in the scientific publishing business can be realized over the coming years, and it is hoped that the ideas presented here will further the discussion and lead to joint ownership of the current problem by all stakeholders, hastening the identification and adoption of meaningful strategies to control serial costs while ensuring the efficient distribution of the rapidly growing body of scientific knowledge.

Acknowledgements

Cass T. Miller thanks Lucinda Thompson for encouraging his participation in this effort and the organizers and participants of the 2003 Charleston Conference, who encouraged this effort and provided useful comments on preliminary drafts. Both authors thank Janet L. Flowers and Selden Durgom Lamoureux for their encouragement and for suggesting this collaboration. Lara F. Kees and Christopher Windolph have contributed valuable editorial assistance.

Contributors

Cass T. Miller is Professor and Chair of the Department of Environmental Sciences and Engineering at the University of North Carolina at Chapel Hill. He has published nearly 400 works and has served in a variety of editorial and scientific leadership positions over the last two decades.

Julianna C. Harris is a recent graduate of the University of North Carolina at Chapel Hill's School of Information and Library Science.

Notes

1. Mark Rowse, "The Consortium Site License: A Sustainable Model?" Libri 53, 1 (March 2003): 1–10; Julie M. Hurd, "Serials Management: Adrift During a Sea Change?" *Journal of Library Administration* 28, 2 (1999): 77–89.
2. Martha Kyrillidou and Mark Young, "ARL Statistics 2001–02: Research Library Trends Introduction," http://www.arl.org/stats/arlstat/graphs/2002/2002t2.html.
3. Cornell University Task Force, "1998 Journal Price Study of Core Agricultural and Biological Journals," http://jan.mannlib.cornell.edu/jps/jps.htm; Charles Hamaker, "Measures of Cost Effectiveness," *Serials Librarian* 36, 1/2 (1999): 199–205.
4. Lydia L. Lange, "The Impact Factor as a Phantom: Is There a Self-Fulfilling Prophecy Effect of Impact?" *Journal of Documentation* 58, 2 (2002): 175–84; Stephen P. Harter and Thomas E. Nisonger, "ISI's Impact Factor as Misnomer: A Proposed New Measure to Assess Journal Impact," *Journal of the American*

Society of Information Science 48, 12 (December 1997): 1146–48; Henk F. Moed, "Towards Appropriate Indicators of Journal Impact," *Scientometrics* 46, 3 (November–December 1999): 575–89.
5. American Geophysical Union, http://www.agu.org/pubs/inf4aus.html; Soil Science Society of America, http://www.scijournals.org/.
6. Olivia M.A. Madison, "From Journal Cancellation to Library Strategic Visioning Faculty Leadership," *Journal of Library Administration* 28, 4 (1999): 57–70.
7. Gillian Page, Robert Campbell, and Jack Meadows, *Journal Publishing* (Cambridge: Cambridge University Press 1997): 63–64.
8. Richard Poynder, "Continuing Evolution in the World of Scientific Journal Publishing," *Information World Review* 166 (February 2001): 18–19.
9. Howard J. Sanders, "Troubled Times for Scientific Journals," *Chemical and Engineering News* 61 (May 30, 1983): 31–40.
10. John M. Budd, "Serials Prices and Subscriptions in the Social Sciences," *Journal of Scholarly Publishing* 33, (January 2002): 90–101.
11. Carol Tenopir and Donald W. King, *Towards Electronic Journals: Realities for Scientists, Librarians, and Publishers* (Washington, DC: SLA Publishing 2000): 181.
12. John Cox, "Pricing Electronic Information: A Snapshot of New Serials Pricing Models," *Serials Review* 28, 3 (2002): 171–75.
13. Kyrillidou and Young, "ARL Statistics."
14. Leslie Horner Button, "The Good, the Bad, and the Ugly: Forming Consortia and Licensing," *Library Collections, Acquisitions and Technical Services* 23, 2 (Summer 1999): 204–6.
15. Tenopir and King, *Towards Electronic Journals*, 251, 253.
16. Ibid., 268.
17. Albert Henderson, "The Growth of Printed Literature in the Twentieth Century," in Richard E. Abel and Lyman W. Newlin, eds., *Scholarly Publishing: Books, Journals, Publishers, and Libraries in the Twentieth Century* (New York: Wiley 2002): 9–11.
18. Michael Mabe and Mayur Amin, "Growth Dynamics of Scholarly and Scientific Journals," *Scientometrics* 51, 1 (2001): 147–62.
19. Tenopir and King, *Towards Electronic Journals*, 268.
20. Ibid., 391–92.
21. Ibid., 372.
22. Ann Okerson, "Are We There Yet? Online E-Resources Ten Years After," *Library Trends* 48, 4 (Spring 2000): 671–93.
23. Kyrillidou and Young, "ARL Statistics."
24. Jan Merrill-Oldham and Jutta Reed-Scott, "ARL SPEC Kit #242: Library Storage Facilities, Management and Services," http://www.arl.org/spec/242fly.html.
25. SPARC, http://www.arl.org/sparc/home/index.asp; Directory of Open Access Journals, http://www.doaj.org/.
26. Richard E. Quandt, "Scholarly Materials: Paper or Digital?" *Library Trends* 51, 3 (Winter 2003): 349–75.

Scholarship and Silence[1]

Lindsay Waters

Contrast the sound of a newborn crying—the sweetest music on earth—to the cacophony and noise of men (and it's mostly men here) struggling for dominance and encouraging youngsters to publish anything, no matter, as long as it allows them to triumph over their brothers. We have been through a *Dunciad* age, a time of overproduction when sounds stop making sense. We need to get back to the most fundamental issues.

This is not a time for stopgap measures so we can "maintain our standards." Steven Greenblatt has proposed departments of English come up with funds to support graduate students buying books so they will get "hooked on books" and build little libraries of their own. Band-aids don't stop hemorrhaging. It is the time to ask what scholarship is about and—I strongly suggest—to change our standards. What we have is a system with little or no room for individual agency of the departmental members or of the books they might write. When I have delivered this essay as a lecture at different universities, I have been attacked a number of times vociferously by people who tell me I do not understand the system and that I had better "get with the program." How could I be so "retrograde," asked one senior scholar waxing wroth in anger, trembling, face beet red, as to talk about individual responsibility in judgment?

As long as we acquiesce in this system, we will remain inside the whale. Freedom will come when we throw over the need for control, the need to be so totally in control of what can be known, and embrace ignorance. We must be willing to be fooled—mistaken in scientific and humanistic inquiry.

As we look more deeply into the problems betokened by the crisis of the monograph, I believe we have to be willing to ask the most fundamental questions. We have to ask, as scholars like Anthony Grafton and Elizabeth Eisenstein and Marshall McLuhan have helped us ask, what is the relationship between thinking, scholarship, and publication? Why do we assume—as we do—a correlation between loquaciousness and the exercise of intelligence befitting a professor?

I think we need to ponder the question of the relation between scholarship and silence. It is possible to be a great thinker and not publish anything. Heidegger pointed out that Socrates "wrote nothing." We know as scholars that sometimes we can study a body of material intently for years with a hypothesis in mind only to come up with no results, and the right thing to do then is to admit that a serious inquiry led one to conclude that there is nothing to say. Of course, Plato was there to capture what Socrates said. But much more important than noticing the contradiction between Socrates' unease with writing and the fact that he had a very high-level scribe in Plato is the case that philosophy, as we know it and think about it in the West, arose among people who felt acutely the tension between speaking and writing. This is the fault-line where friction between two different modes of intelligence proved to be just right for the emergence of philosophy.

In our scholastic rage to stuff libraries till they burst with publications, something got lost. And what do we do now when, increasingly, libraries do not purchase the books and books do not get read and reviewed but only counted? Here is deafening silence, but I am interested in a pregnant silence, the sort that settles in at the end of Wittgenstein's *Tractatus*. It is OK, and it might even be admirable, to produce nothing when one decides that this is appropriate. Just consider that, as Eli Friedlander writes, "the opposite of silence is not necessarily speaking with sense but, rather, making noise." Now in the academic world what we have is a cacophony, but what we should seek is the symmetry of scholars interested in reading and taking up carefully what their colleagues are producing. Some have suggested that the new possibilities for electronic publishing will alleviate our problems. In the wild ideas of some dreamers the new world of electronic publication will actually be an improvement over books. To think this way is to fail to understand that electronic publication will only make the situation worse. Moreover, it will make things worse in a way that undermines the principles behind the culture of the book.

We had better put an end to such foolish talk and keep pressure on the librarians and ourselves to value the book better.

As some have imagined the electronic book it is an abdication of precisely the sort of responsibility we need to develop now and it makes impossible the act of judgment I have claimed is central to the entire process. As imagined by historian Robert Darnton, the great thing about electronic publication is that it would allow us to "dump unlimited numbers of dissertations onto the Web." The Web allows unprecedented access. This seems to me misleading, but we await results from the AHA project, for which Darnton is an advisor, to publish award-winning dissertations online. It is by no means clear that the Web is a good medium for words. It is fine for pornography, because like all electronic forms of reproduction it does a fine job making the gesture salient the way the hand salute performed over and over in Leni Riefenstahl's *Triumph of the Will* turns humans into mere ornaments of the will of the leader. Those who make books, by contrast, used to have to do so as individuals who stand out from the collective.

Let me explain: At the heart of book making is the gathering, the tying together of materials into a package or a unity that the person or group of people pulling together are prepared to have judged. This is true whether the book is a book of sonnets written by one person or a sacred text like the Bible whose unity was the result of group decisions.

The book is a particular form made possible by the development of the codex. It is an object particularly appropriate for the library, because like a library it allows you to skim ahead or skip backwards. And it has heft. It weighs something. It's got what a dean likes in a publication: It goes bump when it hits a table. You can write on it, but at its essence is the judgment someone or some group made that it formed a unity, and it is this unity that any readers of the book are called upon to judge. Whenever we enter a new book it is with the question, "What unifies the materials the author has brought together in it?" The most clever books keep us guessing, which is why we love novels plotted with ingenuity where the writer holds us in suspense. Benjamin insists the written novel is different in kind from the oral tale, but I am not so sure. There is an absolute symmetry between what the book is in production and what it is in reception—a gathering—and it is this symmetry that makes for the special beauty of the book. If the life of a scholar is a calling, a vocation, it is one that is analogous to the calling a book makes to us to read it and judge it. A book is not, nor ever will be, a dump. The book emerges from silence not from cacophony. The book features the highest signal to noise ratio possible of any means of communication.

I have become over the years most intrigued by the scholars who do not want to publish, who hardly even want to talk about what they know. "One should speak only where one must not be silent," wrote Nietzsche in *Human, All Too Human*. I try to listen to their hesitations, the clutch in the voice, that suggests someone is holding something back that needs to break forth. I try to be as much as possible like Sam Phillips listening to Elvis stammering into sense.[2] Some of them are afraid to speak lest they risk ridicule. Some are timid, but not the way I argue scholars like Stanley Fish are timid when they declare a topic out of bounds that would have wreaked havoc on their argument. Maybe these few I am concerned with might be timid or modest in the face of great questions whose complexity they truly appreciate. Some are simply appalled by all the profusion of publications and do not wish to contribute more to the glut. They can see the truly valuable is likely to be ignored. The true innovators are the ones most likely to be beset with epistemological crises because they have wandered off to places where there are no other travelers. Such people may spend many days of their lives like explorers trying to get to one of the poles, uncertain whether they have because snow obscures the sky and makes getting a precise fix on location impossible. History provides too many examples of the truly bold thinker being resisted. Remember that even bold Picasso held back his *Demoiselles d'Avignon* until six years after he painted it, not wanting to face the opprobrium. Gotta know when to hold 'em, know when to fold 'em. Timing is all.

In our moment of high scholasticism, fewer and fewer schools will tolerate this sort of independence from the increasingly rigid norms for publication. It is as if the schools were saying implicitly that in order to win tenure you have to prove that you are not an independent mind by subjecting yourself to the rules and goals of high productivity. But I think one thing to do is to put new pressure on the book by demanding that it be more substantial before it can be accepted and published. We are tired of McDonald's hamburgers. We want something that is slow cooked. I think we can put more pressure on publishers to find the important books that some of the people who don't want to break the silence could write. It really is often the best who are in no rush to write and publish. There are too many people too eager to publish, and not enough people who are biding their time and letting a project grow great within them. Some of the economists of the Rational Expectations School had the idea that there are times in economic history when it is "time to build." The same is true in the academic world. There are times when it is good to build up ideas, to play with them, and experiment with them and not rush with them to print.

I spend a lot of time among the philosophers, and I know that to a great extent they live in a different world from literary scholars, another group of academics I also know quite intimately. When we talk of oral cultures, one might assume they are populated by primitives. Well, I live in an oral universe as a publisher. I used to be embarrassed about this, but I'll freely admit it today. And so do the philosophers. You'll remember Derrida chastising Plato for his reluctance to enter the culture of writing. There is something about thought—that is, free thought, free speech—that resists being brought into material form. Derrida is another one of our current thinkers who seems like such a rebel, but if you were to look at his critique of Plato and "logocentrism" in the light of my argument I think it becomes plain that he promotes the biases of our age towards print and against the oral. For the sake of setting himself up as the ultimate rebel, another Last Man, he really just played upon our own prejudices in favor of publication, a prejudice I share.

By contrast, most philosophers now and over the ages have been for all practical purposes iconoclasts. A story that hit me hard was about Rogers Albritton, a philosopher who taught at Harvard and UCLA and who just before he died spent some of his precious time shredding all his lecture notes so that kind friends would not edit them and bring them to someone like me to publish. Earlier in his career his friend Donald Davidson conspired with several others admirers of Albritton to put him in a situation where he had to publish something: They campaigned to get him elected the President of the Pacific Division of the American Philosophical Association. One duty of the President is to deliver an address at the annual meeting. Those addresses are always published in the proceedings, and so Albritton was tricked into publishing.

As with Albritton, I have the strongest sense that many of the people who have the most to say are most reluctant to say it. And I think the academy should enlist the publishers to try to get some of the silent people to talk. Forget the blabbermouths. They will find their way. Heidegger writes that "all great Western thinkers after Socrates, with all their greatness, had to be fugitives." That which has not yet reached the point of being formulated in the minds of people flickers and teases us just beyond reach of words until we find the words to give body to thought. Some profound thinkers like to linger at the margins of thought: "Heard melodies are sweet, but those unheard/ Are sweeter." The intelligent person wants to express a thought, but first of all wants to explore it and knows one has to be delicate. Thinking can be like catching lightning bugs and not like watching a lightning storm. Some of the greatest thinkers hesitated before speaking. John Rawls was a stutterer who was—I know from trying with no luck for years—most uneager to bring his work into print. Judgment plays a very important role in thinking and deciding what is fit for articulating before a public in lecture or writing. Many brilliant souls judge their work too harshly. In the era of scarcity that seems upon us, publishers might be newly charged to scour the world of learning in quest of those pregnant with thought whose hitherto unformulated ideas need help finding shape on paper.

Some of my greatest joys of the present moment are books that are written and done by scholars I am still shocked I managed to extract books from. I have come to understand that the reason these authors did not want to take the time to get their thoughts down on paper is because they are so impatient. Their minds are so fast they can hardly stand the slowness of conversation, but that they can manage. It's print that's the problem. Isn't that putting things too strongly? No. There is a conflict that deeply intelligent people still feel and will always feel between the authoritarianism of print and the authority one seeks by speaking and publishing. In his rush to show he is so clever, Derrida—very much Oedipus in this—misses something that Plato knows in his bones: that it was in the play or tension that the people of his time felt (uniquely in the West? I think not: Philosophy in China, I have been told, originated at the same fault line) between orality and literacy that Western philosophy emerged. What was Plato's objection to writing? The power to rule over us in silence because people defer to its authority. Here is a potentially lethal silence. We need to keep alive the necessity of making a judgment between the times when it is wise to be silent and when it is wise to talk (see *Phaedrus*). When we scholars defer to the demands of administrators and the procedures of scholarly publishers, as when we outsource tenure decisions, we betray a craven attitude to authority that does not become us. The perennial problem is that humans are always tempted to defer absolutely to masters and thereby to become slaves to others or to their own earlier thoughts as reified in writing or print; they are not challenged to become or remain the masters of their own minds, as they must be when they must make up their minds and speak on the spot in dialogue with others themselves, entering the space of reason as free people.

I think our present mania for publication is a great insult to the dignity of thought, the dignity upon which the authority society might bestow on us is based. Deep thought does not always announce itself in shouts, but sometimes in whispers.

We need to reorient the humanities within the university. Departments have to tell the administrators, in some nice but forceful way, "no." They have to take back the governance of the community of scholars the way some journal editors are now seizing back their journals from rapacious publishers who want to gouge university libraries. In the humanities we have to root out an attitude of complacency in front of the system whether it comes from the administrators or from ourselves (as it does to some considerable extent). We have to be ready to explain ourselves and not find it insulting when we are asked to do so and luxuriate in the aestheticized helplessness to which we have become habituated. And we have to dare look at new things and develop new theories. Humanists have to counter the iconoclastic attitude about books and art that has come to dominate the humanities. We have to embrace art once again and show how the interaction of readers, viewers, and listeners can precipitate the sorts of experiences that allow our souls to spring forth into momentary glory. Experience is for the humanist what experiments are for the scientist, the key events we seek to explore.

If the humanities are about judgment, they are about that judgment that something is new in my interaction with some artistic objects. When we are ready to explain ourselves and when we are ready again to encounter the artwork, that is, when we set our eyes once again upon the prize of the aesthetic experience, we will find students and we will find the support we so desperately need to do our work.

Indeed, I believe, the same general issues are at play in the work of scholarship across the board in the academy. To foster innovation we need all of us in our different realms to foster individual judgment.

Contributor

Lindsay Waters is Executive Editor for the Humanities at Harvard University Press. His essay "The Crisis in English Studies: A Response to Walter Jackson Bate," appeared in *Scholarly Publishing* in 1983. His book *Against Authoritarian Aesthetics: Towards a Poetics of Experience [Mei Xue Quan Wei Zhu Yi Pi Pan]*, translated into Putong Hua by Ang Zhihui, appeared from Peking University Press in 2000. He is currently at work on a book on the nature of the aesthetic experience. He holds a Ph.D. in English from the University of Chicago, where he wrote a dissertation on Byron and the Italian connection.

Notes

1. Excerpted from *Enemies of Promise: Publishing, Perishing, and the Eclipse of Scholarship* by Lindsay Waters (Chicago: Prickly Paradigm Press 2004): 77–87. All rights reserved. Reprinted with permission from the author and from Prickly Paradigm Press, LLC, 5629 South University Avenue, Chicago, IL 60637, *www.prickly-paradigm.com*.
2. See *ibid.*, 60–7.

The Futures of Scholarly Publishing[1]

Cathy N. Davidson

When people expect to get something for nothing, they are sure to be cheated.
—P.T. Barnum, *Struggles and Triumphs*

I will return to that quote from P.T. Barnum later in this paper. To begin, however, I'd like to thank ACLS for organizing this panel on "Crises and Opportunities: The Future(s) of Scholarly Publishing." Those multiple plurals—the emphasis on crises *and* opportunities, and that injunction to imagine our "futures"—signal that we are finally beyond the panic response to "*the* crisis in scholarly publishing." Not that the crisis is over. If anything, it has intensified. However, we now know more than we did in the past, there is less hysteria, and we have an opportunity to make some decisions that could reshape, and potentially save, the best aspects of academic publishing—which means the best academic research.

A key feature of academic publishing is that it touches on so many aspects of our academic lives, since it is the chief evaluating and credentialing mechanism upon which the reward system of academe is based. University press publishing has many portals, and, as individuals, we enter variously as students, scholars, teachers, mentors, editors, and administrators. Institutionally, we also have different relationships to scholarly publishing—as professional organizations, private universities, public universities, libraries, electronic publishers, and a range of different presses. It is important to have all of these—individually and institutionally—represented in our discussion because this forecloses the possibility of thinking there is some utopian "elsewhere" where there *is* no problem. There is a problem, and we are all part of it. Kate Torrey, Director of the University of North Carolina Press, likes to say, "we all breathe the same air." The 'we' in that sentence is not just those in the world of university press publishing but all of us who, in multiple ways, have been rewarded in our professional lives because of work that has been supported by underpaid, understaffed, and overworked scholarly publishers. If we are part of the problem, we all must collectively, and more equitably, contribute to the solution.

At the risk of belaboring the obvious, I am going to linger on this notion of collective responsibility, inclusive decision making, and profession-wide resolutions. I believe we are at a turning point where many of us want to find systemic and strategic solutions and move beyond hand-wringing, finger-pointing, and blame-pinning. Pinning the blame is a shell game that constantly diverts our attention from the ever-travelling pea, leaving us baffled, guessing, and typically looking in one place when the "real problem" resides elsewhere.

A sampling of the essays written on this topic over the last three or four years makes it abundantly clear that we do not need more diagnoses of the problem. We've had plenty of those. The problem is that we have tied tenure to the publication of a scholarly book. No, others say: uncoupling tenure from books cannot solve the problem because journals are in trouble, too. Others suggest that the problem is the scholarly monograph itself, or that the problem is curtailed library spending on humanities books. The problem is price-gouging by commercial publishers of science journals, forcing libraries to spend less money on humanities and social science publications. The problem is chain bookstores, the dwindling number of independent bookstores, and the increasing conservatism of those that remain. The problem is electronic booksellers like Amazon.com, with their heavy discounting and selling of used books. The problem is that books cost too much to produce. The problem is that electronic publishing is too expensive and doesn't work for monographs. The problem is shrinking subsidies to presses in the wake of cutbacks to higher education for state universities. The problem is shrinking subsidies to presses in light of dwindling returns on endowments and diminished philanthropy at private universities. The problem is that many universities that depend upon academic publications (books or journal articles) to award tenure don't have presses of their own—they are "mooching off" everyone else. The problem is the corporatizing of the university. The problem is the sciences. The problem is the changing demographics of higher education: there are fewer assistant professors and graduate students, who are the primary book buyers (as well as the primary authors of articles in refereed journals). The problem is that the course pack has been substituted for the assigned secondary classroom text. The problem is that the jargon of postmodern critical theory has shrunk the audience for the humanities. The problem is that the critical theory boom has ended, and no one is excitedly reading every new book any more. The problem is that, since 9/11, people are watching CNN and not buying books, trade or academic. The problem is that university press books are underpriced relative to their production costs. The problem is that university press books cost too much relative to the income of their target audience. The problem is too many books. The problem is too few books. The problem is too many books of one kind and too few of another. The problem is that students don't know how to read any more.

The problem is that almost all of the above are *part* of the problem. Fixating on parts means that we never arrive at an overarching solution.

Furthermore, while those are some of the shifting problems, even the victims change in other arguments: It's the humanities. It's the humanities and the book-oriented social science fields. It's junior professors in literature. It's junior professors in foreign literatures or working on pre-modern topics. It's junior professors at non-elite institutions in foreign literatures who work on pre-modern topics.... Or maybe it's just the French!

If the insights of today's panel are to amount to anything, we must stop thinking of these problems and the sufferers as ever and always elsewhere. After all, these are the most basic aspects of scholarship, the foundation of our profession. The bottom line is that scholarly publishing isn't financially feasible as a business model—never was, never was intended to be, and should not be. *If scholarship paid, we wouldn't need university presses.*

Members of this panel have been asked to reevaluate big issues such as the reward structures of our profession in light of new technologies, collaborative models of authorship, non-print forms of publication, and so forth. All of these are vitally important. My reservation about having such a discussion, however, is the timing. I am not in favor of uncoupling book publishing from tenure. But I do want to uncouple discussions of reevaluating tenure requirements from the current economic crisis in publishing. A university press book and several refereed articles have been the price of admission to tenure for a good four decades. It is impossible to change overnight the standard of excellence in a profession as hierarchical and decentralized as ours. But we need to stabilize the losses in the publishing business now. Separately, without the sense of economic ruin so near, we can engage in serious conversations about what kind of profession we want. Coupling an economic exigency with a philosophical reassessment is the proverbial apples and oranges, and it will lead to bad business decisions and inequitable professional fixes.

* * *

In the remainder of this paper, I am going to propose a number of ways in which the current costs of publishing can be distributed more equitably. Before I do, however, I want to make two personal declarations. The first has to do with being vice provost at a research university. When you are part of the provost's office, which oversees not only all the costs of doing academic business but also the tenure process, it is impossible not to see to what degree the fates of publishing, libraries, and scholarship are intertwined. A provost trying to save money by asking her university press to bring in more revenue (making cost a major goal in book acquisition) is in an untenable position if she is also trying to maintain the same quality-based publishing standards for her faculty. At the same time, no university has enough money to fund everything, and every university wants to maintain its standards. So every provost is in an impossible and seemingly insoluble double-bind. One of my goals today is to provide practical solutions to help universities move beyond this impasse.

My second personal declaration is affective. I like the scholarly books I'm reading these days. I know it is more sophisticated to make jaded remarks about the decline in the quality of scholarship, but I don't believe there has been a decline. In fact, when Oxford University Press asked me to write a substantial new introduction to a reissue of *Revolution and the Word*,[2] reframing its argument and content for a new generation of readers, I embarked on a two-year crash course in books and articles written on eighteenth- and early-nineteenth-century American history and culture over the last fifteen years. As embarrassing as it may be, I will confess: reading scholarship as voraciously as any graduate student preparing for a prelim has been an exhilarating and even inspiring experience. The future of our profession is in good hands—if there is a future. I have been especially excited by the dozens of serious, scholarly first books I've read by junior scholars scrambling their way towards tenure. Then again, why would that be surprising? I myself was a junior scholar when I was researching and writing *Revolution and the Word*.

Because I am married to an editor and work in the provost's office, I am not allowed to have a connection to my own university press these days. However, simply being a scholar and an adviser of graduate students makes me intensely aware of the dire straits of scholarly publishing. Indeed, my recommendations have almost nothing to do with "saving" university press publishing. Quite frankly, I am not interested in propping up fragile university press publishing businesses if what they offer is simply a watered-down version of trade publishing. I've published several books with trade publishers; they do a good job getting those books out to a large, general readership. My motivation in being on this panel at ACLS is to find ways to save the kind of scholarship that academics are trained to write and that is the basis of teaching and research at colleges and universities. At present, university press publishing provides the most careful, impartial, and efficient system of brokering, networking, evaluating, editing, publishing, and distributing serious scholarship. It does this exceptionally well when its acquisition programs are not skewed by economic pressures. In the future, we may come up with better and more cost-efficient ways to publish books. At present, if we believe in the value of scholarship, then we who hold leadership roles in our profession must devise the best ways to support university press publishing and rally the support of the profession as a whole.

And we need to act now. The costs of scholarly publishing are rising along with all academic costs. The more serious, rigorous, and specialized our scholarship, the more likely it is to lose money. Beleaguered publishers should not have to bear the brunt of the lose-lose economics of scholarship. Nor should strapped universities be required to bail out university presses every year as the economics of scholarly publishing fall further and further from the possibility of breaking even.

What we need is acknowledgement that scholarly publishing costs more than we are spending on it. It requires substantial subsidies and new ideas about where those infusions of capital might come from and how costs might be dispersed more equitably among those who benefit most from scholarly publishing—namely, scholars themselves. I hope that we can leave here today with a mandate to push Carlos Alonso's recommendations[3] further, create whatever task forces we need to create an action plan, and give ourselves a timeline by which to institute profession-wide change.

In that spirit, I'm going to throw out ten small, practical, and workable ideas for how to distribute the economic burden of scholarly publishing. Not all of these ideas are new; all need to be tested; some might be tried and then discarded if they prove untenable. I offer them less as solutions than as potential models for thinking about our collective responsibility. No one model will work. The point is to spark ideas, galvanize energies, and then sit down together and see what we can do.

1. Paying Our Dues

What if we involved all of our professional associations in a combined, considered, and well-publicized effort on behalf of scholarly publishing, emphasizing the responsibility of every individual and institutional member of the profession to the greater good that is academic research? The American Association of Universities (AAU) could, for example, pass a recommendation that every member of the profession who is tenured or coming up for tenure should be a dues-paying member of at least one national ACLS-affiliated association plus one other interdisciplinary, sub-field, or regional organization. This should be extended to the sciences, as well, since the outrageous costs of scientific journals are a key part of the problem. The dues should be sliding (as they generally are), based on salary. And a percentage of the total dues should be reserved for book subsidies that would be given to university presses, as should a portion of conference fees from any conference where a book prize is awarded. The details of how the subsidy would be implemented require working out. Carlos Alonso has already set forth some viable ideas in his March 2003 *PMLA* Editor's Column[4] and in his talk today. Other fields may want to refine the process within their own structures. There might, for example, be book prizes in various sub-fields and interdisciplinary cross-fields, and prize money could be awarded to all university presses entering the contest as well as shared between the winning author and the press. This is essentially a reverse entrance fee to subsidize publishing in the field in which the prize is awarded. Since publishers have lists in certain areas, this would be one way of supporting the kind of work the prize is designed to honor. While this could happen with manuscripts before publication, that, it seems to me, duplicates work better done by publishers and doesn't really address the larger issue. A title subsidy isn't sufficient to support a whole list; you need a developed list in an area for all kinds of reasons studied by scholars in the field of history of the book—a network of reviewers, a reliable standard of peer evaluation, a target market to help in distribution (whether that be a booth at a conference or a mailing list). The reverse entrance fee allows for block or list subsidies, ensuring the health of the field and not simply of the winning entrant. It is a truism of publishers that those books that win the "best book" prizes in their fields often lose the most money. Making prize money available to publishers could help support those books that receive the most scholarly esteem without penalizing their publishers.

Of course, as with all of these suggestions, another professional organization represented here today—the American Association of University Presses (AAUP)—would also have to take a responsible leadership role. If offering subsidies encourages publishers to see this as a boon (not a survival strategy) and as encouragement to expand their size, operations, and costs, then five years out we would be back in the same losing situation in which we find ourselves now, only more heavily taxed. Any profession-wide effort on behalf of scholarly publishing would have to come with equal assurances from AAUP's members that they would also earnestly address the situation and work in a coordinated fashion to stabilize the economics of scholarly publishing. I imagine this would require agreements among university presses: a challenging prospect, since university press publishing's lack of a vigorous profit motive does not prevent it from being extremely competitive. And that's a good thing, since the competition among publishers is one way that we ensure quality, rigor, progress, and the promotion of cutting-edge thinking. It requires others more conversant with the business of academic publishing to figure out how to preserve competition, control expansion, and agree on methods for revenue sharing. If the NCAA can figure that out, the AAUP should be able to come up with something satisfactory.

2. Publishing Electronically

We're learning, fast, that electronic publishing isn't easy and isn't cheap. It does not represent the entire alternative to conventional publishing, and it will not solve the publishing crisis. Will it work in certain situations? Is it sometimes cost-effective? Yes. My colleague John Unsworth is in a far better position than I to comment on this subject, and so I'm going to defer to him but simply mark electronic publication as a solution that has been tried and found wanting—though I would want to try it again, under a different business model and with different expectations.

Among the many worthy possibilities for electronic publishing right now I would include the creation and preservation of more machine-readable databases, multimedia data banks, genetic texts, and multilingual editions of texts. Printing-on-demand (POD) publishing ventures are a promising way of gaining access to books no longer in print and hold possibilities for the future in small fields that will never be able to "break even" under any financing model. There is also much work to be done with preservation of "born digital" materials, meta-standards for archiving and searching, collaborative multi-site and multinational projects with open source access for any who wishes to contribute, and many exciting electronic publishing projects. None of these, at present, offers all that university presses do, and most of these electronic projects require either volunteer labor or considerable subsidies of their own. They are thus a wonderful addition to the scholarly arsenal but are by no means a "solution" to the crisis in scholarly publishing.

3. Start-Up Packages

Several people have suggested book subsidies as part of start-up packages for junior faculty in book publishing fields analogous to start-up packages in the sciences. I'd like to refine that model a bit, since, in my role as a vice provost overseeing interdisciplinary research centers across Duke's eight schools, I'm always aware of escalating costs throughout the university and skeptical of plans that simply add costs to existing structures. Added costs in one area mean reduced expenditures in another. Add-on subsidies pit the university press against, for example, the new humanities center. Why make that bargain?

A strategic way of promoting the start-up package idea (without adding to already overtaxed budgets) is for ACLS or AAU to make a recommendation that universities take their 2004–2005 salary levels—across the board, in all fields—and subtract $500 in order to create a publishing subsidy pool. New as well as current (i.e., junior and senior) faculty members could be guaranteed a publishing subsidy drawn from this pool. I'd suggest $10,000 per book in book publishing fields, and a field-specific sliding amount for journal publications, to be awarded to a book that has already successfully completed the review process by a university press (rather than a commercial enterprise). Such a distributed cost works out about right given attrition rates of untenured faculty members, those who do not ever draw from the publishing-subsidy pool, and investment possibilities for the pool itself. Needless to say, I would prefer that faculty salaries continue to rise *and* that there be a book-subsidy pool, but that is not realistic in the present economy.

This strategic reallocation of existing resources would be an excellent investment for the university as well as for the individual scholar. This year, one of my former students (an Americanist, by the way) received a dozen form rejections saying, "we do not publish first books in literature." He wasn't able to find a press that would read his manuscript. And if no one is publishing first books, how will he ever publish a second one? I'm sure everyone in this room has a similar story to tell. I know my student would have preferred a modest decline in his assistant professor salary if it would have given him a weapon in the battle to enter our profession. I see no reason why this arrangement could not be adapted to senior as well as junior faculty—and it might even be an incentive for those struggling with that crucial post-promotion book. Some universities (Michigan, Cornell, and, to a lesser extent, Emory) provide subsidies to their faculty already. If this became a nation-wide policy, with costs distributed in a way similar to what I am suggesting, it could make an enormous difference. With a $10,000 subsidy per book, 100 books a year would receive a $1 million revenue infusion. That could go a long way toward ending the red ink for publishers and their universities.

4. Scaled Subsidies

For those universities and colleges requiring scholarly books and journals for tenure and promotion but without university presses of their own, book subsidies should be twice as much: $20,000 per book and perhaps $1,000 per scholarly article. How they pay for it could be on the model suggested above or in other ways that suit their own institutional funding structures and resources. The point must be made, however, that we need to take collective responsibility for the good now provided to the entire profession by those universities that do subsidize scholarly publishing.

5. Tax Write-Offs in Lieu of Royalties

Many of us receive tiny checks every year from our publishers. One of my first books brings in somewhere between $37 and $50 a year. What if, instead of a check, university presses sent a royalty statement and gave authors an option: either request the check or send back the statement and ask that it be converted from income into a tax-deductible gift to help subsidize first books or books in a given field. The same could be done for advances. It's ridiculous how we currently make decisions on which publisher to go with over a $500 advance on a book that will lose $5,000. Or, again, instead of offering manuscript reviewers the choice between so many books or the whopping sum of $150, why not provide the option of a tax-deductible contribution? Each book so subsidized would have an acknowledgment indicating that "A subsidy for the publication of this book was made possible by generous authors committed to the survival of university press publishing." Their gifts would be small tokens in a larger project of cultural change.

6. Elimination of Course Packs

University press books are often less expensive than course packs and entail less hassle than all the copyright issues of today's course packs. Furthermore, it is good for everyone, including instructors, to read a whole book occasionally.

7. Battling the Commercial Science Publishers

I'm not sure that, in the end, it would help university presses economically to take on commercial science publishers such as Elsevier, but it would be good on many levels if academic presses were publishing science journals and charging less than the current astronomical subscription rates. A library subscription to *Brain Research*, for example, costs approximately $20,000 a year, while *Bioorganic and Medicinal Chemistry Letters* runs closer to $30,000. A "takeover" by university press publishing would (a) be a fairer and less costly system for scientists, thus helping to make scientists, too, appreciative of the role served by university presses; (b) help libraries put their expenses back in line; and (c) in so doing, help the bottom line of universities—again, a greater good.

8. Using the University's Teaching and Research Mission to Promote Scholarly Books

Every university home page should have links to university press books that deal with topics of importance to courses, initiatives, conferences, invited speakers, and so forth. Click here and go to a centralized online bookstore comprising a consortium of university press publishers. If such a publishing venture were found to violate antitrust laws, then all university web sites could bypass Amazon.com (with its heavy discounting) and go directly to the University of Chicago's legendary Seminary Co-Op Bookstore—surely one of the nation's most valiant supporters of scholarly publishing.

9. Data Collecting

In the current conversation about "the crisis," book publishing is often presented by university administrators as if it were an add-on to the already expensive fields of the humanities and narrative social sciences—those fields considered to be "soft," "weak sisters," "incapable of supporting themselves." I'm not so sure. I want the data. What if all of our associations worked together to challenge our business schools to try to model the full economics of the modern university? How much do the book publishing fields cost a university? If we are going to talk about the corporatizing of universities, let's see "the books"—and not an Arthur Andersen–style cooking of those books, but real costs, real expenses: buildings, M&O, salaries, start-up packages, labs, post-docs, staff, cost-sharing, ICRs, and all the apparatus of the science-and technology-fields driven by "external funds." How much does that photonics or free electron lab really cost? How much tuition revenue is brought in by the sciences as opposed to liberal arts teaching in book publishing fields? It may turn out English departments are cash cows—in which case, it is only right and just that literary scholarship yield some rewards in the form of book subsidies for all its institutional heavy lifting. In the corporate rhetoric of the university, the liberal arts often seem like a pariah. We may, in fact, be the capitalists keeping the system afloat.

10. Institutional Branding and Public Relations

I know at least one or two regional universities that became major national players through heavy investing in the humanities and social sciences. It's an easier and more cost-effective way to improve national rankings than by trying to raise the caliber of the science and engineering faculties. It's also an efficient way to change a university's profile or "brand," because controversy is commonplace in the humanities and social sciences—and controversy is publicity. University presses sometimes "fill out" the offerings of their parent institutions. A great list in a specialty area often brands the university in areas where the university may not have faculty or research strengths. It costs far less to build a publishing reputation in a high-prestige area that doesn't have high student enrolment than it does to create a new department. How can university presses receive more credit for this?

Presses can also do more to be interwoven into the fiber of their universities: Targeted alumni catalogues (with gift and naming opportunities, too); alumni book clubs and press discounts; university press books with handsome book plates as the routine prize for service (instead of the dorky five-year pin); gift certificates for the university press in the welcome baskets of incoming students; graduate fellowships paid partly in scrip (say, $500 a year) that could be used to buy university press books—perfect for the online university press co-op suggested above. Even simple kinds of in-house advertising could pay off. Bulletin boards with tearsheets for current books in the field could be posted outside every department, offering graduate students heavy discounts on selected backlist books.

These seem like tiny gestures, but all aid in making presses more visible to their own universities. They all help educate faculty in non–book publishing fields about the importance of the press. What is the overall cost/benefit of the university press in terms of reputation and luster? Provosts should not only be seeing red when the university press is mentioned; they should be seeing an opportunity. I remember a visit by press directors to the provost's Academic Priorities Committee at Duke. They came with about twenty very handsome new books, slid them down the middle of the table, and said, "Here. They're free. Everybody take one!" And the scramble was on. It was not hard, after that, to make the case that scholarly publishing was important. Yet a good half of the faculty at the table admitted that, until that moment, they had had no idea what the university press really did. University presses need to make themselves far more visible to the universities that support them.

* * *

Will we, today, solve "the crisis in academic publishing?" No. If we go out and form task forces and action committees, if we manage to work together in a model of collective action, will we make the problem go away? I don't think so. *But we don't have to.* What I'm proposing is something far more modest and bold: That we put into effect adjustments that will *improve* the situation for the present. After that, we must persist in collective watchfulness to ensure that these adjustments are working, and that they are not having unanticipated negative results in one sector that will eventually hurt every sector.

Right now, we are putting far too much effort into analysis of the problem and not enough into change. We must learn from the plug-and-play model of business. We need to try one thing—and then try another. We are not in an environment where long-range planning makes sense, because all of the conditions are in flux at once: market conditions, tax structures, demographics, state spending, technology infrastructure, new methods of evaluating productivity, and so on. We must anticipate ways that the economics of publishing might change again (as they most assuredly will) and have the dexterity and the mandate to adapt accordingly.

Universities do not have unlimited resources; if they did, we wouldn't be holding this panel today. We can't keep shifting the blame, and we can't keep looking for individual fixes and then lament when another press loses its intellectual mission, lays off its literature editor, or curtails its monographs. We academics cannot continue to see ourselves as innocents in a process whose fate is decided by others. Innocence is not bliss—it is professional suicide. The problem of university press publishing is *our* problem, and we must solve it. I believe that professional associations, such as the collective body represented by ACLS, must take leadership roles. It undermines all we stand for as a profession if the only way scholarly presses can survive is by looking for books that sell. French history is less valuable than Latin American history because it doesn't sell as well? That's preposterous. Until we realize, as individuals and institutions, that we cannot expect something for nothing, the current situation will deteriorate even further. And then, as P.T. Barnum predicted, we shall all be cheated.

Contributor

Cathy N. Davidson is Vice Provost for Interdisciplinary Studies and Ruth F. DeVarney Professor of English, Duke University.

Notes

1. This paper was originally presented at the Annual Meeting of the American Council of Learned Societies on May 10, 2003, and is published by permission of ACLS. This paper also appears as ACLS occasional paper No. 56. A condensed version was published as "The Economic Burden of Scholarly Publishing," *The Chronicle Review* of *The Chronicle of Higher Education* (October 3, 2003): B7–B10. Cathy Davidson also served as a guest host for a "Colloquy Live" chat hosted by *The Chronicle of Higher Education* called "In Search of Solutions for Scholarly Publishing." The transcript of the chat is available at *http://chronicle.com/colloquylive/2003/10/publishing*.

    The author would like to thank Steve Cohn, Deborah Jakubs, Alice Kaplan, Peter Lange, and Ken Wissoker of Duke University for their help (including energetic disagreement) in researching this essay.
2. Cathy N. Davidson, *Revolution and the Word: The Rise of the Novel in America*, 2nd ed. (New York: Oxford University Press 2004).
3. Carlos J. Alonso, "Having a Spine: Facing the Crisis in Scholarly Publishing," *PMLA* 118, 2 (March 2003): 217–23. A talk based on this column formed part of the panel discussion at the ACLS (see note 1 above).
4. *Ibid.*

The Changing Market for University Press Books in the United States: 1997–2002

Albert N. Greco, Robert M. Wharton, and Hooman Estelami

What was the market for university press books in the United States between 1997 and 2002? What impact did shifts in the general reader market and the creation of library electronic reserve capabilities have on university press net publishers' revenues? What impact did Internet bookselling sites have on new and used frontlist titles? The study reported here reviewed the published literature and statistical data sets. We detected (a) a significant shift in the traditional channels of distribution and (b) the emergence of a sophisticated used book market that undermined both frontlist and backlist sales. Based on a review of the empirical data, we present a series of recommendations for the university press community designed to capitalize on the inherent competitive advantages of university presses.

Introduction

Since the early 1970s, there have been myriad articles, reports, and presentations at scholarly and professional conferences about "the crisis in scholarly communications."[1] Many individuals chastised university presses. They insisted that the "obvious" reduction in scholarly output by these presses placed the entire academic community at risk, since new faculty members could not get their monographs published, which adversely affected their ability to get hired, tenured, or promoted. Other observers blamed the "serials crisis," alleging that steep increases in journal subscription prices—especially in the science, technical, and medical (STM) fields—sapped library budgets, triggering a precipitous decline in the purchase of university press books. Still others accused university administrators of failing to provide the research support, travel budgets, and reduced teaching loads critically necessary to support first-rate research.

While all of these opinions and concerns have merit, very few individuals have studied the actual market for university press books in the United States. In this article we will (a) evaluate the published literature; (b) review a variety of data sets covering the years 1997 through 2002 published by the Book Industry Study Group, Inc. (BISG), in their annual series *Book Industry Trends*, as well as data from the US Department of Commerce to analyze the actual market for university press books (all totals are in US dollars); and (c) address the following questions:

1) Was there, during this period, a substantive shift in the market for university press books?
2) Were there changes in the general reader market (i.e., the trade book market for educated readers) during those years?
3) Did Internet bookselling sites cut into frontlist sales?
4) Did the creation of library electronic reserve (E-RES) systems affect university presses?
5) What steps can be taken to strengthen the role of university presses in the academic community?

Review of the Literature

Most of the recent marketing and econometric research has centered on "value chains," supply and demand, pricing, competition, and distribution issues.

"Value chains" (i.e., the collection of various activities in a firm that permits it to compete within an industry) have received a significant amount of attention by scholars. Michael Porter maintains that "companies' strategies for competing in an industry can differ in a variety of ways." These include specialization; brand identification; channel selection; product quality; cost position; and price policy.[2] David Walters and Mark Rainbird stress the "micro approach," specifically the need to reduce expenditures in the management of "value chains."[3]

Abdullah Al-Mudimigh, Mohamed Zairir, and Abdel Moneim Ahmed analysed the merits and limitation of the supply-side management of value chains, developing a model emphasizing corporate agility and speed in creating effective competitive advantages.[4] John Humphrey and Hubert Schmitz, as well as Claus Steinle and Holger Schiele, have investigated the potential impact of "corporate clustering" as a competitive strategy.[5]

Other researchers, including Jeffrey Dubin, have used empirical research techniques to study the shifting nature of supply and demand.[6] Jacek Cukrowski and Ernest Aksen investigated the relationship between perfect competition and trade issues.⁷ Kostas Axarloglou studied the impact of cyclicality and new product introduction.⁸

Market demand issues have been evaluated by a number of researchers. Corrado Benassi, Alessandra Chirco, and Marcella Scrimitore analyzed the theoretical relationships between income concentration levels and market demand.⁹ Benassi and Chirco also evaluated the impact of personal income and market demand.¹⁰ Auke Leen provides a historical overview of key market demand development.¹¹ Rod Combs investigated the relationship between emerging technologies and market demand.¹²

A number of university press directors have offered their opinions about the changing state of scholarly publishing. Jack Goellner studied the financial issues plaguing libraries and the concomitant impact on the entire scholarly publishing community: "For book publishers, not only did the library pie get smaller, but the slice for books got narrower."¹³ Marsh Jeanneret describes the business model he inherited at the University of Toronto Press, which was based essentially on using profits from its general publishing and printing programs, as well as research grants (i.e., subventions), to support the publication of important scholarly books. "Perhaps I should have perceived the unsoundness of this formula from the outset, but I did not. Its principal weakness was that it failed to link future levels of scholarly publishing to the possible needs of research writing in the future."¹⁴ August Fruge directed the University of California Press during a period of impressive growth, yet he had to confront economic and marketing issues. He writes candidly, "We concentrated on Farquhar's small book program and tried to make it into a first-rate scholarly press."¹⁵

Communications scholars have also contributed to the published literature. Walter Powell describes the intricate and pivotal relationship between financial and marketing considerations at university presses: "However much authors may regret it, the fact is that publishing is not an eleemosynary institution."¹⁶

Robin Peek and Gregory Newby investigated the impact of technology on scholarly communications, pondering how publishing could change because of the electronic dissemination of content.¹⁷ Jason Epstein also stresses the inevitable impact of technology, especially print-on-demand, on publishing.¹⁸ Thomas Ehrmann, Floria Haas, and Rainer Harms analyzed the importance of e-commerce in the online book market, which, they argue, "assumes a vital role in the strategic management of most enterprises"—issues also addressed by Alexis Weedon.¹⁹

Albert Greco evaluated marketing practices and procedures, offering an overview for researchers of trade and university press books.[20]

A number of academics have studied the shifting terrain of the book as a "cultural" or "commercial" endeavor, issues that permeate numerous discussions in the university press community. Jacques Barzun's study on reading books, and the various obstacles facing readers, provides a historical overview of the "multiple satisfactions that come from getting to know the contents of another mind through the channel of a printed work."[21] Michael Robinson and Ray Olszewski's work on books in the marketplace of ideas and "mechanisms that can promote entry while not disrupting efficient market operations" builds on earlier econometric and book publishing theories, notably their nuanced theories regarding whether the publishing "industry's structure unduly restricts new authors' ability to publish."[22] Powell addresses the thorny issue of competition in the book trade, which he agreed has a "current urgency." But he argues that "many of today's complaints are not new," deflating the positions of Ben Bagdikian and others.[23] Ann Haugland analyzed theories "about books as culture and books as mass market commodities," deciding that scholars and industry experts "cannot ignore the importance of the commercial concerns of the industry."[24] Joseph Moran maintains that electronic commerce has the potential to create a shift in "power" and "influence" away from the conglomerates toward smaller publishers eager to locate serious readers; "the growth of interactive multimedia may also encourage publishers to develop forms of promotion that locate different types of readership more exactly."[25]

Laura Miller investigated the modern bookseller who, "aided by the latest technology, provides independent-minded readers with an extensive choice of reading material," an issue of concern to university press authors and publishers.[26] Nina Ziv, who analyzed the organizational structure of the book industry, insists that modern technologies and bookselling outlets "will ultimately enable the industry to regenerate its businesses, reach a new generation of readers, and create an environment that is more conducive to innovation."[27]

The best study of the book publishing industry, and of the debate between the "cultural" and "commercial" mission of book publishing, remains Lewis Coser, Charles Kadushin, and Walter Powell's classic *Books: The Culture and Commerce of Publishing*.[28] While the book is based on an analysis of substantive sociological and economic issues in the late 1970s and early 1980s, the authors frame the issues that have broadened our understanding of the various missions of book publishers.

The Market for University Press Books:
Net Publishers' Revenues Some Historical Background

An analysis of BISG's university press net publishers' revenue data for 1985–96 makes it apparent that between 1985 and 1996, total revenues hovered near the $3.6 billion mark; the entire U.S. book industry topped $185.9 billion during those same years.

In 1985, university presses generated $182.5 million in net publishers' revenues, accounting for a 1.78-percent share of the U.S. book market. Double-digit results were generated in four of the next five years. The pace of the late 1980s flattened in the 1990s, paralleling trends in the broader U.S. book marketplace. Yet the results for 1990 (+2 percent), 1991 (+2.02 percent), and 1992 (+2.08 percent) were still striking. After a dip in 1993, the presses experienced a period of uneven growth patterns: flat in 1993, up in 1994 and 1995, and down somewhat in 1996.

Overall, university press net publishers' revenues were up 113.7 percent between 1985 and 1997, outpacing the performance of the entire book industry (+100.08 percent). Table 1 outlines these trends.

Table 1
Total University Press Net Publishers' Revenues, 1985–96

Year	University press revenues ($ million)	Percent change	U.S. book industry revenues ($ million)	Percent change	University press market share of U.S. book industry
1985	182.5	–	10,280.9	–	1.78
1986	204.0	11.78	10,860.3	5.64	1.88
1987	219.2	7.45	11,897.1	9.55	1.84
1988	245.0	11.77	13,008.3	9.34	1.88
1989	275.6	12.49	14,501.3	11.48	1.90
1990	305.7	10.92	15,278.7	5.36	2.00
1991	325.0	6.31	16,062.8	5.13	2.02
1992	350.0	7.69	16,850.6	4.90	2.08
1993	350.0	0.00	17,949.5	6.52	1.95
1994	370.0	5.71	18,767.8	4.56	1.97
1995	385.0	4.05	19,827.1	5.64	1.94
1996	390.0	1.30	20,570.3	3.75	1.90
1985–96	3602.0	113.70	185,854.7	100.08	1.94

Source: Book Industry Study Group, Book Industry Trends, various years. All numbers have been rounded and may not add up to 100 percent.

Revenues in 1997–2002

Between 1997 and 1999, press revenues totalled $1.28 billion. In 2000, however, the upward trend evident since 1985 flattened out, with no increase in revenues. Negative numbers were tallied in 2001 (-1.56 percent), and the data for 2002 were up only 0.23 percent. Overall, the presses experienced a 1.33 percent decline between 2000 and 2002 (during this same period, the U.S. book industry posted a 6.07 percent growth rate). In addition, the university press share of the total book market declined to 1.7 percent by 2002. Overall, the university press total of $2.62 billion accounted for 1.84 percent of all U.S. book revenues ($142.3 billion) during those six years. Table 2 outlines these trends.

We have included some macroeconomic datasets in the Appendices for readers interested in comparing changes in the U.S. economy between 1985 and 2002. Appendix 1 lists data on the Consumer Price Index (CPI) for 1985 through 2002, with annual percentage changes and the value of the US dollar in constant 2002 dollars. Appendix 2 lists actual university press net publishers' revenues (for 1985 through 2002) as well as net publishers' revenues in constant 2002 dollars. Appendix 3 lists gross domestic product (GDP) data in actual dollars and constant 2002 dollars for 1985 through 2002.

Channels of Distribution

University press books are sold through a variety of channels: (1) the export market; (2) general retailers (e.g., chain and independent bookstores); (3) university and college bookstores (i.e., course adoptions);

Table 2
Total University Press Net Publishers' Revenues, 1997–2002

Year	University press revenues ($ million)	Percent change	U.S. book industry revenues ($ million)	Percent change	University press market share of U.S. book industry
1997	400.0	2.56	20,972.7	1.96	1.91
1998	430.0	7.50	22,340.6	6.52	1.92
1999	450.0	4.65	23,758.6	6.35	1.89
2000	450.0	0.00	24,577.2	3.45	1.83
2001	443.0	-1.56	24,564.0	-0.05	1.80
2002	444.0	0.23	26,068.2	6.12	1.70
1997–2002	2,617.0	11.00	142,281.3	24.30	1.84

Source: Book Industry Study Group, *Book Industry Trends*, various years.

(4) libraries and institutions; (5) high school adoptions; (6) direct to consumers (via e-mail, fax, catalogues, Web sites, toll-free numbers, direct mailings, etc.); and (7) "other" sales (i.e., any sale that cannot be categorized into one of the channels listed above).

University press books, both hardbound and paperback, are adopted for classroom use by college and university instructors. In the college bookstore world, a "college adoption" refers to any book required for student use in a junior or community college, a four-year college or university, or a graduate or professional school. So any university press book, whether it is a traditional 800-page economics textbook or a biography of Emily Dickinson, that is required for a course is viewed as a "textbook" by college bookstore personnel.

This fact posed a methodological problem for our study, since there was no way to ascertain whether a specific book sold in the college bookstore channel was a "textbook." Our review of various data sets, as well as discussions and visits with publishers and industry experts, indicated that very few university presses publish traditional "textbooks." Yankee Book Peddler (YBP), a major distributor of university press books to libraries, estimates that no more than 8 percent of all university press titles are traditional textbooks. So we assumed that the vast majority of net dollars and net units generated in this channel were from scholarly frontlist and backlist cloth and paperback books rather than from "textbooks."

Between 1997 and 2000, the university press community experienced steady growth rates in every channel. Exports increased 15.1 percent, just eclipsing the pace of general retailers (+14.79 percent) and college bookstores (+14.77 percent). Libraries and institutions were up 15.61 percent, high schools were up 15.07 percent, and sales directly to consumers were up +14.61 percent. The amorphous "other" category also increased (+15 percent). However, total net revenues by channel sagged in every channel by 2001. Table 3 outlines these trends.

Hardbound Books

We analyzed the markets for hardbound and paperback books separately. The pattern described above is clearly evident in the hardbound sector. Between 1997 and 2000, total sales increased 12.99 percent; exports kept pace, with a 13.04 percent growth rate. As for domestic sales, general retailers (+12.96 percent), colleges (+12.97 percent), libraries (+12.88 percent), high schools (+14.63 percent), and sales directly to consumers (+13 percent) were all on the upswing. In 2001, slippage was evident in every channel, depressing the gains of 1997–2000. Data for

Table 3
Total University Press Net Publishers' Revenues by Channel of Distribution, 1997–2002

Channels of distribution	1997 ($ million)	1998 ($ million)	1999 ($ million)	2000 ($ million)	2001 ($ million)	2002 ($ million)	Percent change 1997–2002
All sales	400.0	430.0	450.0	460.0	443.0	444.0	11.00
Export sales	51.0	54.8	57.2	58.7	56.6	56.7	11.18
Domestic sales (Total)	349.0	375.2	392.8	401.2	386.4	387.3	10.97
General Retailers	92.6	99.6	103.8	106.3	102.4	102.6	10.80
College bookstores	96.8	104.1	108.6	111.1	107.0	107.3	10.85
Libraries and institutions	105.7	113.6	119.8	122.2	117.5	117.7	11.35
High schools	7.3	7.8	8.2	8.4	8.0	8.1	10.96
Direct to consumers	44.5	47.9	49.9	51.0	49.3	49.4	11.01
Other	2.0	2.2	2.4	2.3	2.2	2.1	5.00

Source: Book Industry Study Group, *Book Industry Trends 2003*. All numbers have been rounded and may not add up to 100 percent.

Table 4
Hardbound University Press Net Publishers' Revenues by Channel of Distribution, 1997–2002

Channels of distribution	1997 ($ million)	1998 ($ million)	1999 ($ million)	2000 ($ million)	2001 ($ million)	2002 ($ million)	Percent change 1997–2002
All sales	193.2	207.7	217.4	218.3	214.5	214.5	11.02
Export sales	27.6	29.7	31.0	31.2	30.7	30.7	11.23
Domestic sales (Total)	165.6	178.0	186.4	187.1	183.8	183.8	10.99
General retailers	35.5	38.2	39.9	40.1	39.4	39.4	10.99
College bookstores	34.7	37.3	38.9	39.2	38.5	38.5	10.95
Libraries and institutions	68.3	73.4	76.9	77.1	75.8	75.8	10.98
High schools	4.1	4.4	4.6	4.7	4.8	4.6	12.20
Direct to consumers	22.3	24.0	25.1	25.2	24.8	24.8	11.21
Other	0.7	0.8	0.8	0.8	0.8	0.7	0.00

Source: Book Industry Study Group, *Book Industry Trends 2003*. All numbers have been rounded and may not add up to 100 percent.

2001 and 2002 are, in essence, identical because of rounding. See Table 4 for an outline of these events.

Paperback Books

A similar pattern is evident in university press paperback books between 1997 and 2002. Sharp growth rates were recorded across the board between 1997 and 2000. Starting in 2001, either no growth or flat rates are evident (again, because of rounding, the tallies for 2001 and 2002 are remarkably close). Paperbacks avoided the steep declines of cloth books during these years, however. Table 5 outlines these trends.

Clearly, the shift in the market for university press books was not confined to only one sector. This is a troubling development, since the big three channels (general retailers, college bookstores, and the library market) all posted declines. Softness in the market could be traced to a number of tribulations, including the impact of the Internet stock market bubble, the recession, a decline in consumer confidence, and the September 11 attack on the United States. Other possible factors include an overabundance of books in the marketplace, higher than normal return rates, library cutbacks, or consumer/end-user indifference toward the available titles.

Table 5
Paperbound University Press Net Publishers' Revenues by
Channel of Distribution, 1997–2002

Channels of distribution	1997 ($ million)	1998 ($ million)	1999 ($ million)	2000 ($ million)	2001 ($ million)	2002 ($ million)	Percent change 1997–2002
All sales	206.8	222.3	232.6	231.7	228.5	229.5	10.98
Export sales	19.5	21.0	21.7	21.7	21.6	21.7	11.28
Domestic sales (Total)	187.3	201.3	210.9	210.0	206.9	207.8	10.95
General retailers	69.2	74.4	78.0	77.7	76.5	76.6	10.69
College bookstores	78.0	83.8	88.0	87.5	86.1	86.6	11.03
Libraries and institutions	15.0	16.1	17.0	16.9	16.5	16.6	10.67
High schools	2.4	2.7	2.7	2.7	2.6	2.7	12.50
Direct to consumers	21.1	22.6	23.3	23.4	23.3	23.4	10.90
Other	1.6	1.7	1.9	1.8	1.8	1.8	12.50

Source: Book Industry Study Group, *Book Industry Trends 2003*. All numbers have been rounded and may not add up to 100 percent.

In essence, it is impossible to ascertain whether only one of these explanations triggered the declines in hardcover and paper net revenues. In reality, the weakening in the university press revenue stream was probably caused by a combination of all of these variables.

The Market for University Press Books: Net Publisher Units

Publishers pay their bills in dollars; but net publishers' unit data reveal the real state of any publishing operation. Were there corresponding drops in net publishers' units between 1997 and 2002?

Our review of the data revealed an erosion in unit sales of university press books. The peak year for total net publisher units was 1999; a downward spiral emerged in 2000, one full year before any softness in net publishers' dollars was evident.

There was an across-the-board decline in total university press units in every channel. Total net units declined 3.13 percent between 1999 and 2000; exports dipped 7.14 percent. General retailers (-2.86 percent), college bookstores (-4.26 percent), and libraries (-1.92 percent) posted declines; the other categories were flat. Table 6 outlines these trends.

Table 6
Total University Press Net Publishers' Units by
Channel of Distribution, 1997–2002

Channels of distribution	1997 (millions of units)	1998 (millions of units)	1999 (millions of units)	2000 (millions of units)	2001 (millions of units)	2002 (millions of units)	Percent change 1997–2002
All sales	28.3	29.7	32.0	31.0	29.5	28.5	0.71
Export sales	3.5	3.7	4.2	3.9	3.8	3.6	2.86
Domestic sales (Total)	24.8	26.0	27.8	27.1	25.7	24.9	0.40
General retailers	9.6	10.0	10.5	10.2	9.8	9.7	1.04
College bookstores	8.6	9.1	9.4	9.0	8.7	8.4	-2.33
Libraries and institutions	4.4	4.6	5.2	5.1	4.7	4.5	2.27
High schools	0.3	0.3	0.5	0.5	0.4	0.3	0.00
Direct to consumers	1.6	1.7	1.9	1.9	1.8	1.6	0.00
Other	0.3	0.3	0.4	0.3	0.3	0.3	0.00

Source: Book Industry Study Group, *Book Industry Trends 2003.* All numbers have been rounded and may not add up to 100 percent.

The Changing Market for University Press Books in the United States 59

Table 7
Hardbound University Press Net Publishers' Units by Channel of Distribution, 1997–2002

Channels of distribution	1997 (millions of units)	1998 (millions of units)	1999 (millions of units)	2000 (millions of units)	2001 (millions of units)	2002 (millions of units)	Percent change 1997–2002
All sales	8.6	9.0	9.7	9.5	9.0	8.7	1.16
Export sales	1.2	1.3	1.4	1.3	1.3	1.3	8.33
Domestic Sales (Total)	7.4	7.7	8.3	8.2	7.7	7.4	0.00
General retailers	2.3	2.5	2.6	2.6	2.5	2.4	4.35
College bookstores	1.3	1.4	1.5	1.5	1.4	1.3	0.00
Libraries and institutions	2.7	2.8	3.1	3.0	2.8	2.7	0.00
High schools	0.2	0.2	0.3	0.3	0.2	0.2	0.00
Direct to consumers	0.6	0.7	0.7	0.7	0.7	0.7	16.67
Other	0.1	0.1	0.1	0.1	0.1	0.1	0.00

Source: Book Industry Study Group, *Book Industry Trends 2003.* All numbers have been rounded and may not add up to 100 percent.

Hardbound Books

The pattern for hardbound books was uneven. All sales increased 12.79 percent between 1997 and 1999, and then units declined steadily through 2002, dropping 10.31 percent between 1999 and 2002. This pattern was evident in overall domestic sales (-10.84 percent), college sales (-13.33 percent), and sales to libraries and institutions (-12.9 percent); the other categories posted flat results. Table 7 outlines these trends.

Paperbound Books

Paperbacks, long the backbone of the college adoption market, showed the steepest declines. All sales were up 13.2 percent between 1997 and 1999; then units declined 11.21 percent between 1999 and 2002. Between 1997 and 2002, exports sagged (-4.35 percent), as did the totals for direct sales to consumers (-10 percent). The other channels generated small increases or were flat. Table 8 highlights these trends.

What happened to the sale of university press books in almost every channel of distribution?

Table 8
Paperbound University Press Net Publishers' Units by Channel of Distribution, 1997–2002

Channels of distribution	1997 (millions of units)	1998 (millions of units)	1999 (millions of units)	2000 (millions of units)	2001 (millions of units)	2002 (millions of units)	Percent change 1997–2002
All sales	19.7	20.7	22.3	21.5	20.8	19.8	0.51
Export sales	2.3	2.3	2.7	2.5	2.5	2.2	-4.35
Domestic sales (Total)	17.4	18.4	19.6	19.0	18.3	17.6	1.15
General retailers	7.3	7.9	8.2	7.9	7.7	7.5	2.74
College bookstores	7.5	8.0	8.4	8.1	8.0	7.7	2.67
Libraries and institutions	1.2	1.3	1.4	1.4	1.3	1.2	0.00
High schools	0.1	0.1	0.2	0.2	0.1	0.1	0.00
Direct to consumers	1.0	0.9	1.2	1.1	1.0	0.9	-10.00
Other	0.2	0.2	0.2	0.2	0.2	0.2	0.00

Source: Book Industry Study Group, *Book Industry Trends 2003*. All numbers have been rounded and may not add up to 100 percent.

An Analysis of Some of the Channels of Distribution

Export Books

University presses publish important books, many of which have export sales potential; but this is an exceptionally difficult market to penetrate. Commercial presses have full-time sales representatives touring important export markets in Europe and the Pacific Rim once or, more commonly, twice a year. Few university presses have sales representatives of their own visiting these markets; instead, the vast majority relies on independent sales reps (often representing a cluster of university presses) to sell their books abroad, which is not the most effective way to tap into this market.

Of course, currency conversion rates can pose serious problems. When, for example, the U.S. dollar rises against the Philippine peso, exports to the Philippines decline. The "Asian currency contagion" (the banking and currency financial crisis that gripped Japan, Indonesia, and most of the Pacific Rim in 1997) undermined sales to many nations in the Pacific Rim and Asia in the late 1990s.

Some of these problems are clearly beyond the control of university presses; but it is possible that the entire university press community has the cumulative means to craft an innovative marketing campaign to try to penetrate an exceptionally important channel of distribution for all publishers, big and small. While additional research on this issue is needed, we believe this market has the potential to make up for slippage in the domestic market, for the following reasons: (1) English is the international language in a number of academic fields; (2) a sizable number of American academics have developed sophisticated research projects in the sciences (areas of great interest abroad); and (2) there have been impressive and innovative research studies in many areas of the humanities and social sciences (again, areas of interest abroad).

High Schools and Direct Sales to Consumers

The high school book market must be considered. Public schools rarely rely on university press books; however, many independent (i.e., "private") schools use university press books in various courses in the humanities and social sciences. A coordinated marketing campaign, combined with attendance at the annual meeting of the National Association of Independent Schools (NAIS), could stimulate sales in this burgeoning market.

The direct-to-consumer sector is primed for growth. Clearly, Internet sales of books have increased sharply since 1997; and catalogues, fax, and toll-free numbers offer opportunities. A coordinated university press campaign in these four sub-markets could mine an important but sagging form of distribution.

General Retailers

Throughout the 1980s and 1990s, many university presses believed that the general reader market was "the market of the future"; as a result, they shifted financial and editorial resources to develop consumer (i.e., adult trade) book lines.

This strategy paid off for a cluster of presses. However, a seismic shift in the marketplace took place in the 1980s and 1990s. The wide acceptance of cable television and VCRs in the 1980s and the emergence of the Internet, satellite television, and DVDs in the 1990s triggered a substantive shift in entertainment usage and expenditure patterns. The end result was a decline in consumer book usage (i.e., hours per person per year). The average individual over the age of 18 spent 123 hours reading consumer books in 1996. In the years that followed years, the number of hours declined steadily, reaching 109 in 2002 (down 11.38 percent). The prognosis for the years 2003 through 2006 is equally unsettling, and additional declines are anticipated. Table 9 outlines this trend.

Table 9
Consumer (Trade) Book Usage, 1996–2006

Year	Consumer book usage (hours per person per year)	Percent change from previous year	Percent of total media usage
1996	123	–	3.67
1997	118	-4.07	3.55
1998	118	0	3.55
1999	119	0.85	3.48
2000	109	-8.4	3.12
2001	106	-2.75	2.99
2002	109	-2.83	3.02
2003	108	-0.92	2.95
*2004	107	-0.93	2.85
*2005	106	-0.93	2.78
*2006	106	0	2.72
*2007	105	-0.94	2.66
*2008	104	-0.95	2.56
1996–2002	-11.38%	–	–
2003–8	-1.8%	–	–

Source: Veronis Suhler Stevenson, *Communications Industry Forecast 2004–2008* (New York: Veronis Suhler Stevenson 2004), 55.

* Indicates estimate. All numbers have been rounded and may not add up to 100 percent.

Table 10
Consumer (Trade) Book Expenditures, 1996–2006

Year	Consumer book expenditures (dollars per person per year)	Percent change from previous year	Percent of total media expenditures
1996	80.98	–	16.09
1997	80.54	-0.54	15.18
1998	82.75	2.74	14.62
1999	87.34	5.55	14.33
2000	86.13	-1.39	13.63
2001	84.45	-1.95	12.44
2002	87.51	3.62	11.86
2003	89.68	2.48	11.53
*2004	90.30	0.69	10.94
*2005	91.49	1.32	10.50
*2006	92.72	1.34	10.06
*2007	93.02	0.32	9.55
*2008	93.70	0.73	9.10
1996–2002	7.46%	–	–
2003–8	5.40%	–	–

Source: Veronis Suhler Stevenson, *Communications Industry Forecast 2004–2008* (New York: Veronis Suhler Stevenson 2004), 53.

* Indicates estimate. All numbers have been rounded and may not add up to 100 percent.

Consumer book expenditures, on the other hand, were up 7.46 percent between 1996 and 2002, with projected increases for 2003 through 2006. The increases in dollars compensated for (and partially hid) declines in unit sales, a fact readily evident in the data published in *Book Industry Trends*. Table 10 outlines these trends.

College Bookstores

A review of data released by the National Center for Education Statistics indicates the potential for real growth in the college and university bookstore sector.[29] Undergraduate enrolments were up 7.88 percent between 1997 and 2002, with graduate schools lagging slightly at 6.39 percent. Table 11 outlines these trends.

Starting in the late 1990s, and readily evident by 2002, the sale of university press backlist books posted declines because of two unrelated events.

First, a review of the data from the National Association of College Stores (NACS) reveals that departmental gross margins are higher for used texts (on average 34.4 percent) than for new textbooks (22.93 percent). Used books accounted for $1.6 billion (20.51 percent) of all college bookstore sales in 2001/2. Our conversations with college bookstore representatives and publishing leaders indicate conclusively that additional growth in used texts is anticipated. Table 12 outlines this trend.

Second, the prevailing consensus of college bookstore representatives and the publishing community is that a newly published required book for college or graduate school students has a sell-through rate of 90 percent

Table 11
Total College and Graduate School Enrolments, 1997–2002

Year	Undergraduate (thousands)	Graduate (thousands)	Total higher education enrolment (thousands)
1997	12,451	1,753	14,502
1998	12,437	1,768	14,507
1999	12,681	1,807	14,791
2000	13,155	1,850	15,312
2001	13,278	1,852	15,442
2002	13,432	1,865	15,608
Percent change 1997–2002	7.88	6.39	7.63

Source: U.S. Department of Commerce, Economics and Statistics Division, Bureau of the Census, *The Statistical Abstract of the United States: 2004–2005* (Washington, DC: GPO 2004), 136. All numbers have been rounded and may not add up to 100 percent.

Table 12
College Bookstore Market Financial Data, 2001–2

Departmental gross margins

	Average	25th percentile	Median	75th percentile
New textbooks	22.93	20.01	22.90	25.73
Custom-published materials	25.49	19.54	23.90	30.51
Used textbooks	34.40	31.30	34.85	37.73
Total course "books"	26.11	23.10	25.70	28.41
General trade books	28.04	22.82	28.59	34.20

College bookstore market

	Total revenues
All course materials	$7.8 billion
General/trade books	$378 million
Student supplies	$611 million
Computer products	$849 million
Insignia merchandise	$552 million

Textbook/course pack market

	Total revenues	Percent of total revenues
New textbooks	$6.1 billion	78.21
Used textbooks	$1.6 billion	20.51
Course packs	$100 million	1.28
Total course materials	$7.8 billion	100

Source: The National Association of College Stores, *http://www.nacs.org*. All numbers have been rounded and may not add up to 100 percent.

in the first year, dropping to 45 percent in the second year and only 10 percent in the third year. Some students will not buy a required book; two or more students sometimes purchase one copy of a book and share it (or make copies of the entire book and share the copies).

Both these events have affected university sales, especially the emergence of a sophisticated, nationally coordinated used book network able to supply used books to college and commercial bookstores.

The Emergence of the Used Book Channel

Starting in 2000, we conducted a series of discussions with a cross-section of book publishers. One intriguing thread emerged during many of those interviews and discussions: backlist sales were either flat or down. At first, we attributed sales fluctuations to the impact of the economic climate. Many academics and general readers purchase books, including university press books, with discretionary income. Data related to previous recessions in the late 1980s and early 1990s show that consumers reduced their expenditures on certain items whenever a recession hung over the nation or there was a decline in consumer confidence levels (as measured by the University of Michigan's monthly surveys).[30]

One publisher mentioned that several books not yet published by her press were available on used book sites. She believed that these sites were involved in a "futures" market. Presses release title information prior to a book's publication date; this publisher maintained that these used book sites had obtained this information and were offering the books prior to the publication date, at new and used prices, to gauge the potential market for specific titles. The Internet retailers would then obtain copies if consumers indicated an interest in purchasing a specific title.

We visited a number of commercial (i.e., non-university) bookstores in several major metropolitan markets (including New York/New Jersey, Boston/Cambridge, Chicago, Kansas City, and San Francisco) to determine the availability of books in several specific book categories: business, economics, U.S. history, and sociology. We often found new and used books placed side by side on shelves, and we discovered that many of these stores also purchased used books. We then surveyed a number of college bookstores in the same metropolitan areas, again scanning the shelves for books, and again we discovered a number of used books.

We discussed the used book market with representatives from three used book companies. Their *modus operandi* was intriguing. They called on faculty members to inquire if they had any books for sale. Using handheld computers programmed with ISBNs and prices, they scanned each book's ISBN, determined the value of the book, and recorded its price. They paid cash for any book they purchased, and no receipt was given to record the purchase.

A Study of Internet Bookselling Sites

We decided to undertake a systematic study of the Internet's new and used frontlist bookselling sites to ascertain their impact on university press book sales.

We visited www.Amazon.com, www.BN.com, and several dozen other Web sites and ran a few titles though their "regular" (i.e., not the used book) sites. We found many new titles offered for sale as "used" books within days of their publication date. We then clicked onto the www.Amazon.com used book site and typed "university press books" into the search engine; more than 1,000 used university press books were listed for sale.

We compiled a complete list of all university presses in North America. We deleted all presses not affiliated with a university in Canada or the United States (e.g., presses that are part of a museum or a research think tank). We selected at random seven of these presses, which we identified as university presses A, B, C, D, E, F, and G. Six of these presses were in the United States and one in Canada; two of the seven were at private universities. Based on our review of North American university presses, we created a list of four press categories (very large, large, medium, and small); our sample of seven presses included no very large presses; four large presses; two medium-sized presses; and one small press.

The randomness of the selection process, and the sizes and affiliations of the seven presses, indicate that they constitute a representative sample of all North American university presses.

We collected a complete master list of all new frontlist cloth and paperback books (each title with a unique ISBN) published by these seven presses during the spring of 2001 (348 books) and the spring of 2002 (369 titles), for a total of 717 titles. A book issued in a split run (i.e., in both cloth and paperback formats) was counted as two titles, since each book had a unique ISBN; both formats were analyzed in the study.

The master lists were compiled in March 2001 (for the spring 2001 list) and March 2002 (for the spring 2002 list). Since a whole list is never released at the same time, we ran the titles through Internet Shopbots (a computerized shopping robot service) in mid-March 2001 (for the spring 2001 list) and mid- to late March 2002 (for the Spring 2002 list) to determine both new and used prices for all new frontlist cloth and paperback books at the various Internet bookselling sites. Not every university press book in our study was found on every site, and not every new frontlist book was available at used prices on these sites. All of the data were aggregated and analyzed using the analysis of variance (ANOVA) procedure, (which analyzes the variance within a data set).

Our research indicated that some new frontlist books had been on the market for up to three months; others had been on the market for a matter of weeks; and some were yet to be released (though some appeared as "futures"). This allowed us to gauge the rapidity with which used new frontlist books were becoming available in the marketplace.

The use of Shopbots to study bookselling is a well-established market research procedure. Karen Clay, Ramayya Krishnan, and Eric Wolff investigated the prices of 399 books available at various online bookstores between August 1999 and January 2000. Their research revealed that "more competition led to lower prices and to lower price dispersion."[31] In another study, Clay, Krishnan, and Danny Fernandes addressed issues related to the impact of information on book prices at both online sites and traditional bookstores. "Using data collected in April 1999 on the prices of 107 books in thirteen online and two physical bookstores," they write, "we find similar average prices online and in physical stores and substantive price dispersion online."[32]

Michael D. Smith and Erik Brynjolfsson investigated online bookselling patterns at thirty-three online sites over a sixty-nine-day period. "Although each retailer offers a homogenous product," they write, "we find that brand is an important determinant of consumer choice.... In particular, we find that consumers use brand as a proxy for retailer credibility in non-contractible aspects of the product and service bundle, such as shipping reliability."[33]

The Results: 2001 Frontlist Titles

The Shopbots generated data on the 2001 frontlist books from a number of Internet sites, including A1 Books (www.a1books.com), Amazon.com, Alphacraze (www.alphacraze.com), 1Bookstreet (www.1bookstreet.com), Barnes & Noble (www.barnesandnoble.com), BooksAMillion (www.booksamillion.com), Buy.com, ClassBooks.com, Ecampus.com, FatBrain.com, Half.com, PageOne.com, Powell's (www.powells.com), TextbookX.com, and Wal-Mart (www.walmart.com).

On average, the prices of new university press books on the Internet sites were 6 percent lower that the suggested retail price (SRP). Taking into account the cost of shipping and handling (S&H), however, the prices on the Internet were 7 percent higher than the SRP. See Table 13 for a complete list of these sites and detailed information about the data.

Significant variations in new book prices were evident across Internet booksellers, and major variations in new book prices were observed across publishers. The heaviest Internet discounting was on books published by Press E. See Table 14 for details.

We also analyzed the discount rate for 473 authors. These rates differed significantly, but no apparent pattern was discovered. While data on specific authors were collected, we cannot release this data, since the authors and the presses could then be identified.

Sales taxes were not computed because (1) not every Internet site studied is legally obligated to charge and remit sales taxes and (2) sales taxes vary significantly from one location to another. Since it was patently

Table 13
Average Ratio of Internet Price to Suggested Retail Price (SRP), 2001

Internet outlet*	Price / SRP	(Price + S&H) / SRP	S&H / price (percent)
A1 Books	0.90 (0.14)**	1.05 (0.13)	17 (8)
Amazon.com	0.96 (0.33)	1.12 (0.34)	17 (9)
Alphacraze	0.91 (0.14)	1.05 (0.14)	16 (7)
1 Bookstreet	1.05 (0.16)	1.05 (0.16)	0 (1)
Barnes & Noble.com	0.97 (0.06)	1.10 (0.08)	13 (6)
Books A Million	0.88 (0.12)	1.03 (0.12)	17 (9)
Buy.com	0.92 (0.12)	1.04 (0.12)	13 (6)
ClassBooks.com	1.00 (0.02)	1.12 (0.06)	12 (5)
Ecampus.com	0.77 (0.07)	0.90 (0.08)	18 (5)
FatBrain.com	0.98 (0.06)	1.11 (0.21)	14 (5)
Half.com	0.87 (0.22)	0.96 (0.10)	12 (10)
PageOne.com	0.82 (0.09)	1.10 (0.16)	34 (9)
Powell's	0.95 (0.14)	1.06 (0.10)	13 (8)
TextbookX.com	0.82 (0.10)	0.97 (0.10)	19 (7)
Wal-Mart	0.75 (0.07)	0.90 (0.12)	20 (8)

* Discount differences across sites were tested through ANOVA and found to be significant at $p < 0.01$.
** Numbers in parentheses are standard deviations.

Table 14
Average Ratio of Internet Price to SRP for Each University Press, 2001

University press*	Price / SRP	(Price + S&H) / SRP	S&H / price (percent)
A	1.43 (1.25)**	1.55	10
B	0.91 (0.10)	1.05	17
C	0.96 (0.30)	1.08	14
D	0.92 (0.08)	1.06	15
E	0.86 (0.12)	0.99	16
F	0.99 (0.09)	1.08	10
G	0.95 (0.11)	1.07	13

* Discount differences across publishers were tested through ANOVA and found to be significant at $p < 0.01$.
** Numbers in parentheses are standard deviations.

unfair to use one location as a barometer in calculating total costs, we disregarded all sales taxes.

However, taking into account the cost of S&H (which averaged 14.5 percent of the selling price), we observed no significant variations in discounting of new books as a function of format (cloth versus paperback). For used frontlist books, significant variations in Internet discounting were observed once the cost of S&H was included. On average, the book price was more heavily discounted for cloth books than for paperback books. See Table 15 for details.

The Results: 2002 Frontlist Titles

For 2002, prices for new university press books on the Internet were, on average, 7 percent lower than the SRP (see Table 16 for detailed information). Taking into consideration the cost of S&H, however, the net prices on the Internet were 3 percent higher than the SRP. Shipping and handling, on average, accounted for 12 percent of the price of the book.

Compared to 2001, higher levels of variation in the new book prices were evident across the Internet sites. The average new book discount (versus the SRP) ranged from 31 percent (at A1 Books) to 6 percent (at Barnes & Noble.com). Significant variations in new book prices were also observed across publishers. The heaviest Internet discounting occurred for presses C and G (average discount: 12 percent) and the least for presses A and F (average discount: 1 percent). Again, Internet discounts varied significantly across authors. See Table 17 for detailed data.

Table 15
Ratio of Internet Prices by Format (Cloth versus Paperback) for New and Used Frontlist Books, 2001

	Cloth	Paperback	Cloth versus paperback difference
New books			
Price / SRP	0.97	0.91	Significant at $p < 0.05$
(Price + S&H) / SRP	1.05	1.09	Not significant
S&H / Price	9%	20%	Significant at $p < 0.01$
Used books			
Price / SRP	0.77	0.76	Not significant
(Price + S&H) / SRP	0.88	0.98	Significant at $p < 0.01$
S&H / Price	16%	31%	Significant at $p < 0.01$

Table 16
Average Ratio of Internet Price to SRP, 2002

Internet outlet*	Price / SRP	(Price + S&H) / SRP	S&H / price (percent)
A1 Books	0.69 (0.04)**	0.86 (0.08)	26 (10%)
Amazon.com	0.93 (0.13)	1.07 (0.13)	15 (9)
Alphacraze	0.91 (0.10)	1.05 (0.11)	16 (8)
1 Bookstreet	N/A	N/A	N/A
Barnes & Noble.com	0.94 (0.12)	1.08 (0.14)	16 (10)
Books A Million	0.93 (0.12)	1.04 (0.13)	13 (11)
Buy.com	0.90 (0.16)	0.89 (0.09)	0 (0)
ClassBooks.com***	1.33	1.51	14
Ecampus.com	0.79 (0.10)	0.88 (0.09)	13 (8)
FatBrain.com	N/A	N/A	N/A
Half.com	0.89 (0.28)	0.98 (0.27)	13 (7)
PageOne.com	0.86 (0.10)	1.09 (0.11)	32 (9)
Powell's	0.92 (0.21)	1.07 (0.24)	16 (5)
TextbookX.com	0.80 (0.09)	0.92 (0.09)	18 (9)
Wal-Mart	N/A	N/A	N/A
BiggerBooks.com	0.77 (0.09)	0.88 (0.09)	16 (8)

* Discount differences across sites were tested through ANOVA and found to be significant at $p < 0.01$.
** Numbers in parentheses are standard deviations.
*** ClassBooks.com data are based on a limited number of observations.

Table 17
Average Ratio of Internet Price to SRP for Each University Press, 2002

University press	*Price / SRP	(Price + S&H) / SRP	S&H / price (percent)
A	0.99 (0.02)**	1.08	9
B	0.90 (0.12)	1.03	16
C	0.88 (0.11)	0.99	12
D	0.95 (0.13)	1.06	12
E	0.95 (0.08)	1.03	11
F	0.99 (0.01)	1.07	10
G	0.88 (0.14)	1.03	20

* Discount differences across publishers were tested through ANOVA and found to be significant at $p < 0.05$.
** Numbers in parentheses are standard deviations.

No significant variations in discounting of new books were observed as a function of format. However, statistically significant differences were evident when the cost of S&H was taken into account. In general, cloth books were found to be more heavily discounted when S&H was factored into the calculation.

For used new frontlist titles, significant variations in Internet discounting were observed. On average, taking into account S&H, the net selling price was more heavily discounted (versus the SRP) for cloth copies than for paperback books. This observation is consistent with the results observed for new books (see Table 18).

A detailed analysis of the seven presses revealed that the prices for used copies of new frontlist cloth books in 2001 and 2002 were competitive and, in some instances, highly competitive (excluding S&H), with three of the seven presses experiencing large discount rates. Table 19 provides detailed data on the new and used average prices for cloth books in 2001 and 2002.

Discount rates for paperback books in 2001 and 2002 were higher, overall, than cloth discounts during those same years. Table 20 outlines this trend.

We also analyzed data on the range of options available to consumers using online bookselling sites. Selecting one of the seven presses in the study at random, we identified the first five books (cloth or paperback) with both new and used frontlist titles in the spring 2001 list and the first five books (again, cloth or paperback) with both new and used frontlist titles in the spring 2002 list. The average SRP for these ten books was $48.45; the average used price for a new frontlist book at the sites list-

Table 18
Ratio of Internet Prices by Format (Cloth versus Paperback) for New and Used Frontlist Books, 2002

	Cloth	Paperback	Cloth versus paperback difference
New books			
Price / SRP	0.92	0.93	Not significant
(Price + S&H) / SRP	1.00	1.09	Significant at $p < 0.01$
S&H / price	8%	19%	Significant at $p < 0.01$
Used books			
Price / SRP	0.49	0.56	Not significant
(Price + S&H) / SRP	0.59	0.75	Significant at $p < 0.05$
S&H / price	19%	25%	Significant at $p < 0.01$

Table 19
University Press Sample of New and Used Cloth Prices, 2001 and 2002

Press	2001			2002		
	Average new cloth book prices (US$)	Average used book prices (US$)	Used price as a percentage of new book price	Average new cloth book prices (US$)	Average used book prices (US$)	Used price as a percentage of new book price
A	44.46	44.46	0	45.78	N/A	N/A
B	34.28	20.18	42	36.07	22.38	61
C	32.45	18.47	76	36.60	31.29	17
D	44.71	36.79	22	46.65	37.94	19
E	54.09	46.29	25	60.27	51.74	17
F	78.08	70.03	12	69.78	56.07	25
G	55.19	39.56	40	34.55	14.70	135

All percentages have been rounded and may not add up to 100 percent.

Table 20
University Press Sample of New and Used Paperback Prices, 2001 and 2002

Press	2001			2002		
	Average new cloth book prices (US$)	Average used book prices (US$)	Used price as a percentage of new book price	Average new cloth book prices (US$)	Average used book prices (US$)	Used price as a percentage of new book price
A	24.78	N/A	N/A	29.95	N/A	N/A
B	17.41	13.66	31	20.36	12.20	67
C	22.86	13.70	67	15.35	14.86	3
D	18.78	15.05	34	19.73	15.58	27
E	20.16	16.73	20	25.94	19.95	30
F	27.17	20.67	32	28.32	26.78	6
G	21.58	14.70	47	23.94	13.88	70

All percentages have been rounded and may not add up to 100 percent.

ing these ten titles was $37.58, a difference of 22 percent ($10.87). The sale of these ten titles as used books cost this press hundreds of dollars in lost revenues (see Table 21).

Our analysis of the data also indicates that used copies of new frontlist books were available relatively quickly after the books' publication dates. For example, by mid- to late March 2002, the following presses faced a deluge of used books flooding the market:

- Press B: 70 percent of new cloth books were available at used prices
- Press C: 23 percent of new cloth books and 50 percent of new paperback books were available at used prices
- Press E: 69 percent of new cloth books and 71 percent of new paperback books were available at used prices
- Press F: 53 percent of new cloth books and 36 percent of new paperback books were available at used prices
- Press G: 47 percent of new cloth books and 75 percent of new paperback books were available at used prices

The Electronic Reserves (E-RES) System

Libraries have used reserve reading systems for decades. Faculty members placed books, book chapters, and articles (along with other materials) on reserve; students could then sign out reserve materials for a limited period, perhaps a few hours, but could not remove them from either the reserve reading room or the library.

While this system worked, inherent restrictions limited its usefulness. Students could not access the materials they needed when the library was closed, and some students found it difficult to access the library, perhaps because of physical or geographical limitations or work requirements.

Table 21
Representative Sample of New and Used Cloth Frontlist Book Prices, 2001–2

Book category	SRP	Used price	Percentage difference
Psychology	55.00	42.95	22
Film Studies	70.00	51.00	27
African Studies	35.00	20.00	47
Economics	27.50	24.00	13
Political Science	55.00	25.00	55
Economics	35.00	21.50	39
Legal Studies	42.00	37.62	1
History	40.00	29.95	25
Women's Studies	65.00	64.35	1
Sociology	60.00	59.40	1
Ten-book average	48.45	37.58	22

Source: Average new and used prices at Amazon.com for the first ten books with new and used cloth frontlist books at one medium-sized press in our seven-press random survey. The S&H fee for new and used frontlist books was $4.48; if an order reached a fixed minimum dollar amount of $25, then S&H was free. All books in this cluster had free S&H. All numbers have been rounded off and may not add up to 100 percent.

The emergence of computer networks has changed the reserve system. Now a faculty member can place a book's chapter(s) or articles on "electronic reserve" (E-RES). The documents are scanned into a computer system, and students can access, read, and download any materials in the library on computer terminals or access the documents at any time from a remote location (an undergraduate student in a dorm room on campus, a graduate student 1,000 miles away from his or her university, etc.), assuming the student has agreed to comply with the copyright statement on the E-RES system.

Clearly, the landscape of research has changed positively, allowing students and faculty members unfettered access to a vast array of academic and research materials. Yet the "law of unexpected consequences" has emerged, as it often does. Since a faculty member can create an entire course using only E-RES, the potential impact of lost book sales is significant. However, the E-RES system is so new that empirical data on usage patterns do not exist. This new development merits close monitoring by the entire university press community.

Used Books and E-RES

Exceptionally sophisticated Internet sites, quickly stocked with new and used frontlist cloth and paperback books, provide value for students and consumers. Changes in the library reserve system have helped turn the library into a veritable twenty-four-hour, seven-days-a-week resource center that will be an invaluable boon to students and faculty members.

At the end of the day, however, the sale of used books at highly competitive prices is undermining frontlist, and ultimately decimating backlist, university press book sales; and the real impact of the E-RES system has yet to be ascertained.

One fact is known. Used book sales are sapping the ability of many presses to develop and maintain lists; and, inevitably, this means that fewer presses will have the resources needed to issue that pivotal monograph for an untenured assistant professor in the humanities or social sciences.

Conclusions and Recommendations

University presses publish substantive works that broaden our understanding of the world and enrich our appreciation for the diverse ideas and culture of our society and our world. It has been argued that a university press book (or a journal article published by a university press, for that matter) is "the coin of the realm" in academic circles, since these peer-reviewed publications are highly prized by authors and widely recognized by department chairs, deans, and provosts as critically important documents in the complex hiring, tenure, promotion, and merit pay evaluations of faculty.

It is also true that these presses compete in the marketplace of ideas for authors, manuscripts, and sales. All too frequently, this "tournament" involves competition with commercial academic publishers who have deep financial resources, cooperative marketing dollars, budgets for advertisements and author tours, and broad domestic and global distribution networks. Clearly, a struggle with commercial houses is inevitable for many university presses.

Based on our discussions, a review of the published literature, and a detailed analysis of various statistical data sets, we believe that university presses have a number of significant competitive advantages over commercial academic publishing houses; we also believe university presses should maximize these advantages.

Accordingly, we suggest that the university press community consider the following options (and also seek appropriate funding from foundations and university provosts):

1) Launch a series of seminars on college campuses (under the aegis of university press directors, librarians, and provosts) to highlight the role of university presses in the transmission of knowledge and to generate support for university presses, especially among provosts. The intended audiences include tenured and tenure-track faculty members; graduate students; academic administrators (department chairs, deans, provosts, etc.); and librarians. Possible workshop topics include

    - "the role university presses play in the publication of books in the humanities, the social sciences, and the mathematics/science areas."
    - "what university press editors look for in manuscripts in the humanities, social sciences, and mathematics/science areas."
    - "how to get your manuscript ready for a university press."
    - "the pivotal role of copyright protection for authors."
    - "the future of print and the electronic distribution of content."
    - "the economics of scholarly publishing," including the costs associated with plant, PPB, distribution and warehousing, and so on (in essence, the P & L); the impact of the "serials crisis" on presses, authors, and libraries; and the fact that the supply of books in certain academic fields is increasing faster than the demand from readers in those fields.

- "the important role university presses play in the intellectual life of the university," especially as publishers of titles in "smaller academic fields."

2) Urge universities to create an "office of scholarly communication" (under the aegis of the provost) to assist faculty members and graduate students in their publishing activities.

3) Evaluate the following areas:
   - the important and growing export market for university press books.
   - export marketing and sales consortia to broaden the reach of all university presses into the export marketplace.
   - advertisements in college alumni magazines highlighting frontlist and backlist books (we know from other research studies that adults above the age of thirty-five are avid readers, and this market is rarely tapped by university presses in alumni magazine advertisements)
   - the use of E-RES on college campuses.
   - the important "independent" school (i.e., "private high school") market for university press books.

The economics of publishing are harsh and unforgiving, but they are understandable. University presses should make sure that all members of the university community understand the economics of publishing as well as the inherent strengths of university presses and the constraints they face in fulfilling their lofty mission: to publish and disseminate the best possible scholarship.

Contributors

Albert N. Greco is professor of marketing at Fordham University's Graduate School of Business Administration. He is the author of *The Book Publishing Industry* (Lawrence Earlbaum 2005) and other books and articles about the publishing industry.

Robert M. Wharton is professor of management systems and area chair of management systems at Fordham University's Graduate School of Business Administration. He is the author of numerous statistical papers.

Hooman Estelami is associate professor of marketing and co-director of the pricing center at Fordham University's Graduate School of Business

Administration. His research papers have appeared in major marketing journals, and he is associate editor of the *Journal of Product and Brand Management.*

Notes

1. Chester Kerr, "The Kerr Report: Revisited," *Journal of Scholarly Publishing* 1, 1 (October 1969): 8–10; Albert N. Greco, "University Presses and the Trade Book Market," *Book Research Quarterly* 3, 4(Winter 1987/1988): 24–53; Chester Kerr, "A National Enquiry into the Production and Dissemination of Scholarly Knowledge," *Journal of Scholarly Publishing* 7, 1 (October 1975): 7; Daniel J. Levant, "Marketing in the Crunch," *Journal of Scholarly Publishing* 4, 4 (July 1973): 302; William C. Becker, "The Crisis—One Year Later," *Journal of Scholarly Publishing* 4, 4 (July 1973): 291–302; Mary M. Case, "University Presses: Balancing Academic and Market Values," *ARL* 193 (August 1997), available at *http://www.arl.org/newsltr/193/up.html*; Scott Smallwood, "The Crumbling Intellectual Foundation," *Chronicle of Higher Education* (September 20, 2002): B6; R. Stephen Humphreys, "Why Do We Write Stuff That Even Our Colleagues Don't Want to Read?" in *The Specialized Scholarly Monograph in Crisis, or, How Can I Get Tenure If You Won't Publish My Book: The Papers*, available at *http://www.arl.org/scomm/epub/papers/humphreys.html*; Willis G. Regier, "5 Problems and 9 Solutions for University Presses," *Chronicle of Higher Education* (June 13, 2003): B7; Robert Darnton, "The New Age of the Book," *The New York Review of Books* (March 18, 1999): 5–7.
2. Michael Porter, *Competitive Strategy: Techniques for Analyzing Industries and Competitors* (New York: Free Press 1980), 126–9.
3. David Walters and Mark Rainbird, "The Demand Chain as an Integral Component of the Value Chain," *Journal of Consumer Marketing* 21, 7 (July 2004): 465–76.
4. Abdullah Al-Mudimigh, Mohamed Zairir, and Abdel Moneim M. Ahmed, "Extending the Concept of Supply Chain: The Effective Management of Value Chains," *International Journal of Production Economics* 87, 3 (February 2004): 309–20.
5. John Humphrey and Hubert Schmitz, "How Does Insertion in Global Value Chains Affect Upgrading in Industrial Clusters?" *Regional Studies* 36, 9 (December 2002): 1017–27; Claus Steinle and Holger Schiele, "When Do Industries Cluster? A Proposal on How to Assess an Industry's Propensity to Concentrate at a Single Region or Nation," *Research Policy* 31, 6 (August 2002): 849–58.
6. Jeffrey A. Dubin, *Studies in Consumer Demand: Econometric Methods Applied to Market Data* (Norwell, MA: Kluwer 1998), 15–82.
7. Jacek Cukrowski and Ernest Aksen, "Perfect Competition and Intra-Industry Trade," *Economic Letters* 78, 1 (January 2003): 101–8.
8. Kostas Axarloglou, "The Cyclicality of New Product Introductions," *Journal of Business* 76, 1 (January 2003): 29–48.
9. Corrado Benassi, Alessandra Chirco, and Marcella Scrimitore, "Income Concentration and Market Demand," *Oxford Economic Papers* 54 4 (October 2002): 584–96.
10. Corrado Bennassi, Roberto Cellini, and Alessandra Chirco, "Personal Income Distribution and Market Structure," *German Economic Review* 3, 3 (August 2002): 327–38.
11. Auke R. Leen, "History of the Collective Market Demand Curve in the 20th Century: From Arthur Cecil Pigou to Gary Becker," *Archives of Economic History* 13, 2 (July–December 2001): 75–88.

12. Rod Combs, *Technology and the Market: Demand, Users, and Innovation* (Cheltenham, UK: ASEAT Conference Proceedings Series 2001), 57–74.
13. Jack G. Goellner, "The Impact of the Library Budget Crisis on Scholarly Publishing in the United States," in Richard E. Abel and Lyman W. Newlin, eds., *Scholarly Publishing: Books, Journals, Publishers, and Libraries in the Twentieth Century* (New York: John Wiley & Sons 2002): 273–6, 274.
14. Marsh Jeanneret, *God and Mammon: Universities as Publishers* (Urbana: University of Illinois Press 1989), 313.
15. August Fruge, *A Skeptic Among Scholars: August Fruge on University Publishing* (Berkeley: University of California Press 1993), 67.
16. Walter W. Powell, *Getting into Print: The Decision-Making Process in Scholarly Publishing* (Chicago: University of Chicago Press 1985), 183.
17. Robin P. Peek and Gregory B. Newby, "Introduction," in Robin P. Peek and Gregory B. Newby, eds., *Scholarly Publishing: The Electronic Frontier* (Cambridge: MIT Press 1996): xv–xxii.
18. Jason Epstein, *Book Business: Publishing Past, Present and Future* (New York: W.W. Norton 2001), 1–34.
19. Thomas Ehrmann, Floria Haas, and Rainer Harms, "The Bases of Successful Market Entry: The Liability and Size of Newness in E-Commerce," *International Journal on Media Management* 4, 4 (Winter 2002): 203–11; Alexis Weedon, "The Book Trade and Internet Publishing: A British Perspective," *Convergence* 2, 1 (Spring 1996): 76–102.
20. Albert N. Greco, *The Book Publishing Industry*, 2nd ed. (Mahwah, NJ: Lawrence Erlbaum 2005), 177–206.
21. Jacques Barzun, "The Future of Reading Books," *Journal of Communication* 28, 4 (Autumn 1978): 10–7.
22. Michael J. Robinson and Ray Olszewski, "Books in the Marketplace of Ideas," *Journal of Communication* 30, 2 (Spring 1980): 81–8.
23. Walter W. Powell, "Competition versus Concentration in the Book Trade," *Journal of Communication* 30, 2 (Spring 1980): 89–97; Ben H. Bagdikian, *The New Media Monopoly* (Boston: Beacon Press 2004), 27–54.
24. Ann Haugland, "Books as Culture/Books as Commerce," *Journalism Quarterly* 71, 4 (Winter 1994): 787–99.
25. Joseph Moran, "The Role of Multimedia Conglomerates in American Trade Book Publishing," *Media, Culture, and Society* 19, 3 (July 1997): 441–55.
26. Laura J. Miller, "Cultural Authority and the Use of New Technology in the Book Trade," *Journal of Arts Management, Law, and Society* 28, 4 (Winter 1999): 297–313.
27. Nina D. Ziv, "New Media as Catalysts for Change in the Transformation of the Book Publishing Industry," *International Journal on Media Management* 4, 11 (Summer 2002): 66–74.
28. Lewis A. Coser, Charles Kadushin, and Walter W. Powell, *Books: The Culture and Commerce of Publishing* (Chicago: University of Chicago Press, 1985), ix–xiii, 13–35.
29. U.S. Department of Commerce, Economics and Statistics Division, Bureau of the Census, *The Statistical Abstract of the United States: 2004–2005* (Washington, DC: GPO 2004), 136.
30. James R. Bettman, Mary Frances Luce, and John W. Payne, "Constructive Consumer Choice Processes," *Journal of Consumer Research* 25, 3 (December 1998): 187–217; Gerald J. Tellis and Fred S. Zufryden, "Tackling the Retailer Decision Maze: Which Brands to Discount, How Much, When, and Why?" *Marketing*

Science 14, 3 (Summer 1995): 271–99; Margaret Slade, "Optimal Pricing with Costly Adjustment: Evidence from Retail Grocery Prices," *Review of Economic Studies* 65, 222 (January 1998): 87–107.

31. Karen Clay, Ramayya Krishnan, and Eric Wolff, "Prices and Price Dispersion on the Web: Evidence from the Online Book Industry," *Journal of Industrial Economics* 49, 4 (December 2001): 521–39.
32. Karen Clay, Ramayya Krishnan, and Danny Fernandes, *Journal of Industrial Economics* 50, 3 (September 2002): 351–67.
33. Michael D. Smith and Erik Brynjolfsson, "Consumer Decision-Making at an Internet Shopbot: Brand Still Matters," *Journal of Industrial Economics* 49, 4 (December 2001): 541–58; also see Hal R. Varian, "Buying, Selling, and Renting Information Goods," *Journal of Industrial Economics* 44, 4 (December 2000): 473–88.

Appendix 1
Changes in the Consumer Price Index, 1985–2002

Year	Consumer Price Index	Annual percent change	Value of dollar in constant 2002 dollars
1985	107.6	3.6	0.60
1986	109.6	1.9	0.61
1987	113.6	3.6	0.63
1988	118.3	4.1	0.66
1989	124.0	4.8	0.69
1990	130.7	5.4	0.73
1991	136.2	4.2	0.76
1992	140.3	3.0	0.78
1993	144.5	3.0	0.80
1994	148.2	2.6	0.82
1995	152.4	2.8	0.85
1996	156.9	2.9	0.87
1997	160.5	2.3	0.89
1998	163.0	1.6	0.91
1999	166.6	2.2	0.93
2000	172.2	3.4	0.96
2001	177.1	2.8	0.98
2002	179.9	1.6	1.00

Source: U.S. Department of Commerce, Economics and Statistics Administration, Bureau of the Census, *The Statistical Abstract of the United States* (Washington, DC: GPO 2004), 463. Base year: 1982–1984 = 100.

Appendix 2
Value of University Press Net Publishers' Revenues in Actual and Constant 2002 Dollars

Year	Actual net publishers' revenues ($ millions)	Net publishers' revenues in constant 2002 dollars($ millions)
1985	185.2	265.6
1986	204.0	270.5
1987	219.2	280.4
1988	245.0	292.0
1989	275.6	306.0
1990	305.7	322.6
1991	325.0	336.2
1992	350.0	346.3
1993	350.0	356.6
1994	370.0	365.8
1995	385.0	376.1
1996	390.0	387.2
1997	400.0	396.1
1998	430.0	402.3
1999	450.0	411.2
2000	450.0	425.0
2001	443.0	437.1
2002	444.0	444.0

Source: Book Industry Study Group, *Book Industry Trends*, various issues. All numbers have been rounded and may not add up to 100 percent.

Appendix 3
The U.S. Gross Domestic Product (GDP), 1985–2002, in Actual and Constant 2002 dollars

Year	Actual GDP dollars ($ billion)	Constant 2002 dollars ($ billion)
1985	4,220.3	6,268.7
1986	4,462.8	6,385.2
1987	4,739.5	6,618.2
1988	5,103.8	6,892.0
1989	5,484.4	7,224.1
1990	5,803.1	7,614.5
1991	5,995.9	7,938.9
1992	6,337.7	8,173.7
1993	6,657.4	8,418.4
1994	7,072.2	8,634.0
1995	7,397.7	8,878.7
1996	7,816.9	9,140.8
1997	8,304.3	9,350.6
1998	8,747.0	9,496.2
1999	9,268.4	9,706.0
2000	9,867.0	10,032.2
2001	10,100.8	10,317.7
2002	10,480.8	10,480.8

Source: U.S. Department of Commerce, Economics and Statistics Administration, Bureau of the Census, *The Statistical Abstract of the United States* (Washington, DC: GPO 2004), 425. All numbers have been rounded and may not add up to 100 percent.

A University Press Publishing Consortium for Africa: Lessons from Academic Libraries

Kwasi Darko-Ampem

This article presents the results of a case study of the policies and practices of six African university presses. Based on the findings, it posits the formation of a consortium of African university presses. It borrows heavily from consortium formation in the library world.

1. Introduction and Background

The modern university press was essentially developed in the English-speaking world, first at the universities of Oxford and Cambridge in England and, centuries later, in the United States and the nations of the British Commonwealth. Beginning with Oxford in 1478, university press publishing has come into its own in the past two centuries, particularly in the United States, where at least 100 university presses now operate as part of the Association of American University Presses (AAUP). The AAUP, established in 1937 by twelve presses, had 111 members (including six international non-American) in 1994 but now boasts of 125 members.[1]

The establishment of university presses in Africa, Asia, and Latin America began in the early 1900s; in fact, India's oldest university press, in Calcutta, was founded in 1908. The university press is a relatively new institution in Africa, as indeed is university education. With the exception of universities established in Egypt (970 in Cairo), Sierra Leone (1827 in Fourah Bay), Liberia (1862), and Sudan (1912 in Omdurman), most African universities were founded around the time of independence in the mid-1960s. In the former British colonies, apart from the early beginning at Fourah Bay in 1827, there were no universities till 1948, and no university presses till the University of Ibadan, Nigeria, established the nucleus of one in 1952.

Within the range of activities associated with the traditional concept of a university, the university press plays the role of publisher of the results of teaching and research. In a report on his own university for the 1917/18 academic year, President Butler of Columbia University in New York stated that:

> A university has three functions to perform. It is to conserve knowledge; to advance knowledge; and to disseminate knowledge. It falls short of the full realization of its aim unless, having provided for the conservation and advancement of knowledge, it makes provision for its dissemination as well.[2]

The purpose of the university press is to provide a publishing outlet for research by faculty members of its own and other universities and to extend the instructional function of its parent institution by publishing and disseminating knowledge and scholarship as widely and as economically as possible to both scholars and the educated public. It publishes learned books of small sales potential, with a limited possibility of financial returns, that commercial publishers cannot profitably undertake and gains favorable publicity and prestige for the university of which it is a part.

Scholarly publishing, usually the main business of a university press, is concerned with those publications that report research findings, comment on academic matters, or, in general, are aimed at an audience of intellectuals. K.M. Ganu defines scholarly publishing by function, stating that it involves

> the publication of original works of research that may come in the form of books and journal articles that contribute to knowledge; the publication of works that seek to reinterpret established fields of study or knowledge; and the publication of textbooks for use in the universities.[3]

The case is put otherwise by Gene Hawes, who equates the scholarly press to the university press:

> Most typically, the university press book is written by a scholar to communicate information and ideas in his/her professional field. It conveys new knowledge or new interpretations, preeminently the results of his/her own research. Its audience includes anyone who needs to know what the scholar has discovered. But it will typically seem difficult to understand or unimportant to any one without some background in the author's subject.[4]

Far-sighted leaders such as Daniel Coit Gilman and William Rainey Harper, respectively the first presidents of the Johns Hopkins University and the University of Chicago, perceived that teaching and research were not enough but that the findings of the investigations must be made available both to others engaged in similar pursuits and to an interested public. Since most commercial publishers were loath to publish books comprehensible only to the highly educated reader, the solution lay with the university press.

This article presents the results of a case study of the policies and practices of six African university presses. Based on the study's findings, it posits the formation of a consortium as a means of banding together to cut costs in all presses' operations. Lessons from consortium formation are borrowed from the library world, where cooperation is known to have begun in the early 1950s and reached a peak in the 1990s. In the following five sections, the article addresses knowledge creation and higher education, sets out the results of the case study, explores library consortia and publishing consortia, and proposes a model for an African universities consortium.

2. Knowledge Creation and Higher Education

The accumulation and application of knowledge have become major factors in economic development and are increasingly at the core of a country's competitive advantage in the global economy. The role of tertiary education in the construction of knowledge economies and democratic societies is more influential than ever. Indeed, tertiary education is central to the creation of the intellectual capacity on which knowledge production and utilization depend and to the promotion of lifelong learning practices necessary to update individuals' knowledge and skills.[5]

While universities do not have a monopoly on either the creation or the dissemination of knowledge, they are, especially in the Third World, the key institutions in this process. With very few exceptions, universities stand at the center of the scientific and intellectual process in many nations, especially those of the developing world.[6]

It was with this view that delegates to the Association of African Universities (AAU) 10th General Conference called on African universities to give priority to effective and positive participation in the global creation, exchange, and application of knowledge. This places urgent demands for the development of mechanisms to publish and disseminate high-level knowledge in Africa (and developing countries) on scholarly publishers, particularly university presses.

Scholarly publishing used to be the "core business" of the university press, to the exclusion of all other types of publishing. However, increased financial stringency and cutbacks in library funding have seen university presses adopt survival tactics and strategies including publishing trade books. In North America, B.G. Jones has shown that environmental influences, including falling direct sales to libraries and falling university subsidies since 1980, have forced many university presses to find means of attaining or maintaining self-sufficiency.[7] One of these survival strategies is expansion into more profitable areas outside scholarly monograph publishing, such as publishing trade books.

3. The Case Study: University Publishing in Sub-Saharan African Countries

The literature affirms that the slow development of Africa's publishing industry has been largely attributed to the continent's stunted economy.[8] Ruth Makotsi has observed that "where the economy of particular countries has improved, publishing has often been strengthened alongside other sectors."[9] Citing the case of Zambia in 1987, G.J. Williams echoes this point, noting that:

> The Zambian economy has, unfortunately[,] continued in its decline. The National Book Development Council has never become functional and the state of publishing in the country—a decade or so later—is undoubtedly now at a much lower ebb than it was in 1977. The depressed state of the national economy is a major factor contributing to the dismal state of publishing in Zambia in the mid eighties.[10]

In an article on periodical subscriptions in Ghanaian university libraries, R. Arkaifie indicates how academic journal subscription numbers are inextricably linked to the economic fortunes of the country. Taking one of the country's three premier universities, he points out that while in 1975 it had a subscription list of some 1,400 titles, in 1987 its list was about 450, thanks to a government rescue project under the Educational Sector Adjustment Credit with funding from the World Bank.[11] Set against these odds is the fact that indigenous publishing does not have roots in Africa, and circumstances during the colonial era and its aftermath did not favor it.[12]

In the specific case of Ghana, the Ghana Universities Press was established in 1962 after the acceptance of the recommendations of the Report of the Commission on University Education in Ghana 1960–1961, which noted that:

> We were impressed with the importance, for the development of university education in Ghana, of the production of new literature, both textbooks and works of scholarship, to consolidate recent advances in African studies, to make available the results of scientific research, and to re-interpret established fields of study. The setting up of a University Press would be a means of encouraging local writers and accelerating the production of books. It should also be possible, through the University Press, to subsidize important publications which cannot be produced on economic basis.[13]

Its objective was to publish scholarly works from the universities and the Council for Scientific and Industrial Research. Challenges that still persist are a shortage of assessors (because university lecturers find the honorarium paid by the GUP too meager); seasoned freelance proofreaders; and funding, which was identified as the greatest constraint. Ganu reports that "the government continues to subsidize scholarly publications by providing subvention to cover staff salaries and a limited range of operational expenses."[14]

By the mid-1970s, there were close to thirty academic journals published, mostly by the East African Literature Bureau (EALB) and East African Publishing House.[15] The Kenya Literature Bureau replaced the EALB in 1979, two years after the break-up of the East African Community in 1977. Nearly all these journals stopped publishing in 1977, when the bureau folded up and the local publishing industry began experiencing problems. Of the four public universities in Kenya—Nairobi, Moi, Kenyatta, and Egerton—only Nairobi has a university press. It was set up in 1984 with a sizeable grant from British American Tobacco (BAT). Until 1991 it had published only one title, a sign that all was not well with its management. The press was then revitalized and produced nearly twenty new titles in the early 1990s. Based on the response to the study questionnaire, however, it has not been able to sustain any of these titles.

Tertiary and higher educational institutions in Nigeria experience acute book and journal shortages, both at the individual student and library acquisition levels. The 1990 Book Sector Study pointed out that "production costs have increased by 700 percent in the last five years, but prices have increased by only 450 percent over the same period."[16] In the view of S.B. Bankole, a combination of factors, including the economy, political instability, and downright interference in the administration of the universities by government agencies such as the Ministry of Education and the National Universities Commission, do not create the right atmosphere for scholarship.[17]

For the six-year period 1987 to 1992, funding declined from 2.26 percent of the total national budget to 1.45 percent. Paradoxically, student population increased from 147,799 to 290,610 during the same period.[18] Not unexpectedly, the campus presses received scant attention from university administrators responsible for allocating funds. In 1995, F.A. Adesanoye thus identified funding as the major problem facing university publishers, conceding that African scholarly presses will continue to receive less and less funding, and called for cooperation among scholarly publishers in Africa.

The Ibadan University Press was established in 1952 and became a full-fledged publishing house in 1955. Many of the fairly old universities, including Ahmadu Bello, Jos, Lagos, Maiduguri, Obafemi Awolowo (formerly Ife), Nigeria, and Port-Harcourt, have established their own presses. The leading houses in terms of title output are Ibadan, Lagos and Ife (both established in 1980), and Maiduguri (established in 1988).[19] In South Africa, the leading university presses are Witwatersrand, Natal, the University of South Africa (Unisa), and Cape Town. Witwatersrand, the oldest and largest university press in Africa, was established in 1922,[20] and Unisa Press has been publishing since 1957.[21] The University of Cape Town Press was established in 1993; it is now owned by a commercial publisher, Juta & Co., a "unique combination of academic and commercial interest [which] represents a consolidation of academic excellence and integrity with sound business and commercial direction and resourcing."[22]

Tertiary education in Zimbabwe is about seventy-five years old, having started with the Polytechnics of Bulawayo and Harare, both founded in 1927. The University of Zimbabwe does not have an official university press, but it established a publications office in 1972 and, since the mid-1980s, has published between three and five titles each year under the imprint of University of Zimbabwe Publications.[23]

The presses covered in this study were the Ghana Universities Press (Accra), the University of Zimbabwe Press (Harare), the University of South Africa Press (Pretoria), the University of Cape Town Press (Cape Town), the University of Zambia Press (Lusaka), and the University Press of Nairobi (Nairobi). The selected presses are from countries that have the most vibrant publishing industries in the sub-region.[24] Furthermore, the ten African countries represented by their national publishing associations at the International Publishers Association include all but one of the five countries covered in the study, together with Egypt, Morocco, Sudan, Tanzania, and Uganda.[25] The University of Zambia Press came in as a last-minute substitute for the presses in Nigeria, which responded to the preliminary questions only.

Founding dates

The study found that the presses were founded between 1957 and 1993, evidence that university publishing in Africa is a recent phenomenon, emerging after African countries won political independence from colonial rule. Outside South Africa, university publishing in sub-Saharan Africa actually started in 1955, with the university of Ibadan, Nigeria.

In general, African university presses (AUPs) were founded to provide publishing avenues for researchers of the newly independent African states.

Press policies/publishing agenda

Two presses stated that their mission is to provide quality publications that contribute to the development of southern Africa and empower the region's people. One of the directors stated that the press will "continually strive to maintain our position as the region's leading publisher of academic and scholarly works—books for empowerment." Another mission statement read, "by publishing outstanding research work, scholarly journals and textbooks of high academic merit ... and to market and distribute these products." Three presses without written mission or vision statements responded in various terms that they are committed to publishing high-quality, relevant, and competitively priced publications; revitalizing research; exhibiting high standards of book publishing; boosting morale by ending dependence on foreign books; and maintaining a reputable imprint through quality publications. All six presses publish substantially in the social sciences and humanities, and one press has an impressive list in art and architecture.

Annual sales figures

The presses are able to sell between 20 and 65 percent of their production. The least successful in terms of sales sold just one fifth of its production; however, together with the rest, this press reported that the trend in sales has increased over the years. The press with 40 percent average annual sales said that sale figures, which increased from 1986 to 1990, have decreased over the ten-year period between 1991 and 2000.

Assessment over fifteen years: 1986–2000

Not all the presses in the study were successful at selling the books they publish, because selling less than 60 percent of the books published may not be enough to recover production costs.

Most of the presses studied do not appear to have a clearly defined subject focus. This may be interpreted to mean that their lists are not focused, a factor that could partially explain the difficulty they face in marketing their books.

The lack of cooperation among university presses also could be a factor; without joint distribution strategies, it may be difficult to market books outside one's own country.

Manuscript acquisition and editorial boards

None of the presses has a formal written policy on manuscript acquisition. According to the survey, the size and composition of editorial boards vary widely: two to five members for one press, six to nine for two, ten to thirteen for another, and fourteen or more for the remaining two. Membership is split between faculty only, faculty and non-university members, and faculty and other university staff.

Kinds of books published

The presses publish research monographs, undergraduate textbooks, school textbooks, professional books, trade books, reference works, and research journals. The main publishing categories are undergraduate textbooks and research monographs. For the majority of the presses (four out of six), the most important publishing category in terms of revenue is undergraduate textbooks.

Marketing and distribution

All six presses identified the bookseller as the single most important distribution channel. Four stated that this channel brings in 70 to 90 percent of their sales. Four of the six presses gave direct sales as the most popular means of selling their works, followed by review copies, cited as the second most important by three presses. The third place on their marketing plans is shared by scholarly journal advertising and conferences and conventions.

What deficiencies exist in their operations?

Lack of cooperation among the AUPs, low sales, lack of written policies, and non-specialized areas (lack of list building) were identified as deficiencies. Two presses did not have any form of cooperation with any press at all. The remaining four do have partnerships with other presses, but these are mainly with presses outside the continent, in particular Europe and North America. Inter-African press cooperation is very low on the agenda of most of the presses surveyed.

The mission and vision statements of the presses surveyed were silent on the idea of "determining a publishing agenda," and, as a result, their lists cover very broad subject areas, including engineering and technology. This lack of focus may partially explain the difficulty they face in marketing their books. A lack of written policies and manuals on press procedures and operations may lead to a loss of corporate knowledge when experienced staff leave the press or resign at short notice. Successful marketing in publishing is built around the principle of having a "family" of books that can be promoted and sold across the board to a fairly coherent readership. Furthermore, titles that do not have continent-wide appeal can be sold only within their country of origin. The lack of cooperation among university presses also could be a factor; as mentioned above, without joint distribution strategies, it may be difficult to market one country's books in any other country.

Model of an African university press in the twenty-first century?

Views on an African model were divided between those who favored AUPs remaining modelled after their European counterparts, on the one hand, and, on the other hand, those who advocated a unique African model. One director replied "yes" to an African model, "but on condition that we respond appropriately to our circumstances," while another proffered a joint partnership with a commercial publisher. The scholarly/commercial publisher relation makes economic sense, since the latter takes care of funding—one of the most pressing needs of the scholarly publisher. The scholarly publisher brings into the relationship the high and stringent academic standards required of every scholarly press.

Comments from those who do not subscribe to a unique African model included the following:

European models are okay and AUPs can do equally well based on these

No, basic business principles should determine decisions, that is quality publishing with profit-making in mind.

Two presses were for the idea, two opposed it, and two did not respond to the question. In the context of their views on an African model, cooperation among AUPs must be seen as fundamental to strengthening their programs and even to their basic existence.

Conclusions and recommendations

Subject specialization must be emphasized, based on the press's publishing heritage or tradition, the evident strengths of the parent university, the sales potential of various fields of inquiry, or the scholarly interests of the editors. The existing internal structures of each press may be retained, but the overall arrangement within the university set-up requires modification into a charitable trust. As a trust, each press will operate with as much autonomy as enjoyed by a private company, but administration will be vested in trustees who will promote the objectives of the press rather than maximizing profit. This structure may attract donor funding for the publication of non-profitable works.

In adopting an existing model, however, it is necessary to consider factors such as adequate staffing, equipment, and investment capital that are basic to any sustainable publishing industry. Serious thought should be given to publishing consortia. AUPs do not have press publishing areas or press lists that define the subject areas in which each press concentrates its publishing. Apart from its marketing implications, a well-defined list helps a press build its reputation in a given field, making it the first choice for prospective authors.

4. Library Consortia

What is a consortium?

In the simplest terms, a library consortium defines activities engaged in jointly by a group of libraries for the purposes of improving services or cutting costs. Library literature has traced the gains in the formation of consortia among libraries as the potential for improving access to the joint collections of participating libraries, stretching limited resources, improving staff competencies, and addressing common needs arising from developments in information technology. Cooperation among libraries started mainly with inter-library lending, but the formation of consortia, beginning in the early 1980s and reaching an all-time high in the mid-1990s, was necessitated by economic factors.[26] Perhaps the real sign that library consortia had "arrived" was the establishment of a group of more than fifty organizations from the United States and other countries into the semiformal entity known as the International Coalition of Library Consortia (ICOLC). The organization has been meeting twice yearly since 1997 in North America. The European ICOLC has been holding separate meetings once a year since 1999.[27]

Library resource sharing may be established by means of informal or formal agreements or by contract and may operate locally, nationally, or internationally. The resources shared may be collections, bibliographic data, personnel, planning activities, and so on. Library consortia or co-operative ventures have grown from a peripheral and limited position of resource sharing to an integrated system-wide resource sharing. This has been made possible by developments in electronic access. Academic libraries now have improved access to catalogue information that reflects the holdings of many individual libraries. In addition, electronic access enables customers to initiate their own searches of remote catalogues and make requests for information. Furthermore, most libraries have achieved a certain level of local system and networking sophistication; the cost of printed resources, especially periodicals, continue to rise, and institutions are looking for ways to cut costs. These factors explain why consortia have become attractive.

Reasons for consortium formation

In the words of William Potter:

> While the chief reason for academic libraries to form consortia has been to share existing physical resources, a new trend is becoming evident or at least much pronounced. Libraries are forming alliances for the purpose of identifying and addressing common needs arising from developments in information technology, especially the growing importance of the Internet and the World Wide Web.[28]

Barbara Allen and Arnold Hirshon indicate that "the most important development for academic libraries during the current decade has been the move from organizational self-sufficiency to a collaborative survival mode as personified by the growth of library consortia."[29] They posit that what brings libraries together is a desire to engage in resource sharing or reduce some common costs. Based on their experiences, surveys, and discussions with other consortium leaders, they believe that there are some key organizational imperatives that have been driving individual libraries and their consortia toward increased cooperation, especially in the 1990s. Among the factors they cite specifically in the case of academic libraries are reductions in funding, emerging changes in the publishing industry, the rapid growth of information technology, and an emphasis on improving the quality of services.

In Allen and Hirshon's view, beginning in the mid- to late 1980s and accelerating in the 1990s, new library consortia developed for three primary reasons:

- to leverage resources by sharing existing collections or resources through virtual union catalogues;
- to reduce the cost of member library operations through group purchase price for information products; and
- to bring pressure to bear on information providers, especially publishers, about the need to reduce the rate of rise in the cost of information.

In his article on trends in academic library consortia, Potter identifies two main reasons for the formation of consortia. He cites the sharing of existing physical resources as the chief reason and the purpose of identifying and addressing common needs arising from developments in information technology as the other. Specifically, he mentions the growing importance of the Internet and the World Wide Web, with the possibility of offering a variety of electronic resources across the Internet.[30] Many established systems are also working to offer electronic resources, grafting them onto existing programs. The newer consortia also address the need to share physical resources; but these newer consortia are focused more on electronic resources. They recognize that electronic resources will be increasingly important and that there are benefits in banding together to offer them, using the leverage of a group and the advantage of a common funding source.

The benefits of cooperation are summed up by G.E. Evans to include the potential for improving access; making available a greater range of materials, or better depth in a subject area; stretching limited resources; sharing resources, leading to gains such as staff training and specialization; actively advertising the consortium's presence and services by directing clients to appropriate sources of information; improvement in the working relationships among cooperating libraries; and the opportunity to share problems and solutions, which in turn, improves each participant's capabilities.[31]

Types of consortia

During the last three decades, libraries have developed a variety of organizational models to support the different kinds of resource-sharing programs that have evolved. Designing an organizational infrastructure appropriate for the participants and the resources being shared can further the success of any kind of library cooperation. At one end of the spectrum are loosely affiliated "buying clubs" where libraries come together primarily to share a discounted rate on electronic (or other) resources. At the other end are consortia that are tightly integrated organizations sharing a variety of resources, requiring long-term commitment and collaborative decision making at all staff levels.

Although consortia may come together to reduce common costs, the new consortia of the 1990s were not simply "buying clubs." The most successful have developed an institutional strategic alliance in which a heightened level of resource sharing binds the member institutions together. There is no one model for these but, rather, a broad continuum from highly decentralized to highly centralized organizations. The categories include loosely knit federations, multi-type/multi-state networks, tightly knit federations, and centrally funded state-wide consortia.[32]

Each model is premised upon different values, objectives, and political realities of its membership. Consortia can also evolve from one model to another as their members become more comfortable with one another and develop a collective agenda.

The consortium of large North East Research Libraries (NERL) has among its objectives to jointly license substantial electronic resources, such as full-text journals, databases, and large literary works, at advantageous terms and rates. Both D.J. Foskett and R. Carr indicate that in 1982 libraries in the United Kingdom formed a Consortium of University Research Libraries (CURL) to share computerized cataloguing or bibliographic information.[33] The libraries in this consortium included major libraries at the Universities of London, Glasgow, Edinburgh, Oxford, Cambridge, Leeds, and Manchester. Although most of these libraries were already computerized, they had a problem of sharing catalogue information. The problem was caused by lack of common cataloguing standards and different levels of automation, coupled with incompatibility in hardware and software and a lack of coordinated policies. The University Grants Committee, later the Higher Education Funding Council, then provided funding and established the Joint Academic Network (JANET) to link the computer centers of all U.K. universities, allowing bibliographic access to the records of one library by another.

Financial constraints and a shift in the missions of higher education institutions, which emphasize research, are among the major reasons for the formation of library consortia. D. Kohl admits that these constraints, in turn, affect academic libraries, which are already constrained in their mission to support teaching, learning, and research. He describes OhioLINK, a highly integrated consortium of higher institutions whose main focus is sharing of electronic access.[34] Other consortium activities are the physical delivery of materials; electronic delivery of journal articles; and integrated collection development. Kohl's research on OhioLINK reveals that the consortium began as a measure to address budget constraints and sky-rocketing serials prices, as well as the problem of space that had affected Ohio academic libraries.[35] Based on the recommendations of the Ohio Board of Regents (OBR), the state encouraged cooperative storage of materials and the use of electronic technology to interconnect academic libraries.

The OhioLINK system was designed to link local systems to a common and central system. Through this system, the Ohio academic libraries share a union catalogue of holdings information for participating academic libraries, Gopher Internet access, and commercial or information databases. In addition to these services, OhioLINK provides customer-initiated circulation services whereby customers can search and initiate their own requests for materials not available locally from remote databases. Materials are usually delivered within forty-eight hours through a contracted twenty-four-hour delivery service. For this consortium to fully function, OhioLINK has a central funding system where subsidies are provided for automation on local campuses. Further, a governance structure in the form of a governing board has been set in place to decide on policy and expenditure issues as well as implementing decisions made by the consortium's board.

Lizanne Payne describes one of the most tightly integrated consortia in the United States, the Washington Research Library Consortium. The shared budget covers core services in the areas of cooperative collection development; a library automation system with an online union catalogue and multiple electronic resources; offsite book storage facility and book delivery service; and a separately staffed service organization. There are optional supplemental services such as additional mounted databases beyond those provided by the core budget.[36]

Issues in cooperation

Evans has divided issues in any cooperative effort into six categories: institutional; legal, political, and administrative; technological; physical; people; and knowledge-based.[37] In any cooperative effort, the library's level of funding will not be sufficient to buy as much as was purchased before while also taking on new cooperative obligations. Hence some subject areas will have to be given up or sharply reduced. But when libraries combine their potential using cooperative arrangements that go beyond traditional inter-library loans, there are true gains for everyone. Online public access catalogues (OPACs) connected to the Internet allow staff and users to check the holdings of the participating libraries. Matters of self-sufficiency, collection size and status, and traditions such as special access rules and other library operating practices, as well as the compatibility of library procedures, must be examined during the formative stages of the cooperative venture.

Legal, political, and administrative issues such as the amount of control and influence each member has will have to be determined at the outset. Other issues that need careful thought and attention include technological, physical, and people issues, as well as adjustments to changing needs. For instance, new technologies are costly and may require additional funding; geographic and transportation issues also create problems, although modern technology is making distance less of a problem. Perhaps the greatest barrier to any cooperative venture is people: There are psychological barriers that planners of a cooperative program must overcome.

Change is almost always threatening; as a result, passive resistance, inertia, and indifference can be serious problems at both the planning and implementation stages. As when selling any change, planners must be honest and forthright about possible modifications to workload, for example. Another major difficulty with cooperative plans is the speed with which adjustments can be made to changing institutional needs. Despite this litany of issues and challenges, it is becoming more and more the practice that cooperatives are set as a matter of economic necessity and nothing else.

5. Publishing Consortia

Perhaps publishers could learn from the library world, where consortium formation has sought to solve many problems using economies of scale. Members of AAUP form only a loose association of presses, each of which is autonomous and operates on its own. The adoption of the consortium model would hopefully create the critical mass of resources in terms of personnel, equipment, and funding required to make the participating presses viable. Distribution bottlenecks would be alleviated through joint efforts, and markets for the published works could be broadened.

A living example of a pan-African publishing initiative is Children's Science Publishing in Africa (CHISCI), a consortium of African publishers from nine countries established to co-publish science books for children. The consortium includes presses from Zambia, Uganda, Kenya, Namibia, Tanzania, Botswana, Ghana, Nigeria, and Zimbabwe. The project is based in Nairobi, Kenya, and plans to develop co-editions with U.K.-based Belitha Press. It aims at increasing print runs to make prices affordable to African parents.

The African Network of Scientific and Technological Institutions (ANSTI), a body within UNESCO that promotes collaboration among African institutions engaged in university-level training and research in science and technology, publishes university-level textbooks and has established the ANSTI/UNESCO Engineering Science series. The series is currently made up of eleven titles, including *Fluid Mechanics*, *Strength of Materials*, *Fundamentals of Electrical Engineering*, *Engineering Mechanics*, and *Engineering Thermodynamics*. These textbooks are usually multi-authored and are written by African experts. *Fluid Mechanics*, for example, "is a broad-based textbook for undergraduate Chemical Engineering, Mechanical Engineering and Civil Engineering students. Wherever possible, the author has chosen examples relevant to the African technological and environmental scene." [38]

The Science for Africa/Kawi project, which publishes culturally relevant and popular science books focusing on renewable energy, is being implemented in conjunction with the African Publishers Network (APNET). The African Writers Series[39] was founded in 1962, with Chinua Achebe as Editorial Adviser. For the first twenty years, until the Nigerian foreign exchanges closed in April 1982, it sold 80 percent of copies in Africa. The "Orange Series," as it was nicknamed, was a delight for those who wanted to learn about Africa through the imaginations of its writers. Together with the UNESCO textbook *General History of Africa*, these projects are very bright spots in Africa's coordinated efforts to satisfy the book needs of the continent. All show that with political will, proper funding, and astute coordination, the book situation in Africa could improve.

There have been several initiatives to form editors' or publishers' organizations in Africa. These include the Consortium of African Scholarly Publishers (CASP), formed in 1993 under the leadership of the African Centre for Technology Studies (ACTS) in Kenya, and the African Association of Science Editors (AASE), started in Addis Ababa. Both these organizations folded within about a year of their formation.[40]

Following a workshop that brought African journal publishers together in 1995, the Swedish Agency for Research Co-operation with Developing Countries (SAREC) supported the establishment of the CASP. Although funded in response to an identified priority, CASP became based in an environmental NGO, with a limited publishing program. Communication was sporadic, and little, if any, activity took place. It is impossible to know whether CASP's demise was the result of a lack of suitable commitment from the host or whether a lack of critical mass in scholarly publishing in Africa meant that any such initiative would be difficult to sustain.

The CASP was established in the mid-1990s "to facilitate cooperation between African scholarly publishers." It was to form "a new database, the CASP Inventory of Scholarly Publishers in Africa, which will aid marketing, distribution and co-publications of African scholarly titles," and to work "with scholarly presses and specialists to set up a series of workshops on specialist aspects of publishing." The ACTS, based in Nairobi, was the secretariat of the CASP, "a network of groups interested in improving and promoting scholarly publishing in Africa."[41] The ACTS published the journal *Outlook* as part of the CASP News Digest.

This brilliant initiative may have failed because of low commitment, logistical problems, and lack of coordination. With a bit of hindsight, a second attempt at a consortium should succeed, provided there is a determined effort spearheaded by a pan-African body such as APNET.

6. Proposed Model for an African Consortium of University Presses (A-CUP)

What is proposed here is a close-knit association of presses into consortia along the lines of library consortia. Examples of such press consortia are the Ghana Universities Press (GUP) in Africa and the University Press of New England (UPNE) in the United States. The GUP, one of the presses covered by the present study, is in fact a consortium, established in 1962 to serve Ghana's three premier public universities and its scientific research institutes. Founded in 1970, the UPNE is a unique publishing consortium at Dartmouth College, the host institution. It is an award-winning university press supported by a consortium of five schools: Brandeis University, Dartmouth College, Middlebury College, the University of New Hampshire, and Tufts University. The UPNE has earned a reputation for excellence in scholarly, instructional, reference, literary and artistic, and general-interest books. Many of these are published cooperatively with one of the member institutions and carry a joint imprint. The UPNE also distributes the titles of seven other presses, as well as selected titles from other publishers, including the Library of Congress.[42] As explained earlier, the UNESCO *General History of Africa* textbook, the CHISCI consortium, and the ANSTI/UNESCO Engineering Science series are examples of pan-African cooperative schemes whose programs have continent-wide appeal.

The forty African publishers who attended the 1995 seminar on copublishing held in Addis Ababa, Ethiopia, and co-sponsored by Bellagio agreed in principle that copublishing is good and of particular benefit if it takes place among African publishers. It was noted then, almost ten years ago, that there was only very limited collaboration among publishers in different African countries. This shortcoming, according to the seminar participants, should be remedied because copublishing has the potential to solve problems of small markets, lack of infrastructure, and distribution across national borders in Africa. But the situation has not changed much, if at all, as this study shows. What Jones calls "networking"[43]—copublishing, joining a consortium, and selling or buying publishing rights—is practiced increasingly by all categories of U.S. university presses.

To take history as an example, James Currey "has just completed its most ambitious co-publishing project, the eight paperback volumes of the abridged Unesco *General History of Africa*."[44] The work was produced under the editorship of African historians, including A. Adu Boahen, B.A. Ogot, J.E. Ade Ajayi, J. Ki-Zerbo, and Ali A. Mazrui. Such large-scale cooperation is not beyond the means of other subject experts on the continent. Citing the overall low print runs of publications as an evidence, Walter Bgoya underscores the need for increased cooperation among universities via common course offerings,[45] a point made by Currey when he writes that university books can be developed and used throughout the continent.

The proposed model, known as A-CUP, would be a continent-wide body based at the AAU, in Accra, or at APNET in Abidjan and having sub-regional "nodes" throughout the continent. Existing AUPs would form the basic building blocks of the A-CUP. It should have representation from the west, central/eastern, southern, and northern sub-regions (beyond the sub-Saharan region) to benefit from the rich publishing experiences of countries such as Egypt. The proposed model is structured, at both micro and macro levels, to take care of the AUP as a unit within a university and as part of a network of publishers on the continent. The premise for this model at the *micro level* is fourfold:

- *Specialization*, which should see presses rely on outsourcing and using freelance editors, illustrators, and designers; literary agents; focused press lists; and project management skills. Each press should carefully select and develop its publishing around specific subject areas based on its strengths, but bearing in mind the publishing lists of other presses in the network. Areas of subject specialization may be selected on the basis of the publishing heritage or tradition, the evident strengths of the parent university, the sales potential of various fields of inquiry, and the scholarly interests of the editors. Since most AUPs publish in the arts and humanities, special efforts should be made to designate specific presses as centers for publishing in science and technology. This will be contingent on the prowess of the coordinating agency.
- *Cooperation*, in the form of sharing resources and expertise, establishing a clearing house to register business needs and ideas, and copublication to reduce local development and production costs and widen the dissemination of books in Africa. These activities should cover adaptations, translations, copublishing, coproduction, co-distribution, reciprocal distribution, rights sales, bulk purchase of raw materials, capital investment, and long-term joint ventures. Copublishing arrange-

ments could cover the publication of book series using the relatively small academic community of experts in Africa.
- *Information and communication techologies (ICTs)*, including e-mail and fax, could be at the center of the press infrastructure for exchanging information and transferring documents. The introduction of e-publishing and print-on-demand technologies could be explored and fast-tracked.
- In terms of *structure*, each press could operate as a trust, enjoying much autonomy as a private company but registered as a non-profit organization, and possibly get donor funding for publishing unprofitable works.

At the *macro level*, the success of the model should not be isolated from the economies of African countries, the general infrastructure, and educational policies designed to sustain it. In that respect, appropriate steps should be taken to *set up sub-regional university presses*: Bgoya cites the investigation into the idea of setting up an SADC university press for southern Africa and the little chance of books published in one country finding markets elsewhere in the sub-region, except where there is a common curriculum.[46] Cooperation and regional integration could be hastened through sub-regional bodies such as the Economic Community of West African States (ECOWAS), the Southern African Development Community (SADC), and so on and by relying on continent-wide institutions, such as the African Union (AU), the AAU, and the African Development Bank (ADB). This would essentially break trade barriers between African states, and improve on the distribution of cultural products, including books.

7. Conclusion

University publishing in Africa is barely fifty years old (1955–2002), in its infancy compared to that of the United Kingdom (where it began in Oxford in 1478) and the United States (introduced at Cornell University in 1869). Within this period, almost every African country has established at least one university press, which gives an indication of the importance attached to this kind of publishing by African governments. What must be done is to consolidate these presses, providing the essential link between research and publication in the bid to find solutions to the many problems facing the continent. There are real challenges on the road to sustaining the presses, but these must be seen as opportunities, not threats.

APNET will continue to play a leading role in this endeavor, but whether or not AUPs will survive in the next ten to fifteen years will depend largely on their resolve to take bold initiatives based on cooperation and the adoption of new technologies. This will require the persistence of publishing personnel and a self-conscious book industry (of publishers, binders, printers, and sellers) that understands the broad ramifications of their policies and is able to effectively organize and communicate with governments and the public and provide effective leadership in book development.

Consortium publishing seems to be a sensible means to reduce the financial burden on each individual press or institution and at the same time provide a sustainable source of funding for each institution's publication programs. It may not be out of order for each member press or institution to commit a fixed percentage of its budget towards the operations of a consortium. In the case of academic libraries, the convention has been an annual expenditure of 5 to 6 percent of the total university budget. This figure could also be set aside for publishing the research output of each institution.

Additionally, it could be made mandatory for part of the funding for each research project to be set aside for the publication of the research results. This publishing component could be paid to the press to publish results of the research. Through consortium arrangements, the problems of small markets, low promotions budgets, distribution bottlenecks, and so on could be tackled in a concerted manner, based on economies of scale. The issue of trans-border trade would also receive attention, with serious consideration of new technology, for example, print-on-demand technology to cut down transportation charges and reduce foreign exchange transactions delays. At the apex of this cooperative program should be a well-articulated coordination scheme.

The creation of a viable consortium requires adequate funding, commitment, and shrewd coordination, together with a set of operating standards. Earlier attempts at cooperation may have failed for lack of these requirements. The options now open to AUPs are mergers, consortium formation, or total collapse. Unless current pressures for self-sufficiency are removed, press directors have little choice but to forge alliances that will keep them in business.

Contributor

Kwasi Darko-Ampem currently works as a Senior Librarian in the Department of Library Services, University of Botswana. Prior to his present appointment he worked with the University of Science & Technology, Kumasi, Ghana, from 1986 to 1996. He received a Bachelor of Science degree from the University of Cape Coast, Ghana, in 1977; a Master of

Information Science degree from the University of Ibadan, Nigeria, in 1992; and a Ph.D. in Publishing from the University of Stirling, U.K., in 2003. His research interests are digital libraries, scholarly publishing, library consortia, project management, and information literacy.

Notes

1. S. Meyer, "University Press Publishing," in P.G. Altbach and E.S. Hoshino, eds., *International Book Publishing: An Encyclopedia* (London: Fitzroy Dearborn 1995): 354–363, 358; AAUP At-A-Glance, Association of American University Presses, *http://www.aaupnet.org/news/glance.html*.
2. Cited in A. Irele, "The Challenge of University Publishing in Africa, with Special Reference to Nigeria," in Philip G. Altbach, ed., *Readings on Publishing in Africa and the Third World* (Buffalo, NY: Bellagio 1993): 74–77, 74.
3. K.M. Ganu, "Scholarly Publishing in Ghana: The Role of the Ghana Universities Press," *Journal of Scholarly Publishing* 30, 3 (April 1999): 111–23.
4. Cited in A.G. Brice, "The Scholarly Monograph and the Hereafter," *Scholarly Publishing* 5, 3 (April 1974): 219–25.
5. World Bank, *Constructing Knowledge Societies: New Challenges for Tertiary Education* (World Bank Report No. 24973, January 2002), *http://www-wds.worldbank.org/servlet/WDS_IBank_Servlet?pcont=details&eid=000094946_02102204203142*.
6. Philip G. Altbach, "Third World Scholarly Publishing," *Library Trends* 26, 4 (Spring 1978): 489–504, 489–90.
7. B.G. Jones, *The Restructuring of Scholarly Publishing in the United States* (Ph. D. dissertation, University of Wales, Cardiff 1998).
8. Philip G. Altbach, "Publishing in the Third World: Issues and Trends for the 21st Century," in Philip G. Altbach and Damtew Teferra, eds., *Publishing and Development: A Book of Readings* (Chestnut Hill, MA: Bellagio 1998): 159–90; Ruth Makotsi, *Expanding the Book Trade across Africa: A Study of Current Barriers and Future Potential* (London: ADEA 2000): 2–5, 92–105; G.J. Williams, "Books in Zambia: The Developing Hunger," in Philip G. Altbach, ed., *Readings on Publishing in Africa and the Third World* (Buffalo, NY: Bellagio 1993): 78–82; Hans M. Zell, "Africa," in P.G. Altbach and E.S. Hoshino, eds., *International Book Publishing: An Encyclopedia* (London: Fitzroy Dearborn 1995): 366–73.
9. Makotsi, *ibid.*, 17.
10. Williams, "Books in Zambia," 78.
11. R. Arkaifie, "Periodicals Subscription under Structural Adjustment in Ghanaian University Libraries: An Appraisal," *Library Management* 18, 7 (1997): 316–22.
12. Philip G. Altbach, "A Fair Climate in Africa," *The Bookseller* 16 (Spring 1996): 26–27.
13. Cited in Ganu, "Scholarly Publishing in Ghana," 115.
14. *Ibid.*, 118.
15. H. Chakava, "Kenya," in P.G. Altbach and E.S. Hoshino, eds., *International Book Publishing: An Encyclopedia* (London: Fitzroy Dearborn 1995): 384–96.
16. V. Nwankor, "Nigeria," in P.G. Altbach and E.S. Hoshino, eds., *International Book Publishing: An Encyclopedia* (London: Fitzroy Dearborn 1995):396–415, 400.
17. S.B. Bankole, "Scholarly Publishing in Nigeria: A Dilemma," *Bellagio Publishing Newsletter* 8 (December 1993): 5–7.

18. F.A. Adesanoye, "Scholarly Publishing in Nigeria," in *The Book in Nigeria: Some Current Issues* (Ibadan: Sam Bookman 1995): 73–88, 78.
19. C. Ike, ed., *Directory of Nigerian Book Development* (Enugu: Fourth Dimension/Nigerian Book Foundation 1998).
20. University of the Witwatersrand, All Things Cultural, http://www.wits.ac.za/depts/wcs/resources.shtml.
21. University of South Africa, Unisa Press home page, http://www.unisa.ac.za/default.asp?Cmd=ViewContent&ContentID=247.
22. For the first time in its history, the University of Cape Town Press, a Juta subsidiary managed by Juta Academic, was able to make an extraordinary 55 percent turnaround in its operating profits, according to the Juta Annual Report, 2002.
23. University of Zimbabwe Press, http://www.uz.ac.zw/publications/.
24. Hans M. Zell, "Africa: The Neglected Continent," in Philip G. Altbach, ed., *Publishing and Development in the Third World* (Sevenoaks, U.K.: Hans Zell 1992): 65–76; Damtew Teferra, "The Significance of Information Technology for African journals," in Philip G. Altbach and Damtew Teferra, eds., *Publishing and Development: A Book of Readings* (Chestnut Hill, MA: Bellagio 1998): 39–61; Altbach, "Publishing in the Third World."
25. International Publishers Association, http://www.ipa-uie.org/ipa/ipa_id.htm.
26. R.B. Nfila and K. Darko-Ampem, "Developments in Academic Library Consortia from the 1960s to 2000: A Review of the Literature," *Library Management* 23, 4/5 (2002): 203–12; G.E. Evans, "Management Issues of Co-operative Ventures and Consortia in the USA, part 1," *Library Management* 23, 4/5 (2002): 213–26.
27. International Coalition of Library Consortia (ICOLC), http://www.library.yale.edu/consortia/.
28. Cited in J. Kopp, "Library Consortia and Information Technology: The Past, the Present, and the Promise," *Information Technology & Libraries* 17, 1 (1998): 7–12, 11.
29. Barbara Allen and Arnold Hirshon, "Hanging Together to Avoid Hanging Separately: Opportunities for Academic Library Consortia," *Information Technology & Libraries* 17, 1 (1998): 36–44, 36.
30. W. Potter, "Recent Trends in Statewide Academic Library Consortia," *Library Trends* 45, 3 (1997): 416–34.
31. Evans, "Management Issues of Co-operative Ventures."
32. Allen and Hirshon, "Hanging Together to Avoid Hanging Separately."
33. Cited in Nfila and Darko-Ampem, "Developments in Academic Library Consortia."
34. D. Kohl, "OhioLink: A Vision for the 21st Century," *Library HiTech* 12, 3 (Fall 1994): 39–34.
35. D. Kohl, "Resource Sharing in a Changing Ohio Environment," *Library Trends* 45, 3 (1997): 435–47.
36. L. Payne, "The Washington Research Library Consortium: A Real Organization for a Virtual Library," *Information Technology & Libraries* 17, 1 (1998): 13–17.
37. Evans, "Management Issues of Co-operative Ventures."
38. From the blurb for *Fluid Mechanics* by Olu Ogboja http://www.ansti.org/publications.
39. James Currey was Editor of the African Writers Series from 1967 to 1984. James Currey Publishers are leading academic publishers on Africa and the Caribbean, specializing in archaeology, history, politics, development studies, economics, anthropology, gender studies, literary criticism, theater and film studies. See the James Currey web site, http://www.jamescurrey.co.uk/jcurrey/aboutus.asp?TAG=&CID=jcurrey.

40. See Janet Hussein, "African Association of Editors of Scholarly Journals in the Making," *Bellagio Publishing Network Newsletter* 31 (November 2002): 13; Carole Priestly, "On African Publishing Initiatives," *http://www.inasp.info/pubs/bookchain/profiles/priestley.html*.
41. African Centre for Technology Studies, *http://www.acts.or.ke/*.
42. University Press of New England FAQ, *http://www.dartmouth.edu/acad-isnt/upne/aboutupne.html*.
43. Jones, *The Restructuring of Scholarly Publishing*.
44. J. Currey, "Co-publishing: A Model," in J. Gibbs and J. Mapanje, eds., *African Writers' Handbook* (Oxford: African Books Collective 1999): 220–24, 223.
45. W. Bgoya, "Publishing in Africa: Culture and Development," in J. Gibbs and J. Mapanje, eds., *African Writers' Handbook* (Oxford: African Books Collective 1999): 59–84.
46. *Ibid.*

The Publishing Experiences of Historians[1]

Margaret Stieg Dalton

To obtain the views of scholars on the so-called crisis of the scholarly monograph, a questionnaire was sent to 1,461 historians in doctoral/ research universities asking about experiences in getting their books published and their opinions on a range of issues relating to publication. Included were questions on refereeing, on the changes they have encountered in the publication process since their first book, on electronic publishing, and on expectations of the future. Additional questions related to their practices as readers and buyers of books. Among the major conclusions were that the refereeing process is considered essential and that it accomplishes its purposes successfully; that there exists widespread reluctance to publish in a format that is available only electronically; that the emphasis on the bottom line in university presses has had an impact on the topics historians have chosen to investigate; that there is no agreement on the kind of books that history needs, although many would like to see more attention paid to what individuals who are interested in history but are not themselves scholars would like to read; and that the majority of historians are not finding it more difficult to get their books published than they did earlier in their careers.

Keywords: historians, electronic publishing, monographs, articles, buying patterns

Although the connection between research and publication precedes the founding of the *Journal des Sçavans* by the Académie Française in 1665, that event is usually considered the beginning of the system of modern scholarly communication. An aggregation of conferences, journals, and books—now augmented by the possibilities created by electronic communication—the system has served to disseminate the results of research, as research has grown from the work of a few gentlemen pursuing their intellectual interests to a not-so-small industry. Simultaneously an intellectual, economic, social, and cultural phenomenon, scholarly communication is now a system of great complexity, with stakeholders who include publishers, librarians and booksellers, scholars, and readers, as well as society at large.

Like most systems, the system of scholarly communication is constantly evolving. Its instability in the United States in the last decades of the twentieth century produced cries of a "crisis," most particularly with respect to the form of publishing known as the scholarly monograph.[2] Conferences were held, papers were written, and doubtless the "crisis" was the topic of many a conversation in faculty lounges and clubs. In the flood of words on the topic, however, the scholar's viewpoint has rarely been represented in print. This article is an attempt to fill that gap.[3]

But why historians? Historians were chosen because the scholarly monograph is central to their discipline; at least one is generally required for tenure. In addition, scholarly books in the area of history are central to the programs of almost every university press. An estimate shows that in 1895 at least 7 percent of the books published by university presses in the United States were in the field of history. By 1925 that figure had grown to at least 12 percent; in 1955 it was 15 percent, in 1985 17 percent, and in 2004 22.5 percent.[4] A final reason for the focus on historians is personal. This research builds on thirty years of previous work in scholarly communication, especially the scholarly communication of historians.[5]

For all its importance in their lives, historians have had relatively little to say about the publishing process. When historians write memoirs, they write about their research and their lives, the interesting people they have met, their adventures both scholarly and otherwise, their successes, and their disappointments. Their books are mentioned, but primarily in terms of ideas. Only a few historians' autobiographies have anything to say about publication, and, when they do discuss it, they tend to weigh the merits of a commercial publisher versus a scholarly publisher or to advocate writing for a broad audience, rather than discussing the process itself.[6]

One can protest that those who have written such memoirs belong to a generation remote from present problems and needs, but a 2003 discussion sponsored by the Organization of American Historians demonstrated that at least some of the fundamental concerns about publication have not changed. One contributor to this symposium deplored the lack of progress in engaging public audiences. Another asked pointedly, "Why must so much energy go into creating scholarly obscurity?" At the same time, however, this discussion reflected some of the concerns of the 1990s. The statement "There is so much to read today, too much for any one set of eyes" not only hints at the manifold changes in the character of the academic life[7] but also suggests a reason for the declining sales per title experienced by university presses in recent decades. The declaration that "it is vital that we maintain our tradition of monographic scholarship addressed only to one another" asserts the importance of preserving the endangered publication of specialized scholarly monographs.[8]

To obtain a broad picture of what historians are presently experiencing and thinking with respect to publication, a questionnaire (see Appendix A) was developed and distributed in the spring of 2005 to 1,416 randomly selected individuals from the 4,651 individuals listed on the Web sites of the history departments of those universities in the United States categorized as "doctoral/research universities—extensive" by the Carnegie Foundation. In total, 461 usable responses were returned, an impressive number given the length and complexity of the survey.[9] This high rate of return demonstrates how vital publication is in the life of historians and how concerned they are.

The principal focus of the questionnaire was the scholarly monograph. How do historians proceed when they have a manuscript to publish? What problems do they encounter? Does the need to be published influence them intellectually? What do they think about the process of publication? What do they plan to do in the future? And, finally, do they buy and read the scholarly monographs written by other historians?

The respondents to the questionnaire were predominantly tenured faculty; almost twice as many were full professors as all other ranks combined; only ninety of the 461 (19.6 percent) were untenured. It is highly unlikely, therefore, that any respondent falls into the category about which there is the most concern: those junior faculty who are either being turned down for tenure or, more commonly, leave before coming up for tenure.[10] Such persons could have been included only if they had been rejected by one university but subsequently hired by one of the departments included in the survey. In short, survey respondents are predominantly the successes of the field.

The demographic and intellectual characteristics of the respondents reflect the composition of most history departments. By more than two to one, respondents were male rather than female. Historians of the United States were most common, although historians interested in other parts of the world were well represented. In terms of time period, the most recent dominated: about one-third of respondents specialized in the nineteenth and/or twentieth centuries. Cultural history was the most frequent topical specialization.

Finding a Publisher

The publication of a scholarly book begins with a manuscript. For the vast majority (88.7 percent) of the historians in the survey who had published at least one book, their first book began as their doctoral dissertation. Since a book was essential to tenure and promotion, the necessity for speed precluded any alternative, and, almost invariably, it was a scholarly monograph rather than any other kind of book, although several described their first books as having a broader potential audience than the typical scholarly monograph in history. Most (87.8 percent) did some revision, but a minority (12.2 percent) said they simply submitted the dissertation unrevised. The publication process, however, did not necessarily begin with a *completed* manuscript. Almost one-third of the respondents reported having approached a publisher before their manuscript was completed. From beginning research to submitting to a publisher, the average time elapsed was 6.8 years.

How was a publisher for that first scholarly book selected and then approached? The historians were likely to seek a university press; for historians, "scholarly publisher" is virtually synonymous with "university press," and a substantial 80.5 percent of first scholarly books were published by university presses. In a few cases, no search for a publisher—or choice of publisher—was necessary, because the historian had received a post-doctoral fellowship or a prize that carried with it publication. For the most part, however, when young historians made their choices among publishers, the factor of greatest significance was the specialization of the press (39.2 percent). The prestige of the press ran a close second (34.6 percent). Other influential factors were the quality of the staff of the press or the likelihood of reaching a broad audience; one historian wanted a publisher that would make his publication available in Africa. Once an appropriate press was selected, the press was approached. About half (51.3 percent) of respondents made their own initial contact on their first book; in the remaining cases, contact was initiated by the publisher (28.2 percent) or by the historian's advisor or mentor (20.5 percent). Comments make it clear that personal connections have an important role. A number of respondents mentioned meeting the publisher at a conference; one met his editor at a cocktail party. As for how many publishers were approached, the most common response was only one (43.8 percent); the second most common choice was three to five presses (25.2 percent).

The survey shows that as historians advance in their careers, changes occur. They are less likely to write a scholarly monograph; they are more likely to be approached by a publisher than they were earlier; and they tend to contact fewer publishers. One area that does not change, however, is the number of presses to which they submitted a completed manuscript. The number of presses to which respondents reported submitting their most recent scholarly book is strikingly similar to the equivalent number for their first scholarly book.

Acceptance and Revision[11]

A critical reading by an expert—usually called "reviewing" for a book and "refereeing" for an article—is the hallmark of scholarly publication. Once a publisher expresses an interest in a manuscript, the manuscript is sent to such an expert. The mechanics vary. Sometimes the expert is a member of the publisher's editorial board; sometimes he or she has no affiliation with the publisher. The author may well also have sent the manuscript to colleagues before submitting it to a publisher, although such readings would not meet the publisher's need for an expert evaluation. The manuscripts of the survey respondents were sent by the publisher to an average of 2.7 readers.

The most common form of revision suggested by these outside readers was cosmetic rewriting (40.0 percent). Next most common was the recommendation to treat additional aspects of the topic (20.4 percent). Suggestions of greater attention to related scholarship, more attention to the wider context of the topic, revision or rethinking of the central argument, shortening of the length, and more attention to the theoretical framework were considerably less frequent. Making the requested revisions took an average of nine months.

Satisfaction with this reviewing process is general. Of the 351 respondents who answered the question on how they evaluated the readers' suggestions, 85.5 percent considered them helpful (ranging from mildly helpful to very helpful) and only 2.0 percent considered them inappropriate or wrong. Historians clearly consider review a positive experience; 88.5 percent of respondents believe that their book is a better one, thanks to reviewing and revision.

Not that there was no criticism: different comments on the same book could be at once helpful, indifferent, and wrong. One historian found one reader very helpful and the second reader completely out of line, wanting a book totally different in subject and recommending the use of sources that did not exist. Another described the comments received as "rude, nasty, and obnoxious." Comments could be worthless because of "lack of knowledge."

Change

Because the initial impetus behind this research was the desire to test the reality of the "crisis" in scholarly publishing, several questions on the theme of change were addressed to historians who had had more than one scholarly monograph published. A large number (86.1 percent) reported either that they had had an easier time finding a publisher for their most recent scholarly monograph than for their first scholarly monograph or that the level of difficulty had been about the same. Initial contact with the publisher of the most recent monograph was less likely to have been made by an advisor or mentor or initiated by a direct inquiry from the author and more likely to have come from the publisher.

Many respondents interpreted the question about their perception of changes that had taken place in the publishing process in personal terms. As one historian put it, "I think my experience with the latest book was easy because I have a reputation in my field. Younger scholars appear to have a very hard time finding a publisher." Another saw the role of reputation quite differently: "Reputation of author and earlier work seems not to matter. I think it used to matter."

If one looks at publication in terms of where a historian was published, the picture is one of considerable stability.[12] For seventeen historians, the same press published both their first scholarly monograph and their most recent; fourteen of those presses were university presses, two were trade publishers, and one was a scholarly publisher but not a university press. (The Pipe Roll Society is an example of a scholarly publisher that is not a university press.) When university press publishers are ranked in twenty-two groups in terms of perceived quality,[13] thirty-one historians remained in the same-ranked group for both their first and their latest scholarly monographs; forty-eight published their second monograph with a press of less prestige than their first (on average 4.7 groups lower); and thirty-seven published their most recent monograph with a press of higher reputation (on average 4.6 groups higher).

When addressing what they thought had changed about the process of getting a book published—as opposed to how easy it was for them—historians displayed a considerable range of opinion. Many authors of more than one scholarly monograph felt that not much had changed. Those who did identify changes mentioned differences in production practices and in various intellectual, social, and economic features of publication. On some points there was no consensus: opinion on whether too much or too little is being published was divided, as was opinion on whether there is greater specialization or less specialization of topics.

There was widespread agreement, however, that scholarly publishers increasingly focus on the bottom line. One historian summarized the situation succinctly: "Marketing factors are clearly more important now." Another described publishers as "far more concerned about potential sales than they were 35 years ago." Words like "marketability" and "profitability" were used, and the desire of presses to have an author obtain a subsidy was mentioned. That the production process today is different from what it was earlier was frequently noted. Computers are now ubiquitous; e-mail has brought speedier communication and made regular contact easier. The entire production process, in fact, is clearly faster. Some new practices have had drawbacks. An emphasis on speed, for example, has sometimes meant that authors get less individual attention. In general, less work is done in-house by publishers. Copy-editing in particular is neglected. One respondent summarized the results of these changes as follows:

> As an historian, I'm also concerned by the decreasing standards of book editing, and publishers' tendency to skimp on footnotes, which are fundamental to good historical monographs.

Other changes are more subtle but have important intellectual consequences for the discipline. As one historian stated, "Most presses are under pressure to publish in trendy areas and to generate income." The need for wider audiences has led to a preference for shorter, less specialized books with fewer footnotes. Many historians feel that presses are less willing to publish monographs. There is also general agreement on two points that have important implications for the future of historical scholarship in the United States. First, first-time authors have a harder time than established historians getting a book accepted by a publisher; second, some fields are particularly disadvantaged, notably European history and Latin American history. One suspects that virtually any non-U.S. history topic is similarly handicapped.[14]

Trade publishers do not loom large in the publication of scholarly historical monographs; only 15 percent of the 408 first and most recent monographs written by the 204 historians who answered section D of the survey were published by commercial presses. Of those historians who published at least two monographs, only thirteen published both their first and most recent monographs with a commercial publisher. An additional twenty-two historians published their first monograph with a commercial press and their most recent with a university press; eleven of those university presses ranked in either Group 1 or Group 2 in terms of prestige. A further fifteen historians published their first monograph with a university press—seven of the presses in question were in either Group 1 or Group 2—and their most recent with a trade house.

Scholarly presses that are not university presses have an even smaller role. Only 3 percent, fourteen of the 408 titles, were published by scholarly presses that were not university presses, and, of the eleven individuals involved, only three published both their first and most recent books with such presses.

Electronic Publishing

Electronic publishing, that is, writing in digital form that is disseminated on the World Wide Web, has been a reality since the 1980s. Use of the term "electronic publishing" varies. Electronic publishing can be quite formal, as in a peer-reviewed journal, or it can be completely informal, as on an individual's personal Web site. The electronic publication may be available only in digital form and not on paper, or it may be available in both. Many traditional journals now publish in both paper and digital formats, and many previously published books have been digitized. For the purposes of the survey and of this discussion, the term "electronic publishing" refers an original work that is published *only* in electronic format.

It was recognized early that without scholarly acceptance, electronic publishing can play only a limited and, indeed, questionable, role in scholarly communication.[15] Previous research has established the following points that are relevant to this study:

- that humanists are more reluctant to accept digital publication than natural or social scientists
- that scholarly credibility (i.e., the peer-review process) is essential to acceptance
- that technology has yet to reach a comfortable stage (e.g., some individuals find it unpleasant to read extensive material on a screen)

At the same time, the steadily rising costs, both financial and social—as when a scholar fails to get the manuscript of an article or book accepted—have forced the interested parties (scholars, publishers, and buyers) to consider alternatives to paper. In the field of history, Gutenberg-e, a joint project of Columbia University Press and the American Historical Association to publish outstanding dissertations, is a major pioneering effort.[16]

Like other humanists, historians continue to be reluctant to publish electronically, although they are not uninterested in the new medium. Of those who participated in the survey, only 16.5 percent said that they had published anything in electronic format, and it was clear from comments that most of those publications were book reviews. Responses to the survey item "Whether you have published electronically or not, please describe the circumstances under which you would be willing to publish electronically" make it clear that many, even if they would publish electronically, would do so grudgingly.

A few used their responses to this request to explain why they would not consider it. A perceived lack of prestige, the ease with which an electronic publication can be plagiarized, and concern for long-term preservation were mentioned. One person wrote that he just likes paper, and pointed out that that was why he was returning the survey in its paper form. One respondent expressed his opposition with particular vigor, saying that he would consider electronic publication only "if hell freezes over."

The circumstances under which the respondents said they might consider electronic publication clarify their reservations; many of their conditions appeared as reasons given by those who would not publish electronically. Vague but significant words such as "quality" and "appropriate" appeared frequently. Several thoughtful responses combined intellectual and technological factors; for example:

> I think the simple and honest answer is that I am waiting for some kind of critical mass, that electronic publishing will be recognized to be as important and prestigious as publishing on paper. That said, on a more philosophical level, I think I am waiting for technology that makes it as easy to read on a screen as on paper. Say a high-definition screen in size and weight of a typical book. At present, I find it very hard to read more than a few pages on a screen (and I am not yet forty).

The single most frequently mentioned precondition—raised by forty-two of the 304 who were willing to contemplate electronic publication—was some variation on the theme of prestige. Only if the profession accepts electronic publication as equal in prestige to publication on paper will these historians be willing to publish electronically. That position, however, raises another question: How can the format achieve respectability if historians are unwilling to publish in it? Bound up with prestige is the issue of the credit universities are willing to give for electronic publication; twenty respondents mentioned acceptance by the university as essential to their participation.

A dictionary definition of "prestige" is "standing or weight in the eyes of people."[17] For a publication to have standing in the eyes of historians, peer review is a *sine qua non*. No fewer than thirty-nine of the respondents to the question about the circumstances under which they would be willing to publish electronically used the words "peer review." Others were obviously thinking of it when they used terms such as "rigorous" and "quality."

Another group of responses to this question focused on the audience for the publication. Some historians saw electronic publishing as enabling them to reach a wider audience. Others saw it as appropriate for highly specialized works, with their concomitant narrow audiences, while still others saw it as a way of reaching non-specialists.

Preservation was a major concern; present-day historians are clearly aware that some day they will be history, and they want their contributions to be accessible. This concern appeared in various guises. One historian wanted to be convinced "that [electronic publications] will be available for a century or more, like paper publications." Some would publish electronically if a paper version were also available, which seems a rather qualified form of electronic publication. Some considered storage on JSTOR or Project Muse, or confidence in the stability of the URL, acceptable alternatives.

Authors' rights also figured in responses, both generally and specifically. Assurance that electronically published material would be copyrighted is important to respondents, and this concern sometimes manifested itself as recognition that plagiarism of digital records is very easy. The services provided by a publisher to an author, such as copy-editing and publicity, were also mentioned.

Then there were the practical reasons. A number of historians would acquiesce in electronic publication "if there were no alternative," although the variant "If there were no print outlet of quality" suggests that the virtues of print are not absolute. Another condition that made electronic publishing thinkable for respondents was an invitation, especially if the invitation came from a friend or the topic were appealing. Finally, there is money: several said they would do it if payment could be guaranteed. And every historian may have his price—one optimistic respondent set his at $100,000.

For all that the majority of historians remain reluctant to publish electronically, there is appreciation of the medium's potential. One respondent summarized the new opportunities the digital environment offers as "digitized images, video, sound, hypertext links, etc." Another was on the verge of publishing electronically a database including information on 15,000 people who had worked in a particular area of endeavor, a publication that he believed no publisher would be able to undertake on paper. The opportunity to include copious primary documents and the ability to update work are other attractive possibilities of electronic publication.

Future Publications

Responses to the question asking historians where they expected to concentrate their energies in the future show that the book is still the primary mode of communication. Three quarters of those responding indicated that they expected to concentrate on either scholarly monographs or scholarly treatises; the 18.6 percent who said they intend to write scholarly treatises may well be doing so out of a desire to accommodate university presses' demands for more marketable books. Their reasons for choosing to devote the majority of their efforts to a book rather than an article reflect the profession's values: that many significant historical topics require protracted discussion; that a book is a way of achieving a certain scholarly immortality; that a book is particularly honored by their peers. For some, however, the motivation to write books is simpler. As more than one historian wrote, "I enjoy it."

Those who said they plan to concentrate on articles tended to do so for practical reasons: an article is a smaller investment of time and energy, its format is more suitable for their research, or they believe an article is more likely to be read. One historian, however, described his preference for articles and book chapters as based more in his temperament, his wide-ranging interests, and his short attention span than in any perception that scholarly monographs and treatises are getting harder to publish. Another, a specialist in Renaissance Europe, took the occasion to assert that "I think articles, in general, are a better, more efficient, less *wasteful* format" and that "*MANY* books could be boiled down to articles!" His statement is slightly less colorful than the MLA Task Force Report's assertion that many monographs are really "articles on steroids,"[18] but it addresses the same issue.

For most, publishability is a matter of interest—the majority of historians consider it when choosing a book topic—but it clearly does not lead historians to favor articles over books. As one remarked, "I think about it, but go ahead and write what I want to write anyway." Some historians plan to step outside the traditional formats for historical scholarship. One is interested in making a documentary film, a few want to write history for a popular audience, and several plan historical or other novels.

When those who had not indicated that they would concentrate their efforts on scholarly monographs were asked what might convince them to write one, practical considerations, especially time, figured prominently. Most common, however, was an enticing topic. Adjectives used ranged from "appropriate" to "good," "right," "big," and "juicy."

Whether for intellectual or practical reasons, books, and especially scholarly monographs, are a leading element in the *Weltanschauung* of historians. Scholarly monographs may be more difficult to get published than they used to be, but 80.0 percent of the respondents would encourage their doctoral students just appointed to a tenure-track position to concentrate their energies on writing a monograph.

The preeminence of the book is also apparent in how historians think of their careers. When asked in which of their publications they took the most pride, 86.0 percent listed a book. When asked why, one respondent wrote, "It's a good book!" Another said, "I like the way it turned out. It said things that were important to me." Many responses emphasized the character of the work; that it was "pioneering," "original," or a "classic" were among the more frequent explanations. Quality of research and the sheer amount of work were other reasons for pride, as was a conviction that the work was well written. A sense of accomplishment and personal involvement with the work were often apparent, and several commented that writing it had been fun. One person was pleased because "posterity can argue with me now." Some, of course, found it difficult to make a choice. More than a few were equally proud of all of their publications, although a greater involvement with the most recent or the one currently in progress was also evident.

The reception of that book as a reason for pride was less prominent, but it was not irrelevant. Several historians were proud of a book because it had been reviewed well, had been translated, or was still in print. Some felt that their books had been influential; others mentioned prizes. One individual wrote:

> I have worked on this project for 17 years—since I was 23 years old and in my first year of grad school—and I believe I have discovered and uncovered many connections that have not been synthesized before; plus I think it is well written, very well researched, and honestly, everybody who has read it has told me it is a wonderful, exciting, sometimes funny, and entertaining book that shows how vital gender is to the construction of political discourse. Colleagues who have assigned portions in their classes tell me that gender as an analytical category really "clicks" for students.

But books are not only a source of pride; they are almost invariably a critical factor in building the career of a historian. Of the respondents,

88.3 percent credited a book with having had the most impact on their careers. The most frequently cited effect was that the publication had made their name familiar to other historians in a positive way (46.9 percent); the second most frequently cited effect was that it had helped them to get tenure (33.2 percent). Some mentioned a promotion or a move to a better job. That the monograph had brought opportunities to speak and to consult were among other assorted benefits. The all-pervasive, comprehensive impact a good book can have was summed up by one British historian who wrote that his first book secured his tenure and established him as a legitimate historian in his area of specialty; "without this, nothing else is possible."

When respondents were asked where they would encourage doctoral students just appointed to a tenure-track position to concentrate their efforts, the results again affirmed the primacy of the monograph. Writing a monograph would be recommended by 80.0 percent, writing articles by only 10.0 percent, and teaching by only 4.6 percent. Comments, however, show an appreciation that what is most important varies among colleges and universities. Many supplemented their response with some version of "It depends entirely upon the institution. This cannot be answered in the abstract." It is clear that these professors realize that many who receive doctorates from universities in the "doctoral/research—extensive" category are then getting jobs at institutions where good teaching is more highly valued than research.

Historians as Readers and Buyers

A major contributory cause of the "crisis" of the scholarly monograph is the diversion of library budgets from books to electronic resources and the technology needed to support those resources. Perhaps even more important, however, is the shifting of library funds from books to periodical subscriptions. In the last quarter-century, the rising costs of periodical subscriptions have outrun inflation, a trend only exacerbated by the move to digital delivery, the mode in which libraries now deliver most periodicals. The shrinking of this market is so serious because individual buyers have not for many years been a major market for scholarly monographs. Herbert Bailey, director emeritus of Princeton University Press, in an article in *Scholarly Publishing* published in 1988, traced the decline of book sales at Princeton University Press from 1,660 copies per title of hardback publications in 1969 to 1,003 in 1984.[19] Today university presses expect to sell, on average, fewer than 500 copies per title.[20] Bailey also noted that individual buyers in some fields, such as classics and gender studies, were more likely to buy than those in other fields, such as sociology, suggesting that desire to support the field was a motivating factor.[21]

The figures from this survey bear out the idea that university presses cannot look to individuals as a substantial market for scholarly monographs,[22] nor can journal publishers have much more optimism. The respondents to this survey claimed to have purchased an average of 16.9 scholarly monographs in the preceding six months; they subscribe to an average of 3.8 journals, and to subscribe to any electronic journal is very rare.

Respondents reported that they had read an average of 19.5 scholarly monographs and 34.5 articles in the last six months.[23] Although there is no evidence about the nature of their periodical reading, their reading of monographs is predominantly related to their research.[24] Comparing the two figures, we find that the average of 13.3 monographs read having to do with research and the average of 16.9 monographs bought strongly suggest that respondents' purchases are primarily in the area of their research interests. Certainly, their reading is. Seventy-two of the 368 individuals who answered question F.6 (see Appendix A) reported that 75 percent or more of their reading had to do with research.

The Books History Needs

Some respondents found the task of describing briefly the kind of books history needs impossibly broad, while others considered the answer self-evident. As one put it, "Incisive works based on vast archival research on important topics, duh." A few thought the field was fine and the distribution of kinds of books "just right." With an academic avoidance of the simple answer, others wrote, "it depends." Still others opted for variety: "Many different kinds—there's a place for close study of narrow topics as well as sweeping studies for more general audiences. History can be a big tent." The most poetic version was, "Let a hundred (well-written) flowers bloom."

As might be anticipated, beyond such generalities agreement was limited. Some historians wanted more theory, others less. Some felt that there should be less of the social-science approach, while others wanted more. The need for interdisciplinary work was often mentioned, most elegantly phrased as a need for "field-crossing, nuanced, and analytically complex books." There were those who wanted books on large topics and those who wanted micro-histories; there were those who wanted clear arguments and those who wanted less argumentation. One thing no one wanted was longer books, although a number urged shorter ones.

Where there does appear to be considerable consensus is on what might be called the staples of history. These are the traditions that come from the field's past, some even antedating the development of professional history in the nineteenth century. Probably the most important of these is the conviction that an understanding of history is important for every educated person. Of the 346 individuals who wrestled with this question, eighty, or almost one fourth, mentioned the need to write books that will appeal to an audience beyond the members of the academy, books that present scholarship in accessible ways. The most succinct statement of this view was, "Ones that won't bore the daylights out of my Mom." At the same time, however, many made it clear that these accessible works must maintain scholarly standards; "garbage" is to be avoided.

Good writing was a priority, perhaps a legacy of the time when history was a form of literature. Not all would agree completely with the historian who wrote that "history is a humanity, not a 'social science.' It retains a narrative obligation to its readers," but there is a widely shared conviction that history should be well written. Those sought-after broad audiences, after all, are not going to put up with less. Jargon is to be eschewed, especially "trendy jargon" and "theory jargon."

Research, good research, was less often mentioned, probably because it is taken for granted, although one participant did argue the need for books that are "steeped in sources." The clearest indication that sustained research in archives is inseparable from the historical enterprise was the historian who felt that "general thought provoking works rather than simply well researched" books are needed. The need to include nontraditional sources was also mentioned.

Probably the most varied "needs" perceived were those of topic. The topic could be quite specific, such as twentieth-century popular culture, the Carolingian period, medieval China, or oppressed and dispossessed Middle Eastern peoples; one historian even called for "obscure topics" in Spanish cultural and intellectual history. The topics could also be quite general, such as religion, women's history, or, on one historian's list, sensory history, temporal history, and comparative history. Several historians called for history relevant to current events and policy formation; one described politics and policy as "dangerously neglected topics." Such works would have relevance for every concerned citizen, coordinating with the "history is for everyone" theme. Historians, in short, want "significant" questions to be examined, but what constitutes significance is a matter of individual opinion.

Many historians seemed to be thinking in terms of formats or types of books, which is not surprising in view of the thrust of the questionnaire. Although biographies, collections, textbooks, and oral histories were categories of books mentioned, most commonly, historians wanted some combination of scholarly monographs and scholarly treatises. As one wrote:

> I think we need both the scholarly monograph and the treatise. I think a monograph proves one's ability to conduct original research and follow through on a project; the treatise should be part of one's maturation as a scholar.

Certainly, from the point of view of the field, the two are intertwined. One respondent wrote, with particular clarity:

> I like cross-over books myself, the kind you describe as scholarly treatises. Works like Natalie Davis's *Return of Martin Guerre*, Laurel Ulrich's *Midwife's Tale*, Louis Menand's *Metaphysical Club*, and Timothy Tackett's *When the King Took Flight* offer ways to bridge the specialized research of the academic profession with the general interest of the reading public beyond the university. That being said, however, I don't think these or any other scholarly treatises could exist without the specialized work of the scholarly monographs that came before.

Scholarly treatises clearly have greater market potential, but scholarly monographs are "where contributions are made," even if market forces do not favor them. History does, indeed, need many different kinds of books to fulfil the purposes historians have historically regarded as its responsibility.

"Syntheses" were frequently identified as desirable, a category that seems to mean books of breadth, books that seek to be less specialized and to combine diverse elements into a coherent and readable whole. Probably belonging to this category would be those described as "transnational" or "comparative history" or even as "big picture." A synthesis also implies a quality that several historians explicitly identified: mature judgement and comprehensive knowledge. How a synthesis differs from the questionnaire's category of "scholarly treatise" is not apparent.

Originality is valued, and attention was paid to innovation. Many respondents identified a need for imaginative and thoughtful books, books that are ground-breaking and take new approaches, books that push the intellectual and disciplinary boundaries. One called for "riskier" books.

A few historians clearly believe that books should be written more slowly; "we're all being rushed into print," lamented one. The demand for speed is the result of a tenure process that "forces far too many people to publish books too quickly," not to mention a system of rewards and punishments that requires constant publication. These results led one respondent to call for "fewer but better books."

A number of historians voiced practical considerations. Shorter books were suggested by at least ten individuals, one specifying 125 pages as optimal. Also mentioned was cost. One respondent, a historian of Soviet Central Asia, deplored the absence of $18 paperbacks in his field; Americanists, he noted, are abundantly supplied with them.

Comments

When asked for any comments or insights they might have to offer, 190 historians had something to say. What emerges most clearly from their words is a collective concern for the discipline. Adjectives tended to the pessimistic—"miserable," "dreadful," "depressing," and "a mess" are examples. Most responses concentrated on problems, only a few displaying satisfaction or optimism.

The largest cluster of concerns derives from the increasing dominance of economic considerations in scholarly publishing as university administrators push their presses to be self-sustaining or even profitable. Historians recognize that university presses are being forced to behave as commercial enterprises, but they hardly approve. What Nicholas Murray Butler, later president of Columbia University, wrote in his 1889 proposal to establish a department of publication at Columbia is as true now as it was then: the results of research are "always of a technical character and usually destitute of commercial value."[25] Historians see the consequences of the new emphasis on profit as having led to a loss of diversity of the kind of material published; the need to have a book be "trendy" and the problems of many small fields are among the consequences.

That the impact is most severely felt by junior faculty is also appreciated. With a book the *de facto* if not *de jure* requirement for tenure at any U.S. university in the "doctoral/research—extensive" category and the probationary period for tenure effectively five years, the pressures on anyone who is untenured are enormous. A few historians called for reconsideration of the insistence on a book for tenure, but others defended that first scholarly monograph as the necessary proof of scholarship.

A second group of concerns follows the increasing pressure from universities for what is often referred to as "productivity." Some historians expressed distaste for the emphasis on numbers and its consequence, too many monographs. One summarized the situation this way: "There is a lot of fluff being published—better to publish less and make sure it is significant to the field."

Correlations

Assumptions underlie most research, and this survey was no exception. One such assumption was that historians were finding it more difficult to find a publisher than they previously had (survey item D.4). The findings did not support this. Because ease or difficulty seem likely to be related to various factors, however, responses to this question were correlated with the quality of the university at which the historian was located, with his or her area of specialization and gender, and with the year in which his or her highest degree was received. In none of the cases was there any correlation of statistical significance. In other words, neither the distinction of the university at which a historian is employed; the geographic, temporal, and topical areas in which the historian specializes; whether the historian is male or female; nor when his or her Ph.D. was received shows any sign of affecting the response to the question of whether finding a publisher is easier, harder, or about the same as it was for the first book. The closest any such variation comes to statistical significance is that of gender: 46.0 percent of female historians, as compared to 60.9 percent of their male colleagues, found subsequent publication easier; 18.0 percent of female and 12.2 percent of male respondents found it harder; and 36.0 percent of female and 26.9 percent of male respondents found it about the same.

The question that asked where respondents expected to concentrate their future efforts (survey item E.1) was analyzed in terms of each individual's rank, quality of employing university, areas of specialization, gender, year in which degree was received, and tenure status. In this case there were significant differences in aspiration among ranks, by the year in which the Ph.D. was received, and between the tenured and the untenured. Professors and associate professors were significantly more likely than assistant professors to plan to spend their time on scholarly treatises or articles. Because full and associate professors are also more likely to have received their doctorates earlier than assistant professors, it is no surprise that an earlier doctorate also correlates with greater likelihood of concentrating on scholarly treatises and articles. Similarly, the untenured were more likely to concentrate on scholarly monographs. There was no significant difference among specializations.

The ability to subscribe to journals and to purchase scholarly monographs depends upon both disposable income and inclination. Professors were significantly more likely to subscribe to more journals than associate professors or assistant professors were; those who received their degrees earlier were significantly more likely than those who received them earlier to subscribe to more journals; and tenured respondents were significantly more likely than the untenured to subscribe to more journals. There was no significant difference among specializations, nor among the quality of employing universities. Greater income would appear to be the determining factor where journal subscriptions are concerned.

With respect to purchase of scholarly monographs, on the other hand, the results show the opposite pattern. Assistant professors purchased significantly more scholarly monographs than those of higher rank; those whose degrees are more recent purchased more monographs than those whose degrees were earlier, and the untenured were more likely to buy more monographs than the tenured. Again, the explanation is likely to be the obvious: disposable income is less important than the need of younger faculty to build their personal collections. There were no significant differences among specializations, nor was the quality of the employing university a significant factor.

The question about how many scholarly monographs had been read in the last six months produced no significant differences when analyzed by rank, by specialization, by year in which degree was received, or by tenure status. Historians at the five top-ranked history departments, however, read considerably more scholarly monographs than those at the five bottom-ranked history departments, an average of 22.5 versus 14.9 monographs. This difference is almost, but not quite, statistically significant.

Conclusions

If the results of this perception study were to be summarized in one sentence, that sentence would have to be this: The present faculty at doctoral/research universities—extensively have not themselves suffered from the "crisis" in scholarly publishing, but they share a deep uneasiness. That uneasiness pertains not just to publishing in the future—the only fact about which we can be certain being that it will be different from the present—but to the present itself. There is widespread recognition that junior faculty are experiencing difficulties in getting their work published, that historians in certain areas of history are experiencing difficulties in getting their work published, and that the future of the discipline is being influenced by less-than-welcome external forces. For the most part, however, the senior tenured faculty who primarily responded to this survey have found publishers for their work, even if those publishers were not their first choice.

It has been clear for some time that scholarly publishing is in a time of transition, if not crisis. Like every other area of human experience, scholarly publishing is in continuous transition, but the number and magnitude of the unresolved issues that have accumulated in the last two decades are exceptional. Answers to the following questions have yet to manifest themselves:

- What will be the relative roles of print and electronic publication?
- Will the requirements for tenure be modified, or will the scholarly monograph remain the *sine qua non*?
- What will be the role of the university press *vis-à-vis* commercial presses? With respect to tenure decisions?
- What balance will be struck between marketability and scholarship?

What scholarly publishing in history will be like ten or twenty years from now remains to be seen. Historians seem, however, to be well placed to influence their own future. The field, whether judged by the thoughtful responses to this questionnaire or by the reviews in the latest issue of the *American Historical Review*, is vibrantly alive. Its practitioners share a core of well-defined values, even if their priorities are not necessarily the same. The field benefits from its tradition that history is a matter of interest to the intelligent citizen. Many current historians believe that good history with wide appeal can be written—and they cite pertinent exemplars. This conviction makes them more willing to attempt to accommodate the university presses that are under such pressure to publish more profitable books.

At the same time, historians will be forced to address a number of questions—or will have answers forced upon them. Are they willing to sacrifice some scholarly conventions, such as footnotes and historiographical context, to make their works more attractive to a lay audience?[26] Many current historians call for studies on broader topics and syntheses, but are they willing to sacrifice depth? And what is the proper balance between quantity and quality?

In his memoirs, John Lukacs proclaimed the end of the Age of the Book, that is, the end of the habit of reading books that spread with the spread of printing.[27] Given the central role that the book has played in the dissemination of historical scholarship, books seem unlikely to disappear any time soon. The book of twenty years in the future, however, may well differ significantly from the book that has prevailed in the last century—in its physical format, in the breadth of its subject matter, and in the audience it is designed to attract. Whether the scholarly monograph will be as dominant as it is now appears doubtful, although it clearly plays, and will continue to play, a unique and essential role in historical scholarship.

Contributor

Margaret Stieg Dalton is a professor at the School of Library and Information Studies of the University of Alabama. She has written frequently on the subject of scholarly communications, particularly among historians.

Notes

1. Special thanks go to Dr. Elizabeth Aversa, director of the School of Library and Information Studies, for her generous support on this project. Cherry Quinn, Administrative Specialist; Clay Davis, Manager, Area Computer Services; and Xu Jie (Patrick), my graduate assistant, went above and beyond the call of duty with assistance on the survey. Patrick did all the correlations and statistical calculations. Linda Bathgate, of the publishing firm Lawrence Erlbaum Associates, suggested the important question, "Please describe briefly the kind of books you think the field of history needs" for the questionnaire. The members of the Department of History of the University of Alabama and my acquaintances among library historians performed that necessary favor, pre-testing the paper and electronic versions of the survey.
2. The crisis in the publication of journals is primarily a matter of rapidly rising prices and is particulrly acute in the natural sciences. For books, the issues are more involved. For a definition of the term "scholarly monograph," see the questionnaire (reproduced as Appendix A) that was the basis of this article; the term is defined in the questionnaire's preface.
3. The proceedings of a conference sponsored by the American Council of Learned Societies, the Association of American University Presses, and the Association of Research Libraries provides an introduction to the voluminous literature. Mary M. Case, ed., *The Specialized Scholarly Monograph in Crisis, Or, How Can I Get Tenure If You Won't Publish My Book?* (Washington, DC: Association of Research Libraries, 1999). Robert B. Townsend, "History and the Future of Scholarly Publication," *Perspectives* (October 2003), available at *http://www.historians.org/Perspectives/Issues/2003/0310/0310vie3.htm*, reviews many of the issues with specific application to the field of history. See also Margaret Stieg Dalton, "A System Destabilized: Scholarly Books Today," *Journal of Scholarly Publishing* 37, 4 (July 2006): 251–69.
4. These figures are rough estimates and make no pretense of exactitude. They are based on a study of the publications from four representative university presses at private institutions (Johns Hopkins University, the University of Chicago, Columbia University, and Princeton University) and four representative university presses at public institutions (the University of California, the University of Washington, the University of Illinois, and Louisiana State University). All records in WorldCat in which one of these presses was listed as a publisher were retrieved, and percentages for classification numbers (either Dewey or Library of Congress) in history were calculated. A number of factors require caution. The presses selected

are considered representative; no random sampling was attempted. In addition, only through machine cataloguing, which began with the MARC project in 1967, can one be certain that all university press publications are in WorldCat, although the number not listed is bound to be small. Finally, using classification numbers to determine what publications are in the field of history omits many historical publications. To give one example, Anne M. Butler, *Daughters of Joy, Sisters of Misery: Prostitutes in the American West, 1865–90* (Urbana: University of Illinois Press 1985) is undoubtedly historical, but it is classified in the LoC scheme as HQ ("The Family, Marriage, Women") and by Dewey as 306 ("Culture and Institutions"), and therefore is not included in the figures presented here: only books in the C, D, E, and F categories of the LoC classification scheme and those in the 900s of the Dewey decimal classification system have been counted.

5. E.g., Margaret F. Stieg, "The Information Needs of Historians: Or, How Historians Don't Use Libraries," *College and Research Libraries* 42, 6 (November 1981): 549–60; Margaret F. Stieg, "Refereeing and the Editorial Process: The *American Historical Review* and R.K. Webb," *Scholarly Publishing* 14, 2 (February 1983): 99–122; Margaret F. Stieg, *The Origin and Development of Scholarly Historical Periodicals* (University: University of Alabama Press, 1986); Margaret Stieg Dalton and Laurie Charnigo, "Historians and Their Information Sources," *College and Research Libraries* 65, 5 (September 2004): 400–25.

6. James Thomas Flexner, *Maverick's Progress: An Autobiography* (New York: Fordham University Press, 1996); H. Stuart Hughes, *Gentleman Rebel* (New York: Ticknor & Fields, 1990); John Lukacs, *Confessions of an Original Sinner* (New York: Ticknor & Fields, 1990); Dexter Perkins, *Yield of the Years* (Boston: Little, Brown, 1969).

7. Two obvious factors are the inexorable progress of specialization in academic fields and the heavy emphasis on productivity within universities.

8. "Interchange: The Practice of History," *Journal of American History* 90, 2 (September 2003): 576–611, 577, 588, 590, 594.

9. Approximately twenty completed pre-test questionnaires are included in this figure, slightly reducing the rate of return from the 40.6 percent represented by the total of 461. For a more detailed description of the survey, see Appendix A.

10. The only reliable statistics on this are from modern language departments, where, in the years between 1994/95 and 2003/04, only around 10 percent of tenure applicants were rejected but well over 20 percent of tenure-track faculty left the departments that had originally hired them before coming up for tenure. It seems probable that statistics for history departments are not much different. See Modern Language Association, *Report of the MLA Task Force on Evaluating Scholarship and Promotion* (December 2006), http://www.mla.org/tenure_promotion. This report was issued in 2006 and discussed at the MLA's December 2006 meeting.

11. Because some of the historians surveyed published their first books twenty or more years ago, only information about the acceptance and revision of their most recent book was requested.

12. A total of 204 historians indicated a publisher for both their first scholarly monograph and their most recent.

13. The perception of quality of a university press was considered to be the same as the perceived quality of the program in history. The rankings come from Marvin L. Goldberger, Brenden A. Maher, and Pamela Ebert Flattau, eds., *Research-Doctorate Programs in the United States: Continuity and Change* (Washington, DC: National Academy Press, 1995), Appendix Table P-22, "Relative Rankings for Research-Doctoral Programs in History." History programs are divided into

twenty-two groups of five. The highest-rated programs are those of Yale University, the University of California—Berkeley, Princeton University, Harvard University, and Columbia University. The presses at those universities are therefore Group 1, the highest-ranked university presses. To Group 1 were arbitrarily added the presses of Oxford University and Cambridge University. Both these presses publish a significant number of titles by U.S. historians, and their reputations are generally considered at least equal to those of U.S. institutions in Group 1.

14. The Association of American University Presses (AAUP) produces a subject-area grid that shows the areas in which each AAUP member press has a "strong interest": *Association of American University Presses Subject Area Grid, http://aaupnet. org/resources/AAUPGrid2008.pdf*. Its 128 members are the presses of universities in the United States, but its membership also includes both non-university scholarly presses, such as those of the Brookings Institution and the National Gallery, and non-U.S. university presses such as those of the University of Toronto, Oxford University, and the American University (Cairo). When tabulated, the results show that 93 profess a strong interest in history. Specialties in history are distributed as follows: American history, 83; environmental history, 58; modern history, 58; European history, 51; Latin American history, 39; British history, 33; Asian history, 30; Classical history, 29; Middle Eastern history, 28; ancient history, 27; Canadian history, 22; African history, 22.

15. This discussion is based on William Y. Arms, "Quality Control in Scholarly Publishing on the Web," *Journal of Electronic Publishing* 8, 1 (August 2002), available at *http://www.press.umich.edu/jep/08-01/arms.html*; Margaret A. Boden, "Appraisal of Research," in Karen Brookfield, ed., *Scholarly Communication and Serials Prices* (London: Bowker Saur 1991): 15–23; Jeanne Galvin, "The Next Step in Scholarly Communication: Is the Traditional Journal Dead?" *Electronic Journal of Academic and Special Librarianship* 5, 1 (Spring 2004), available at *http://southernlibrarianship.icaap.org/content/v05n01/galvin_j01.htm* (an excellent summary of the pros and cons); May Katzen, "Electronic Publishing in the Humanities," *Scholarly Publishing* 18, 1 (October 1986): 5–16; Cass T. Miller and Julianna C. Harris, "Scholarly Journal Publication: Conflicting Agendas for Scholars, Publishers, and Institutions," *Journal of Scholarly Publishing* 35, 2 (January 2004): 73–91; Geoffrey Rockwell and Lynne Siemens, "The Credibility of Electronic Publishing," *http://web.mala.bc.ca/hssfc/Final/QuestionnaireR.htm* (a survey of faculty attitudes in Canada); and Aldrin E. Sweeney, "Tenure and Promotion: Should You Publish in Electronic Journals?" *Journal of Electronic Publishing* 6, 2 (December 2000), available at *http://www.press.umich.edu/jep/06-02/sweeney.html* (a survey of faculty attitudes at the University of Florida).

16. Patrick Manning, "Gutenberg-e: Electronic Entry into the Historical Professoriate," *American Historical Review* 109, 5 (December 2004): 1505–26; Kate Wittenberg, "Digital Technology and Historical Scholarship: A Publishing Perspective," *Journal of the Association for History and Computing* 5 (November 2002), available at *http://mcel.pacificu.edu/JAHC/JAHCV3/ARTICLES/wittenberg/wittenberg.html*.

17. *Webster's Seventh New Collegiate Dictionary* (Springfield, MA: G. & C. Merriam 1972), *s.v.* "prestige."

18. *MLA Task Force Report*, 38.

19. Herbert S. Bailey, "The Future of University Press Publishing," *Scholarly Publishing* 19, 2 (January 1988): 63–9.

20. Mary M. Case, "Foreword," in Mary M. Case, ed., *The Specialized Scholarly Monograph in Crisis, Or, How Can I Get Tenure If You Won't Publish My Book?* (Washington, DC: Association of Research Libraries 1999): v–vii; Kate Torrey,

"Welcome and Introduction," in Mary M. Case, ed., *The Specialized Scholarly Monograph in Crisis, Or, How Can I Get Tenure If You Won't Publish My Book?* (Washington, DC: Association of Research Libraries, 1999): 3–8, 8; Joanna Hitchcock, "Reaching Specialized Audiences: The Publisher's Conundrum," in Mary M. Case, ed., *The Specialized Scholarly Monograph in Crisis, Or, How Can I Get Tenure If You Won't Publish My Book?* (Washington, DC: Association of Research Libraries 1999): 25–30, 27; and Marlie Wasserman, "How Much Does It Cost to Publish a Monograph and Why?" in Mary M. Case, ed., *The Specialized Scholarly Monograph in Crisis, Or, How Can I Get Tenure If You Won't Publish My Book?* (Washington, DC: Association of Research Libraries, 1999): 33–40, 36, all note the same sharp decline, and some of their estimates are even lower.

21. Bailey, "The Future of University Press Publishing," 64.
22. If one does the math, it appears that for each title in history published by a university press, a publisher could expect that approximately 98.4 copies would be sold to individual historians. In 2005, according to R.R. Bowker Inc., "Bookwire University Press Production 1993–2004," *http://www.Bookwire.com/university.html*, university presses published 1,599 titles in history. If one multiplies the average number of scholarly monographs purchased in the last six months by the historians who responded to the survey (16.9) by the number of faculty listed in history departments in the "doctoral/research universities—extensive" category, the result is that those 4,651 historians bought 157,203 books per year. Dividing that by the number of titles gives a result of 98.4 copies per title. Admittedly, this figure is very approximate. Not all scholarly monographs that historians might purchase are published by university presses, nor are all books published by university presses scholarly monographs; all historians who might buy books are not located at universities in this category. On the other hand, because of their institutions' focus on research, not to mention their better salaries, these historians are probably more likely than other historians to buy university press publications. The significance of selling 98.4 copies per title would also vary with the publisher's expectations. If the average scholarly monograph sells somewhat fewer than 500 copies, those 98.4 copies represent about 20 percent of total sales.
23. These figures are hardly exact. Many respondents used terms like "a lot" or said they could not remember.
24. Again, this is an estimate. "Most" was a term often employed.
25. Quoted in Gene R. Hawes, *To Advance Knowledge: A Handbook on American University Press Publishing* (New York: American University Press Services, 1967), 32.
26. Only one respondent addressed the general reader's uncomfortable allergy to footnotes. This historian was told by his editor (from one of the elite group of university presses) that footnotes were to be kept as short as possible; he was to avoid discursive footnotes, avoid putting dates in titles and chapter headings, and dwelling too much on scholarly debates, or his book might read like a dissertation. In other words, he was to "avoid making the book too scholarly!" Yet such a book is "what one's 'scholarly' reputation (and thus tenure decision) will be based on."
27. Lukacs, *Confessions of an Original Sinner*, 264.

Appendix A: The Questionnaire

Note: Explanatory material in italics was not part of the questionnaire distributed to historians.

Definitions of some terms used in this questionnaire:

Book: a set of written sheets bound together, either a paperback or hard back; a physical object. Example: your telephone directory.

Scholarly monograph: a book on a narrow topic by a specialist, intended for specialists with an interest in the same field. In history, based on research in primary sources, follows scholarly principles of argument and evidence, e.g., abundant footnotes. Has a limited market. Example: Margaret Stieg, *Laud's Laboratory: The Diocese of Bath and Wells in the Seventeenth Century*.

Scholarly treatise: a book on a broader topic than a monograph, intended for an audience of scholars in the author's field and loosely related fields and [which] may also be read by interested individuals who are not professional scholars. Primary research is not usually a major component; the author builds on the research of others, although he or she has probably done primary research in some aspect of the topic. Follows scholarly principles of argument. Example: James McPherson's *Battle Cry of Freedom*.

Scholarly book: any of the following: scholarly monograph; scholarly treatise; textbook; critical edition of a manuscript; collection of essays or proceedings for which you were the editor.

A. For those who have not yet published a book. *[Because 126 individuals filled in at least one question in this section, but only ninety individuals indicated that they were not tenured, either a significant number of individuals teaching in 2005 had received tenure without publishing a book or some tenured individuals answered questions without realizing that they were intended only for untenured historians.]*

1. Are you currently working on a book?
      50   yes.
      2   no.

2. If you are not currently working on a book, which of the following best describes your reasons for not doing so? After making your choice, skip to section E on page 5. *[Insufficient data to tabulate.]*

      _____   I need publications as soon as possible and it takes too long to get a book written and published.
      _____   it is too hard to get a book published.

_____ the topics in which I'm interested aren't suitable for book-length treatment.
_____ my university values articles more than books.
_____ I find the idea of writing a book too overwhelming.
_____ none of the above. Please describe briefly.

3. If you are working on a book, for how long have you been working on it? (Include research time as well as time spent writing.) _____ *[126 historians filled this in, therefore are presumably working on a book]*

    688.6   sum.
    5.5 yrs average.
    30 yrs highest.
    0.08 yr lowest (one month).

4. What kind of book is it?

105 (82.7 percent)	scholarly monograph.
13 (10.2 percent)	scholarly treatise.
3 (2.4 percent)	textbook.
1 (0.8 percent)	critical edition of a manuscript.
3 (2.4 percent)	collection of essays or proceedings, i.e., you were the editor.
2 (1.6 percent)	other (please specify).

5. If it is a scholarly monograph on which you're working, was it originally your dissertation?

    57   yes
    60   no

6. When you approach a publisher, what will be the most influential factor?

38 (34.9 percent)	overall prestige of the publisher.
46 (42.2 percent)	publisher specializes in the area of my manuscript, e.g., has a series in it.
3 (2.7 percent)	my advisor or mentor recommends this publisher.
7 (6.4 percent)	I think that the publisher will be likely to accept the manuscript.
2 (1.8 percent)	I want a commercial publisher because I can hope to earn some money from the book.
13 (11.9 percent)	other. Please describe briefly.

7. Have you had a manuscript rejected by a publisher after a review?

    26 (21.0 percent)   yes.
    98 (79.0 percent)   no.

8. If you have had a manuscript rejected, by how many publishers was it rejected? *[Insufficient data to tabulate.]*
9. If you are still seeking a publisher for a manuscript that has been rejected, please indicate when you first sent the manuscript out for its first reading by a publisher. *[Insufficient data to tabulate.]*

Please skip to section E on page 5.

B. Your first scholarly book (For those who have published or had accepted for publication at least one book).
1. In which year was your first scholarly book published?
        Average = 1989
2. How would you describe the character of the book?

345 (88.7 percent)	scholarly monograph.
17 (4.4 percent)	scholarly treatise.
1 (0.3 percent)	textbook.
12 (3.1 percent)	critical edition of a manuscript.
13 (3.3 percent)	collection of essays or proceedings, i.e., you were the editor.
1 (0.3 percent)	other.

3. Was your first book your dissertation in either a revised or unrevised version?
        295 (87.8 percent)   yes.
        41 (15.3 percent)   no.
4. If your first book was your dissertation, did you revise it before sending it to a publisher?
        295 (85.5 percent)   yes.
        41 (15.3 percent)   no.
5. Approximately how long did it take to write your first book from beginning research on the topic to its first submission to a publisher? If it was your dissertation, include that time in your estimate.
        Average = 6.8 yrs.
6. Approximately how much time elapsed between the first submission to the publisher that eventually published it and
        acceptance: average = 0.9 yrs
        publication: average = 2.1 yrs
7. At which stage in the process did you first approach a publisher?
        78 (7.9 percent)   with idea or proposal.
        195 (70.3 percent)   with completed manuscript.

107 (21.8 percent) somewhere between idea and completed manuscript stage.

8. What was the most influential factor in your choice of first publisher to approach?

    112 (34.6 percent) overall prestige of the publisher.
    127 (39.2 percent) publisher specialized in the area of my manuscript, e.g., has a series in it.
    57 (17.6 percent) my advisor or mentor recommended this publisher.
    26 (8.0 percent) I thought it likely the publisher would accept the manuscript.
    2 (0.6 percent) I wanted a commercial publisher because I hoped to earn some money from the book.
    0 (0.0 percent) other (please describe briefly).

9. How was the initial contact with the publisher who eventually published your first book made?

    78 (20.5 percent) my advisor/mentor spoke with the publisher.
    195 (51.3 percent) I inquired, either by letter or telephone, if they would be interested.
    107 (28.2 percent) the publisher spoke to me about the possibility of publication.

10. How many publishers do you estimate that you contacted about the possibility of publication, including the one that eventually accepted your manuscript? Please include all modes of communication in your estimate: letter, e-mail, telephone, face-to-face, etc.

    168 (43.8 percent)   1
    69 (17.8 percent)   2
    98 (25.2 percent)   3–5
    37 (9.5 percent)   5–10
    16 (4.1 percent)   More than 10

11. If you can remember, which mode of communication did you use?
        244 (71.3 percent)   letter.
        22 (6.4 percent)   telephone.
        19 (5.6 percent)   e-mail.
        55 (16.1 percent)   face-to-face.
        2 (0.5 percent)   other _____.

12. To how many publishers did you submit the completed manuscript for your first book before its acceptance?
        261 (67.1 percent)   1
        88 (22.6 percent)   2
        35 (8.9 percent)   3–5
        5 (1.2 percent)   More than 5

13. What kind of publisher published your first book?
        313 (80.5 percent)   university press.
        54 (13.9 percent)   commercial publisher.
        8 (2.1 percent)   historical society.
        14 (3.6 percent)   other (please specify).

Please continue on with Section C.

C. The review process on your most recent book, which may be the same thing as your first book (For those who have published or had accepted for publication at least one scholarly book).

1. How would you describe the character of your most recent book?
        256 (65.8 percent)   scholarly monograph.
        57 (14.6 percent)   scholarly treatise.
        21 (5.4 percent)   textbook.
        6 (1.5 percent)   critical edition of a manuscript.
        41 (10.5 percent)   collection of essays or proceedings, i.e., you were the editor.

2. How many readers was the manuscript sent to? *[354 people answered.]*
        2.7   Average
        30   High

3. How would you characterize the suggestions for revision that you received? Check all that apply. *["Single letters" indicates an individual chose only category; "multiple letters" indicates that he or she checked more than one and that the indicated category was one of them.]*

	Single letters	Multiple letters	Total	%
Cosmetic rewriting	132	109	241	40.0
Additional aspects of topic need to be treated	28	98	126	20.4
Greater attention to related scholarship on topic or closely related topic	6	49	55	8.9
More attention to the wider context of the topic, e.g., you're writing about economic developments in nineteenth-century Germany and more treatment of political developments is urged	6	49	55	8.9
Revision/rethinking of the central argument or theory	4	30	34	5.5
More theoretical framework be provided	1	25	26	4.2
Other (please describe)	26	21	47	7.6
Shorten [This category was added when the results were tabulated because so many responses in the "other" category were "shorten"]	9	25	34	5.5

4. Approximately how long did it take you to complete revisions?
   0.75 yrs (9 months)
5. How would you evaluate the readers' suggestions?
   300 (85.5 percent) helpful
   44 (12.5 percent) indifferent. They didn't help the book, they didn't hurt it.
   4 (1.1 percent) inappropriate
   3 (0.9 percent) wrong
6. Do you believe that it is a better book because of the reviewing and revision?
   324 (88.0 percent) yes
   44 (11.9 percent) no
7. At which stage did you receive a contract?
   131 (34.5 percent) after initial proposal.
   146 (38.4 percent) after first review of manuscript but before revision and final acceptance.
   103 (27.1 per cent) after final acceptance.

If you have published or had accepted one book, please skip to Section E; if you have published or had accepted more than one scholarly monograph, please continue on with Section D.

D. Comparing your recent with your previous experience (For those who have published more than one scholarly monograph. Only answer this section if you have had more than one scholarly monograph published or accepted for publication).

1. When was your most recent monograph published?
  Average = May 1999
2. Which publisher published your first scholarly monograph? *[This information was used to determine the prestige of the press.]*
3. Which publisher published your most recent scholarly monograph? *[This information was used to determine the prestige of the press.]*
4. Was it easier or harder to find a publisher for your most recent monograph than it was for your first scholarly monograph?

120 (57.4 percent)	easier
29 (13.9 percent)	harder
60 (28.7 percent)	about the same

5. How was the first contact with the publisher who published this scholarly monograph made?

27 (13.3 percent)	a colleague or mentor spoke with the publisher.
97 (47.8 percent)	I inquired, either by letter or telephone, if they would be interested.
79 (38.9 percent)	the publisher spoke to me about the possibility of publication.

6. How many publishers did you contact about the possibility of publication, including the one that eventually accepted your manuscript?

108 (52.1 percent)	1
47 (22.7 percent)	2
40 (19.3 percent)	3–5
10 (4.8 percent)	5–10
2 (1.0 percent)	More than 10

7. To how many publishers did you submit the completed manuscript for your first book before its acceptance?

145 (70.0 percent)	1
27 (13.0 percent)	2
33 (15.9 percent)	3–5
2 (1.0 percent)	More than 5

8. Please describe briefly what you think has changed about the process of getting a book published?
Please continue on with Section E.

E. Books, articles, and the future (For everyone).

1. Where do you consider yourself most likely to concentrate your energies in the future? Select **one**. *[Many respondents checked more than one category. These checks were included in the totals.]*

289 (56.1 percent)	scholarly monographs.
96 (18.6 percent)	scholarly treatises.
18 (3.5 percent)	textbooks.
8 (1.5 percent)	critical editions of manuscripts.
69 (13.4 percent)	articles.
35 (6.8 percent)	other. Please identify. _____

2. If you checked one of the book formats in question E.1, what is your primary motivation for this choice? *[Many respondents checked more than one category. These checks were included in the totals.]*

21 (4.7 percent)	I believe my choice has the greatest prestige.
73 (16.3 percent)	I believe that if I suceed, I will receive more rewards in terms of promotion and pay; in other words, my department and university prefers this form of publication.
142 (31.6 percent)	I believe that my choice is more likely to have a continuing impact through the years.
192 (42.8 percent)	I believe that the format I have chosen is best for the topics in which I am interested.
3 (0.67 percent)	I believe that the format I have chosen will be easier to get published.
18 (4.0 percent)	Other. Please describe.

3. If you checked "articles" in question E.1, what is your primary motivation?

22 (27.5 percent)	an article is a smaller investment of time and energy.
6 (7.5 percent)	it's easier to get an article published.
9 (11.3 percent)	an article can be published faster.
17 (21.2 percent)	an article is more likely to be read by my colleagues.
26 (32.5 percent)	other.

Please describe.

4. If you did not check "scholarly monograph" in question E.1, what might convince you to write one?

5. Does probable publishability influence your choice of topics when planning a monograph?

233 (59.6 percent)　yes
158 (40.4 percent)　no

6. Have you published an article in an electronic journal or a book in an electronic book program? For the purposes of this question an electronic journal is defined as a journal that is available **only** in electronic format; it does not include a journal like the *American Historical Review* that is available electronically, but is also published in paper. An electronic book program is defined as one that makes available new publications electronically, not one that makes available books previously published in print format.

72 (16.5 percent)　yes
364 (83.4 percent)　no

7. Whether you have published electronically or not, please describe the circumstances under which you would be willing to publish electronically.

8. In which of your publications do you take the most pride?

338 (86.0 percent)	a book, that was published by _____.
44 (11.2 percent)	an article, that appeared in the journal _____.
1 (0.25 percent)	not applicable because I have no publications (if you

check this skip the next three questions).

10 (2.5 percent) other   *[This category was added by a number of respondents because none of the above categories covered their situation.]*

9. Why are you proud of it?

10. In your opinion, which of your publications has had the greatest impact on your career?

    347 (88.3 percent)   a book, that was published by _____

    27 (6.8 percent)   an article, that appeared in the journal _____

    19 (4.8 percent) other   *[This category was added by a number of respondents because none of the above categories covered their situation.]*

11. How would you describe the character of the impact?

    103 (33.2 percent)   most important factor in my receiving tenure.

    56 (9.9 percent)   improved my pay.

    122 (46.9 percent)   made my name familiar to other historians in a positive way.

    9 (1.7 percent)   antagonized other historians.

    26 (8.1 percent)   other. Please describe.

12. Would you encourage your doctoral student who has just been appointed to a tenure track position to concentrate his or her energies on *[Many respondents checked more than one category. Those checks were included in the totals.]*

    44 (10.0 percent)   writing articles.

    379 (80.0 percent)   writing a monograph.

    22 (4.6 percent)   teaching.

    29 (6.1 percent)   other. Please describe.

13. Please describe briefly the kind of books you think the field of history needs.

Please continue on with Section F.

F. Reading of scholarly literature (For everyone)
1. How many scholarly journals do you personally subscribe to?
>Average = 3.8

2. How many of them are electronic journals, that is, journals that are **only** available electronically? *[410 respondents left this blank.]*
>20   0
>27   1
>4   1–2

3. Approximately how many scholarly articles have you read in the last six months? Include articles both from the journals you subscribe to and those you have obtained from other sources.
>Average = 34.5
>Highest value = 1,000

4. Approximately how many scholarly monographs have you bought in the last six months?
>Average = 16.9
>Highest value = 2,000

5. Approximately how many scholarly monographs have you read in the last six months?
>Average = 19.5
>Highest value = 400

6. Of these monographs, how many have to do directly with your research?
>Average = 13.3
>72 of 368 reported that 75 percent or more of their monograph reading had to do with their research.

Please continue on with Section G.

G. Biographical Information
1. Rank
>2   instructor
>92   assistant professor
>123   associate professor
>215   professor
>15   other (Please give your title)

2. Field of specialization, e.g., early twentieth century German cultural history *[Because many identified a specialization that included geographic, temporal, and topical features, or a specialization that fell into more than one group within a category, the totals vary.]*

Geographic specialization
- 179 United States
- 23 Latin America
- 117 Western Europe
- 24 Eastern Europe
- 14 Near East
- 33 Far East
- 13 Africa
- 13 Classical Mediterranean
- 2 Caribbean/Atlantic world
- 9 World
- 15 No geographic specialization, e.g., history of biology

Time-period specialization
- 4 post-1945
- 4 1900–1945
- 33 nineteenth century
- 5 eighteenth century
- 2 sixteenth century
- 0 fifteenth century
- 10 AD 1000–1400
- 2 AD 700–1000
- 1 100 BC–AD 300
- 10 ancient history (to 100 BC)

- 66 twentieth century
- 16 nineteenth and early twentieth centuries
- 12 eighteenth and nineteenth centuries
- 28 seventeenth and eighteenth centuries
- 11 sixteenth and seventeenth centuries
- 2 fifteenth and sixteenth centuries
- 1 AD 100–1400 and fifteenth century
- 21 AD 700–1400

- 27 nineteenth and twentieth centuries
- 32 eighteenth, nineteenth, and early twentieth centuries
- 1 seventeenth, eighteenth, and nineteenth centuries
- 5 sixteenth, seventeenth, and eighteenth centuries
- 1 fifteenth, sixteenth, and seventeenth centuries

1	AD 1000–1400 and fifteenth and sixteenth centuries
5	AD 700–1000, AD 1000–1400, and fifteenth century
1	ancient period, AD 300–1000, AD 1000–1400
2	AD 1700–post-1945
1	AD 1400–1945
1	AD 1000–1945
4	AD 1600–1900
1	AD 1000–1700
1	AD 700–1700

When the results of those who identified multiple time periods are added to single time periods:

99	post-1945
122	1900–1945
147	nineteenth century
61	eighteenth century
68	seventeenth century
28	eighteenth century
13	fifteenth century
42	AD 1000–1400
30	AD 700–1000
1	100 BC–AD 300
10	ancient history (to 100 BC)

Topical specialization

42	cultural history
32	social history
14	political history
21	race/ethnicity (African Americans, Chicano/a, Native Americans)
21	women's history
19	history of science and technology
18	intellectual history
12	religious history
9	economic and business history
9	international relations
6	military history
57	other:

144 The State of Scholarly Publishing

9	environmental history
9	legal history
6	Jewish history
5	urban history
3	history of medicine
3	Holocaust
3	maritime history
2	sport history
2	history of education
2	migration/immigration history
1	imperial history
1	American Revolution
1	rural South
1	Renaissance
1	comparative history
1	population history

3. Please identify the university where you are currently employed so that it will be possible to relate the results of this survey to the relative rankings of graduate programs in history.

4. Gender

291 M
156 F

5. Year in which highest degree was received

Average = 1984.8

54	2000–2004
135	1990–1999
86	1980–1989
114	1970–1979
34	1960–1969
3	1950–1959

6. Year of first tenure track appointment

Average = 1985.6

7. Year in which tenure was awarded. If tenure has not yet been awarded, please indicate by an X. [*352 responded to this question.*]

X 90

Average for those who received tenure = 1987.7

8. If you have left an institution voluntarily, that is, for reasons other than being turned down for tenure, did publications and research enter into you decision in any way? Explain briefly.

9. Number of books published. (If a book has been formally accepted for publication and is now going through production, please include that in the count.)

10	0
97	1
73	2
121	3–5
94	more than 5

10. Number of books published by type (if more than one edition has been published of a particular title, please indicate)

	Total responses	Sum total	Average
Scholarly monograph	361	814	2.6
Scholarly treatise	86	201	2.3
Textbook	82	137	1.6
Critical edition of a manuscript	42	78	1.9
Collection of essays or proceedings, i.e., you were the editor	164	299	1.8
Other (please specify)	[This category was tabulated in other categories.]		
Number of books on which co-author or co-editor	140	338.5	2.4

11. Approximately how many articles have you published?

8	none
10	1
127	2–5
97	6–10
90	11–20
115	more than 20

12. If you are untenured, I would be very grateful if you would give me your name, business address, and e-mail addresses, both personal and professional. In five years I hope to do a follow-up study to this one of the untenured faculty to find out what their experience has been. That will not be possible unless I can query the same individuals. I give you my word that you will never be personally identifiable in any publication or presentation that emerges from this work. I may use a label like "an assistant professor at an Ivy League university" or "a specialist in classical Rome," but that is as specific as I will get, and then, only if it enhances the point I am making.

Please continue on with Section H.

H. Comments
I would appreciate any opinions and/or insights you have to offer on the current state of publishing of historical scholarship.

Electronic Publishing in Archaeology

Jingfeng Xia

Electronic publishing has currently achieved varying degrees of success in different academic disciplines. This article briefly reviews the exercise of electronic publishing in archaeology and introduces some major efforts in its development. By looking at the challenges and opportunities of these digital projects, the article attempts to pinpoint potential directions of development. An involvement of e-print repositories in supporting archaeological scholarly communication is proposed.

Introduction

Electronic publishing has currently achieved varying degrees of success in different academic disciplines. In archaeology, it has been developing for some time and in several directions. Among current practices of electronic publishing in archaeology, the digital dissemination of research *results* is relatively scarce. Most efforts have been made to work on preserving and sharing archaeological *data*. As a result, there are few electronic journals and e-print repositories in this field, but many online databases for archaeological excavations exist. Some museum collections can also be found online.

In general, electronic publishing has not become widely accepted by archaeologists. Information technology is still somewhat marginal to research activities in this respect. This situation could be explained as the result of a "discipline culture,"[1] because information delivery in archaeology is quite different from that in other academic fields. However, it is obvious that a broad and rapid sharing of information, both at the knowledge level and at the data level, is necessary for archaeological research. It is the responsibility of the creators and managers of digital resources to raise scholars' awareness of the new means of scholarly communication. Specifically, the way electronic publishing is designed and maintained will have a crucial impact on the attitudes of archaeologists toward accepting it.

To better assess the development of electronic publishing in archaeology, it is important to understand what scholars in this field really need for their research. It is also essential to become familiar with how scholars in this field have traditionally circulated scientific data and research results.

What Do Archaeological Researchers Need?

Archaeology is such a broad field that its research methods vary from subject to subject, and various technologies have been applied to different types of research. Some areas in archaeology have incorporated the approaches of related fields, developing into interdisciplinary features. For example, geo-archaeology applies the concepts and methods of earth sciences to archaeological inquiries; ethno-archaeology employs ethnographic fieldwork observations among living groups as an analogy for understanding peoples of the past; and experimental archaeology studies faunal remains found at archaeological sites. This article, however, will concentrate on mainstream archaeology (i.e., field archaeology), which represents the conventions of archaeological research.

In doing archaeological research, scholars first go into the field to carry out excavations on prehistoric and historic sites. They dig up cultural as well as biological remains from the soil left by people in the past. Archaeological investigations are considered a principal source of knowledge of prehistoric, ancient, and extinct cultures.[2] In order to reconstruct their history, scholars rely on all the unearthed evidence, such as man-made objects, which can be as small as tools and ornaments or as large as architectural residues. The mainstream studies are particularly interested in interpreting man-made objects for their social and cultural significance.

Archaeological data have several characteristics distinctive from those of other fields. The first characteristic is the individualization of material remains. Although moulding technology was applied to standardize products in some areas at certain times in the past, most of the objects discovered were produced by human hands. It is not an exaggeration, in most cases, to say that no single object is exactly the same as any other. Scholars have found it difficult to use patterned descriptions to precisely elucidate variations of individual objects. They usually trust their own visual inspections of objects rather than counting on the textual narratives of other scholars about those objects in carrying out their analysis.

Second, archaeological data are characterized by their enormous quantity. A typical excavation can yield thousands of pieces of artefacts from one site. Given such massive numbers, neither journal articles nor excavation reports can describe every item from an excavation. Even for the items already covered in a publication, there is often no room to provide full descriptions. It is very common for financial and manpower constraints to prevent such data from further formal publication. A normal practice is for archaeologists to compile a final report to conclude their excavation(s) on a site. The shorter version of such a report may be published as a journal article, while the longer one may not be published at all. Such reports, therefore, will not enter the circulation of data in research activities. Scholars generally become aware of the existence of material discoveries by reading the brief reports or through personal communication. More often than not, they will need to visit particular collections in person in order to visually examine the materials relevant to their own interests. Publications provide less information than is needed.

It is amazing how much energy, time, and money must be invested to bring one item from the soil to publication: discovering it in the soil, measuring its relevance to other objects/features on the site, identifying its geographical stratification, taking it to the lab for clean-up, cataloguing it, repairing it if necessary, drawing and photographing it, and describing it in words. Yet this is only a very simplified version of the cycle. This process has inevitably delayed the availability of data to scholars, to varying extents.

Not only are data processed slowly, but research results are also not easy to get published adequately and promptly. The peer-review process is slow, and the number of scholarly journals is limited. Furthermore, publishers prefer to bring out popular topics that attempt to bridge the gap between professional and lay audiences; pure scientific studies are given lower priority.

The obviously ineffective communication situation in the field of archaeology, as described above, has existed for decades. We must bear in mind that archaeology is a huge discipline, with thousands of researchers working in more than 500 academic departments, museums, and other institutions in the United States alone.[3] Few important universities anywhere in the world are now without archaeology professors and archaeology programs. It should be clear that the communication channels practiced in the field have unfortunately limited its research productivity. What archaeological researchers need are efficient communication platforms that can provide prompt and complete access to excavation materials as well as research results. Electronic publishing is one of the solutions.

How Has Electronic Publishing Affected Archaeological Research?

As early as the mid-1990s, the importance of electronic publishing to support archaeological research was recognized. Logically, it began with attempts to publish raw data from selected archaeological sites. Data were stored in various digital formats, to be shared with the research community. The earliest digital data were delivered on CD-ROM, but soon the Web became a major vehicle in distributing comprehensive information.

The United Kingdom was a pioneer in the development of electronic archaeological publications. It still contributes, along with some other European countries, a major portion of the work involved in archiving and disseminating archaeological data. Not only has its research community become actively involved in the campaign for new means of scholarly communication, the British government has also become aware of its importance in promoting research and preservation and has provided the necessary financial support to facilitate related activities. The Archaeology Data Service (ADS) in York is one of the famous organizations that work on handling data preservation and distribution.[4] Established in 1996, the ADS has endeavored to undertake online data delivery to students and researchers. Through its numerous projects in digital preservation, it has contributed much to the knowledge of archaeologists. Many of its projects are funded by English Heritage, the largest heritage agency in Britain, as well as by other funding agencies.

In the United States, numerous efforts have also been made to create broad and fast ways to circulate archaeological data. The Center for the Study of Architecture/Archaeology (CSA) has been enthusiastic in systems development since 1986. Based at Bryn Mawr College, this center focuses on advancing the use of computer technologies and digital information for architectural history, archaeology, and related disciplines. In addition to the various types of research projects it undertakes, the center publishes quarterly newsletters announcing contemporary developments in digital archiving, both within and outside the center.[5]

The following sections will briefly review the major developments in electronic publishing in archaeology in both Europe and the United States. Both the achievements and the challenges of these development are highlighted. The purpose is to illustrate how different types of electronic publishing have helped archaeological research and what are their potentials and problems.

Online Databases Have Been the Standard

Online databases are considered the standard format for archaeological data sharing. The appearance and rapid improvement of the Web since the mid-1990s have made the creation of online databases possible. The progress of other information technologies adds more value to this method of data sharing. Several projects serve as benchmarks for the development of online databases.

The CSA began to operate the Archaeological Data Archive Project (ADAP) in 1993, working with scholars to bring data sets to the archive. Archaeological databases were placed on the Web, with proper structure to support indexing. The indexes were designed to be machine readable, which, alongside online instructions, made the databases useable.[6] In the interests of preserving scientific data, the project follows a procedure of making three copies of files on CD-ROM, storing them in separate places, and checking their quality every six months to ensure proper data protection. The project had the initial purpose of making people aware of the problems of data preservation. However, it was not very successful in helping scholars deposit their own digital materials into the data archives.[7]

To encourage normal operation of the project, a pilot project, co-sponsored by the National Center for Preservation Technology and Training, was created to gather the necessary experience, provide technical assistance, and monitor the ADAP process.[8] This pilot project involved work done under the auspices of State Historic Preservation Offices in California, Colorado, and Pennsylvania, from each of which four projects were selected for participation. A variety of data types were included, such as databases, CAD models, geographic information systems (GIS) data sets, and images.

In Europe, since 2002, the ADS has managed an international project, the ARENA Archives.[9] Funded by the European Commission to promote awareness of digital preservation among European archaeologists, this project brought together a diverse group of experts from Denmark, Iceland, Norway, Poland, and Romania. To serve the needs of different user groups, the project adopted a new model that allows each digital archive to keep its own characteristics. Some of the archives made available excavation materials in the style initiated by ADS: "They give background and bibliographic information and allow users to download archaeological archives for their own use."[10] Some key sites were represented in these archives with materials in the form of digital images, data files, field survey records, digital mapping, and plans. Not only did archives vary from each other but individual sites in each archive also had different organizations and presentations. The diversity of the archives made them useful to a wider European audience. Also important to the project were the efforts of its members to enhance its usability by attempting to make it an online research and teaching center.

Almost at the same time, English Heritage supported a series of digital projects.[11] Rather than archiving paper copies of reports and databases, these projects adopted a hybrid publication strategy. They maintained digital archives from a group of organizations, including the Museum of London Archaeological Service, Albion Archaeology, the Norfolk Archaeological Unit, the Essex County Council Field Archaeological Group, the Oxford Archaeological Unit, and the Cambridge Archaeological Unit. By offering advice and guidance on the digitization of the archives, the projects were able to provide access to both raw and interpreted data sets, allowing users to search and download. English Heritage has collaborated with the ADS to implement the projects that made these data sets available online through the ADS servers.

In addition to these keystone projects, individual research organizations have also created their own online databases to distribute digital materials. Examples include the Digital Archaeological Archive of Chesapeake Slavery in the United States[12] and the Danebury Project Excavation Digital Archive in England.[13] A variety of Web portals also exists to collect useful online resources for the subject of archaeology, including archaeology.about.com,[14] DANA-WH,[15] archaeology.org,[16] and archNet.[17] These Web portals provide helpful aids for locating links on archaeological topics. Moreover, some individual scholars maintain good Web sites for the purpose of sharing data, research ideas, and other important information.

Basically, online databases represent three major data-dissemination formats: those that are searchable through queries, those that are presented as a series of downloadable files, and those that can be used in both ways. Susan Jones spent time comparing the first two types of databases and pinpointing the advantages and disadvantages of each type. According to her findings, it is hard to tell which type is better than the other: "The 'best' presentation method is dependent upon the goals, stability of the data, and resources of the project."[18] No matter how an online database is organized, it is true that the electronic preservation and dissemination of archaeological *data* have been a ubiquitous practice within the research community. Now, let us turn to the electronic publication of research *results*.

Electronic Journals Keep Coming Up

The first electronic journal for archaeology was *Internet Archaeology*, initiated in 1996.[19] It has published articles of a high academic quality, covering topics from archaeological excavations to GIS surveys. A wide array of multimedia techniques is used to present color images, Virtual Reality Modeling Language (VRML), QuickTime Virtual Reality models, and the like. Within a short time, *Internet Archaeology* has received broad recognition from scholars. As of 2002, it had been used by more than 27,000 individuals from more than 120 countries, symbolizing great success.

About two years later, another electronic journal of archaeology—*Mediterranean Prehistory Online*—was created. This journal originated from the Early Prehistoric Migration project and soon expanded to cover studies in all aspects of Mediterranean prehistory.[20] It then set further expansion plans to broaden the scope of articles in the journal to include a chronological range from the Lower Paleolithic to the dawn of Classical civilization in the Mediterranean Basin. Keeping high academic standards in mind, this journal strives to take advantage of new digital technology and make it accessible to all researchers.

Several other e-journals, such as the *Journal of Social Archaeology*[21] and the *American Journal of Archaeology*,[22] have also been added to the list. It is worth noting that some of these electronic journals have adopted a peer review process to ensure the quality of their publications, but without slowing down their publication speed. As a matter of fact, the time within which articles become available to the public in most electronic journals can be measured in weeks rather than in months, as was previously the case.

In addition to the peer-reviewed journals, some professional associations and research organizations have started to post their newsletters online; an example is the *CSA Newsletter*.[23] Research news, activities, and informal articles can now be shared faster. If these two types of online publications have served the needs of archaeological research in slightly different ways, we will find that a considerable number of electronic publications in archaeology has adopted a very dissimilar approach: one with the public in mind. Or, at least, they are not designed specifically for archaeologists. Selected data are interpreted to favor lay readers for the understanding of particular histories or cultures. Such efforts consist mainly of the practices described below.

Cultural Heritage/Museum Informatics Has a Non-Research Emphasis

The term "cultural heritage informatics" refers to research that aims to preserve and interpret events and figures in history. Archaeological evidences are regarded as part of cultural heritage, and thus part of the informatics research. In particular, because archaeological discoveries constitute the main part of museum collections, a sub-area of cultural heritage informatics—museum informatics—has explored electronic techniques to bring archaeological collections to public attention. The most recent practice of museum informatics includes using the Web as the vehicle for online exhibits.

Museum informatics has benefited from the founding of the International Conference on Hypermedia and Interactivity in Museums (ICHIM) in 1991. ICHIM was initiated with the intention of promoting the potential of interactive multimedia in museum programs.[24] Through its biannual meetings, researchers in cultural/museum informatics are brought together to exchange ideas and create a presence on the Web for their museums.

Major museums have since established a system of digital exhibits. These exhibits are mostly organized under selected topics, using the museums' own collections. Keeping pace with advances in information technologies, the exhibits have become more interactive and multimedia oriented. Visualization has been greatly enhanced, and flexibility to serve different audiences has been increased. Many people find visiting museums only a click away.

Recently, online museums have been developed in two major directions: one that allows art collections to be digitized and displayed on the Internet and one that combines archives with museum collections to describe historical events. The former effort is symbolized by the work of the Art Museum Image Consortium (AMICO), a not-for-profit organization of institutions holding collections of art that collaborate to enable educational use of museum multimedia.[25] Arts, textiles, and other visual collections are moved to the Web for public access.

At the same time, digital projects involving museum collections and archives are encouraged and supported by the Institute of Museum and Library Services (IMLS) under its National Leadership Grant Program in the United States.[26] The Colorado Digitization Program is one project that has successfully carried out collaboration among libraries, museums, historical societies, and archives and has created good practices.[27] Museums in the Online Archive of California is another successful example of such efforts.[28] Similar digital collections can be found on many museums' Web sites, with or without direct support from IMLS.

However, such digital efforts are not really designed for archaeological data sharing. First, digital collections on museums' Web sites are selected for specific exhibition subjects. Like traditional exhibits, they are designed to enhance public understanding of chosen topics, not to facilitate research. Second, the restricted online collections focus primarily on arts and related archival materials. Archaeological discoveries such as potteries, lithic tools, and bronze wares are relatively rare in these presentations. Finally, online collections are not presented in systematic ways. For scientific research, an item may become more informative only when it is associated with other items in an assemblage.

In fact, it is the purpose of most digital museum designs to facilitate easy online visiting for a general audience. Scholarly communication has not been taken into serious consideration in most existing programs. Museums may have found difficulties in presenting their collections on their Web sites; there may be restrictions in terms of financial, technical, and management concerns for individual museums. Difficulties may also come from varied strategies of collection organizations between museums, such as different ways of cataloguing items and implementing metadata.

What are the Challenges and Opportunities?

Standards Ensure Efficient Communication

There are increasing concerns about the exercise of standards in electronic publishing. Standards may apply to the preparation, presentation, or preservation of archaeological data. It is understandable that standards can facilitate scholarly communication. In fact, however, many aspects of current practices lack standards.

Data preparation is typically done by archaeologists through a well-established process of items curation. Preparing data for the Web has brought up new issues in this process in terms of technical and personnel arrangements. New technical tricks of curation have been added in order to satisfy the requirements of online database structure. A result is that some non-archaeologists take part in the process. Because they are less concerned about archaeological research and have limited knowledge of archaeological curation, their participation has inexorably raised questions as to the maintenance of standards. To enhance standards, it may be better to encourage more archaeologists to contribute to related work, and train them in technical skills, than to train others in archaeological specifics.

Data presentation here refers to methods that bring archaeological data to display on the Web. For some years, the diversity of the information technologies has made the task of creating common standards difficult. Various programming schemata have been used to assist in electronic data preservation and presentation. These different schemata have created dialects, making information organization a confusing situation. Scarce resources have not been efficiently used.

In order to improve standards in online publishing in archaeology, several initiatives have been developed. For example, both Spectrum and Categories for the Description Works of Art (CDWA) are intended to be metadata standards for the description of museum collections, and the Visual Resources Association (VRA) core is the metadata schema that handles visual objects specifically, including archaeological materials. Authority control also constitutes an important part of the efforts to enhance standards. The Getty Vocabulary is one of the best-known subject/name authority files in the organization of archaeological material culture.[29]

Recently, Extensible Markup Language (XML) has demonstrated its strength as a standard for working with online data presentation.[30] It also enables scholars to create archaeological data in formats suitable for digital preservation. Designed to be both machine interpretable and human readable, XML not only provides an easy way to describe data but also allows metadata harvesting to ensure cross-domain information flow. Some initiatives, such as HEIRPORT in Britain and XSTAR in the United States, have taken advantage of XML technologies. In Norway, the Museusprosjektet has successfully explored XML capabilities in handling a long-running digitization project.

From the user's perspective, how online archaeological data are presented determines how those data can be used. Both downloadable and searchable presentations require extensive labor. Recently, Harrison Eiteljorg II has proposed a "finding-aid" idea.[31] Obviously, this thought was inspired by archival management in special collections. It could be a viable presentation method allowing scholars to become aware of the existence of wider resources without requiring extensive data preparation. In the future, more data-presentation techniques will be discovered to meet the needs of diverse research projects.

Everything Requires Money

Financial constraints have greatly limited the ability of archaeologists and information professionals to explore new channels of online publishing. Even some existing projects may face problems in maintenance because of the shortage of money. The ADAP is such an example.

As a core project of the CSA, the ADAP found no way to support its archives financially after several years of operation. As a result, it recently ceased offering its services. In response to the demise of the project, the CSA director has made some suggestions for the efforts of future digital archives. In what he calls the business model, he proposes several improvements based on his experience in the ADAP. Not surprisingly, financial capability is one of the most important recommendations. In fact, he advises a depositor-pay model: "every project that produces data for deposit will need to find funds to pay for depositing the data."[32] This is a very unconvincing position because there is no motivation for them to pay. What would lead data depositors to feel they should pay for others to use their processed data?

On the other hand, a pay-to-read model has been used by some electronic journals. After a period of five years of free access to its content, *Internet Archaeology* began to charge for individual subscriptions in December 2001. In answering critics, the journal's editor notes the high costs of producing the publication. These costs may include expenses in file preservation, editing, and peer review as well as computer hardware and software maintenance. "It is about time the community recognized that e-publication does not come for free."[33]

The availability of electronic journals in other academic fields shows that it is possible for e-publication to be free of charge to readers.[34] Even in archaeology, some other electronic journals, such as the *Journal of Social Archaeology*, do not yet charge for access. Nevertheless, it is true that creating and maintaining online archaeological databases does add extra costs. Extensive curation of raw data is necessary for electronic publishing of archaeological data. It may take months, if not years, for archaeologists to complete collection curation of one site. All these jobs require money. Unfortunately, according to Eiteljorg's observation, "I am aware of no archival plan in the U.S. that has found a funding system that could support an on-going archival storage program for digital archaeological data."[35] What, then, are the solutions?

I would argue that two major directions need to be explored in the development of electronic publishing in archaeology. First, it is worth making further efforts to seek reliable funding possibilities. This sounds like a question answering a question. But people are becoming more and more aware of the potential and importance of digital technology, so more funding agencies have offered support for digital initiatives. In the United States, for example, the National Science Foundation has recently sponsored numerous repository projects, both institutional and disciplinary.

Second, it is time to seek alternatives for electronic publishing. Online databases have proven to be excellent in disseminating archaeological data; but they are not the only solution. A dilemma is already obvious: How many individual research organizations or excavation projects, apart from those that are well funded, can afford to establish such a database? We can probably do something else to help facilitate archaeological research.

E-Print Repository Is among the Alternatives

The e-print concept has developed into popular disciplinary and institutional repositories since the early 1990s. Although a variety of e-print applications is currently in use, these applications share many similar characteristics. First, they are all free for download, with the source code open for their own customization. Second, they are easy to configure and maintain. Third, they can accommodate various file formats. And finally, they support metadata harvesting to broaden searchability.

Given these characteristics, the e-print repository is clearly a good alternative to current electronic publications in archaeology. It can save tremendous time, money, and energy for individual scholars and research organizations/projects to build and maintain their own Web sites and online databases. The repository can serve as a centralized platform to contain data from any source of excavations. It is now up to archaeologists, rather than information professionals, to decide on what to upload into the repository. Data can be saved in different formats, according to the convenience of resource creators. For example, data on spreadsheets and Microsoft Access tables are still searchable and downloadable.

Maintaining an e-print repository is relatively inexpensive, as is shown by the practices of existing repositories in other academic fields. The business models of presently successful repositories have shown great viability for this type of digital program. For example, an information and library science repository, E-LIS, has adopted a volunteer management style that has greatly reduced operation costs but provided efficient and effective management.[36] Financial concerns about supporting electronic publishing are minimal here.

A great deal of flexibility is allowed within repository content. Not only can scientific data be saved into an e-print database but research results can also be accommodated. The existing repositories have encouraged the uploading of pre-prints, work before publication, and post-prints, work after publication, as long as copyright issues are properly handled. From this point of view, e-print repository is like an online inventory controlled by its contributors, who are mostly scholars.

Recently, several e-print repositories have been created to support archaeological research. Stevan Harnad proposed to create an archaeology sector in his CogPrints repository (for cognitive sciences).[37] However, because no significant efforts have been made to attract the attention of scholars, few archaeologists are aware of its existence. Another repository is the *Journal of Intercultural and Interdisciplinary Archaeology* Disciplinary Repository (JIIA).[38] Like CogPrints, JIIA has not been successful in gaining the acceptance of the research community. The primary reason is that it was launched in Italy, with Italian as the main language of operation. All other repositories that claim to be for archaeology are only a category subordinate to a broad subject, such as social sciences, or to an institutional repository with an affiliated archaeology program.

Open access is the spirit of e-print repository.[39] Neither contributors nor users pay for services. Any resource will become available immediately after it has been uploaded to the repository database and reviewed by the manager(s). It is necessary to mention that, because of the lack of a peer-review process, users will need to make their own judgments about the quality of the materials in a repository. Yet to relax control over an e-print repository is by no means to lower the value of such a repository as an innovative means of electronic publishing for archaeology.

Conclusion

Electronic publishing has demonstrated its potential to support archaeological research. Archaeologists and information professionals have worked together to explore various ways to digitally preserve and disseminate archaeological data. Numerous projects have been launched to build online databases and exhibits. These endeavors have successfully promoted scholarly communication in the research community.

Yet development problems do exist: financial constraints have threatened the ongoing practices of some digital projects, and standards have been lacking in the operation of certain online resources. Although recommendations have been made by scholars to solve these problems, it is still doubtful whether any of the proposals is viable. An evaluation of the advances in digital technologies makes clear that e-print repositories may become a useful participant in electronic publishing efforts in archaeology. The management models of existing e-print repositories encourage scholars' contributions and are cost efficient. With proper management, e-print repositories will be able not only to handle archaeological data sharing but also to facilitate the exchange of research ideas and results.

Like other academic disciplines, archaeology is eager for innovative approaches of information exchange. It is the task of scholars to keep abreast of the development of modern technology. In particular, information professionals should become more enthusiastic about helping archaeologists build new systems of scholarly communication.

Contributor

Jingfeng Xia is the Reference/Instruction Librarian (Social Sciences) at Rutgers University. His current research interests include applying GIS technologies to library management and scholarly communication, particularly digital repositories.

Notes

1. Ibironke Lawal, "Scholarly Communication: The Use and Non-Use of E-Print Archives for the Dissemination of Scientific Information," *Issues in Science and Technology Librarianship* 36 (Fall 2002), available at: *http://www.istl.org/02-fall/article3.html*.
2. Brian M. Fagan, *Archaeology: A Brief Introduction,* 6th ed. (New York: Longman 1997).
3. American Anthropological Association (AAA), *AAA Guide* (Washington, DC: AAA 2005).
4. William Kilbride, "Digital Preservation Meets Electronic Publishing: Towards an Integrated Resource," *CSA Newsletter* 14, 3 (Winter 2002), available at *http://csanet.org/newsletter/winter02/nlw0203.html*.
5. Harrison Eiteljorg II, "Archiving Archaeological Data: Is There a Viable Business Model for a US Repository?" *CSA Newsletter* 17, 3 (Winter 2005), available at *http://csanet.org/newsletter/winter05/nlw0501.html*.
6. Archaeological Data Archive project, *http://csanet.org/newsletter/nov94/nl119403.html*; "A Database about Databases," *CSA Newsletter* 7, 2 (August 1994), available at *http://csanet.org/newsletter/aug94/nl089408.html*.
7. Eiteljorg, "Archiving Archaeological Data."
8. "Archaeological Data Archive Pilot Project," *CSA Newsletter* 14, 2 (Fall 2001), available at *http://csanet.org/newsletter/fall01/nlf0101.html*.
9. Jon Kenny and William Kilbride, "Networked Access to Digital Archaeological Archives in the European Area," *CSA Newsletter* 15, 2 (Fall 2002), available at: *http://csanet.org/newsletter/fall02/nlf0202.html*.
10. Archaeological Records of Europe—Networked Access (ARENA), *http://ads.ahds.ac.uk/arena*; Jon Kenny and William Kilbride, "Europe's Digital Inheritance: ARENA Archives Launched," *CSA Newsletter* 16, 1 (Spring 2003), available at *http://csanet.org/newsletter/spring03/nls0302.html*.

11. Kilbride, "Digital Preservation."
12. Digital Archaeological Archive of Comparative Slavery (DAACS), *http://www.daacs.org*.
13. The Danebury Excavations Digital Archive, *http://ads.ahds.ac.uk/catalogue/projArch/danebury_var_2003/index.cfm*.
14. Archaeology from about.com, *http://archaeology.about.com*; see also C. Susan Jones, "Access to Archaeological Resources on the Web," *CSA Newsletter* 17, 3 (Winter 2005), available at *http://csanet.org/newsletter/winter05/nlw0504.html*.
15. Digital Archive Network for Anthropology and World Heritage (DANA-WH), *http://www.dana-wh.net/*.
16. *Archaeology, http://www.archaeology.org*; see also Jones, "Access to Archaeological Resources."
17. ArchNet Home Page, *http://archnet.asu.edu/*.
18. C. Susan Jones, "Archaeological Data Preservation Formats on the Web," *CSA Newsletter* 17, 2 (Fall 2004), available at *http://csanet.org/newsletter/fall04/nlf0402.html*.
19. Julian Richards, "*Internet Archaeology* and the Myth of Free Publication," *Learned Publishing* 13, 3 (July 2002): 233–4.
20. Dirk Brandherm, "Scholarly Online Publishing in Archaeology: The Price of Progress," *Mediterranean Prehistory Online* (August 2, 2000), available at *http://www.ruhr-uni-bochum.de/ufg/Personal/Dr__D__Brandherm/Brandherm01.pdf*.
21. *Journal of Social Archaeology, http://jsa.sagepub.com/*.
22. *American Journal of Archaeology, http://www.ajaonline.org/*.
23. *CSA Newsletter, http://csanet.org/newsletter/*.
24. Archimuse Archives and Museum Informatics, *http://www.archimuse.com/*.
25. Art Museum Image Consortium (AMICO), *http://www.amico.org/*; David Bearman, Kelly Richmond, and Jennifer Trant, "Open Concepts: Museum Digital Documentation for Education through the AMICO Library," International Cultural Heritage Meeting, Milan, Italy, September 6, 2001, available at *http://www.amico.org/docs/papers/2001/trant.ichim01.pdf*.
26. Timothy W. Cole and Sarah L. Shreeves, "The IMLS NLG Program: Fostering Collaboration," Library Hi Tech 22, 3 (September 2004): 246–8; Joyce Ray, "Connecting People and Resources: Digital Programs at the Institute of Museum and Library Services," Library Hi Tech 22, 3 (September 2004): 249–53.
27. Brenda Bailey-Hainer and Richard Urban, "The Colorado Digitization Program: A Collaboration Success Story," Library Hi Tech 22, 3 (September 2004): 254–62.
28. Robin Chandler, "Museums in the Online Archive of California (MOAC): Building Digital Collections across Libraries and Museums," First Monday 7, 5 (May 2002), available at *http://www.firstmonday.org/issues/issue7_5/chandler/index.html*; Online Archive of California (OAC), *http://www.oac.cdlib.org/*.
29. The Getty Vocabularies, *http://www.getty.edu/research/conducting_research/vocabularies/*.
30. William Kilbride, "Past, Present and Future: XML, Archaeology and Digital Preservation," CSA Newsletter 17, 3 (Winter 2005), available at *http://csanet.org/newsletter/winter05/nlw0502.html*.
31. Harrison Eiteljorg II, "A Wider Vision of an Archaeological Data Archive," CSA Newsletter 17, 3 (Winter 2005), available at *http://csanet.org/newsletter/winter05/nlw0503.html*.
32. Eiteljorg, "Archiving Archaeological Data."
33. Richards, "Internet Archaeology."
34. For example, in the field of information and library science, D-Lib Magazine, *http://www.dlib.org*, is free to readers.

35. Eiteljorg, "Archiving Archaeological Data."
36. E-LIS: E-prints in Library and Information Science, *http://eprints.rclis.org/*.
37. See Stevan Harnad, "Eprints for Archaeology?" American Scientist Open Access Forum (November 29, 2001), *http://www.ecs.soton.ac.uk/~harnad/Hypermail/Amsci/1685.html*.
38. Journal of Intercultural and Interdisciplinary Archaeology and Archaeological Disciplinary Repository, *http://www.jiia.it/*.
39. See Peter Suber, "Open Access Overview" (March 10, 2006), *http://www.earlham.edu/~peters/fos/overview.htm*.

The Value of Knowledge Created by Individual Scientists and Research Groups

Chen-Chi Chang

Researchers of scholarly communication have often suggested that scientists publish their research findings in academic journals to maximize knowledge creation. However, as the size of journals has increased, investigating the factors affecting the value of such knowledge creation becomes both more difficult and more important. Therefore, this article aims to explore the factors that affect the value of the knowledge created through journal publishing by individual scientists and by research groups. The study surveyed data from an online citation database that includes 160 authors and 4,525 articles. The results of this survey show that single authors' knowledge and previous publishing performance play an important role in the value of the knowledge created. Research productivity and publishing work experience on the part of co-authors increase the value of the knowledge created by research. Thus, this study is important in explaining which factors affect knowledge creation.

Key words: knowledge value, research quality, knowledge creation, research productivity, academic publishing

Introduction

Recent years have seen increased attention to knowledge sharing in the management science literature. Academic publishing is an important means of knowledge sharing among scientists. Scientists publish their research findings and review others' research results in academic journals for maximal effect on present and future research. Academic journals disseminate information to the community and provide quality control, a trusted archive, and author recognition. The number of journals and conferences has been increasing rapidly; the forms of scholarly communication through which scientists can share their knowledge have become very diverse. Journal publishing has grown: not only have the number of articles per issue and the length of individual articles increased, but there has been a marked increase in the number of pages published per scientist.[1] The study reported here may be critically important in laying the groundwork for understanding the value of knowledge. Multiple knowledge domains produce novel combinations that increase the variance of product performance. Extensive experience produces output with a high average performance.[2] This study examines the effects of knowledge and experience on both the mean and variance measures of individual scientists and research groups in terms of knowledge creation and research productivity. Kate Wittenberg points out that scholars and students need more effective access to information and skills to determine the quality and value of that information.[3] Several methods of measuring the quality of research have appeared, some of which remain controversial in spite of reams of research productivity.

The study of research quality measurement has apparently moved from prescriptive to more descriptive and scientific stances. Many research results indicate that researchers have been ranked based on their contribution of articles to leading journals;[4] the quality of research is often measured by the quality of the journal in which the resulting article is published.[5] Research productivity in academic institutions is reflected by the number and quality of articles published by the affiliated faculty. In the past thirty years, the science and technology of research quality measurement have progressed tremendously. Ranking the value of the knowledge created by researchers based on their contributions to leading journals has been increasingly common in recent years.[6] The *impact factor* is the indicator of an academic journal's quality, measuring the degree to which material published in that journal is seen, read, used, built upon, cited, and applied by the contributors' fellow researchers.[7] As Stuart Barnes notes, the real value of a journal is in the dissemination of knowledge for use by others.[8] The research paper has been particularly influential in scholarly communication, as it is cited by referees who are academics in the same field. With the increasing use of Thomson Scientific's Journal Citation Reports, the reliability requirement for impact-factor analysis has become more critical. Much research uses the impact factors published by the Institute for Scientific Information (ISI) to assess the knowledge creation by a given scientist in a given year.[9]

Previous research has measured the value of knowledge focusing on the journal level with the impact factor.[10] As the number of different ways to publish increases, so does the demand for more varied publications. The present study investigates the factors affecting knowledge value creation at the article level with the cited number. Figure 1 depicts three levels of measurement of research quality: knowledge value, journal impact factor, and citation frequency. One of the most fruitful areas of research in this area has been the focus at the article level, which improves the precision of the citation analysis. This study uses the Scopus "cited number" statistic—the number of times a particular paper is cited by other works included in the database—to assess the value of the knowledge creation represented by a given scientist's publications. Scopus is the largest abstract and citation database, it covering more than 15,000 peer-reviewed titles from more than 4,000 international publishers, including open-access journals, conference proceedings, trade publications, and book series. Scopus's content coverage is driven by user demand; a content-selection committee composed of researchers and librarians reviews new sources for inclusion, which helps to ensure that relevant information is not omitted. All titles that conform to academic quality standards, specifically peer review, and are published in a timely manner are considered. Scopus covers titles from all geographical regions, including non-English-language titles, as long as English abstracts can be provided.

Figure 1
Research Quality Measurement Levels

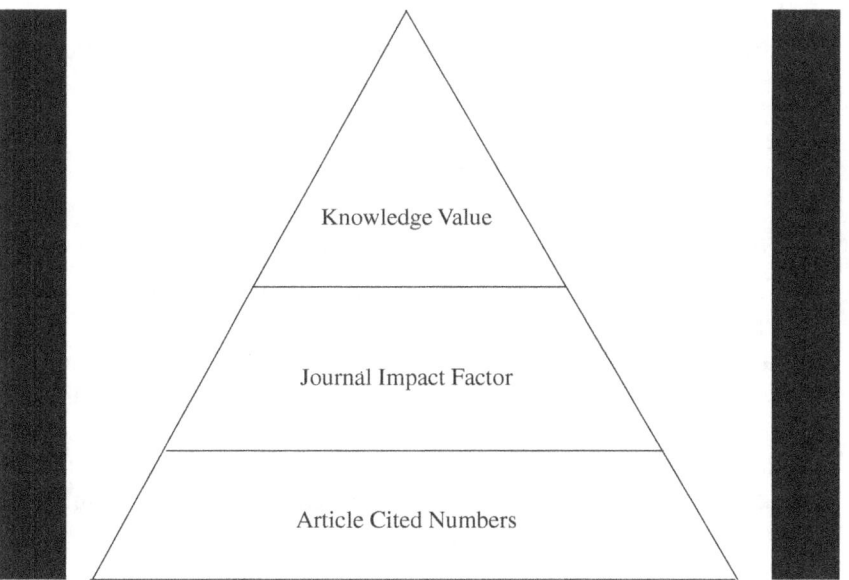

The purpose of this study was to explore how knowledge diversity and experience affect knowledge creation and research productivity. If a research institute were structuring the investigation of a specific research issue, would the quality of the results differ depending on whether the research was done by an individual scientist or by a research group? The evaluation of research productivity has a significant impact on tenure and promotion decisions, salary levels, and mobility, especially in research-oriented institutions. Because research productivity is so important in academic institutions, many studies, published in almost all the major business disciplines, have addressed this issue.[11] The process of writing a research paper is based on the different uses of knowledge; more novel output results when more diverse information and knowledge are applied. The deeper the existing knowledge the researcher uses, the more predictably the resulting paper performs. Too diverse a knowledge base can result in unwieldy and impractical output, while too narrowly focused knowledge can result in a "competence trap," in which new information is disregarded and teams become locked into their old behaviors.[12]

This study covers current and significant issues of knowledge combination and innovation by researchers, university instructors, and students of management science, including knowledge sharing and creativity in research productivity. To ground the theoretical discussion, the next section first describes the academic publishing context that is the focus of the study; I then make predictions based on an analysis of the "cited number" and several variables relating to academic publishing. The results are then presented, with a through description of the creation and evaluation of knowledge. Finally, the results are discussed and conclusions are drawn.

Theory Building

Describing the Publishing Context

The publishing context that was the focus of this study is composed of authors (scholars, university instructors, and students) producing journal articles that are published by commercial or non-profit publishers. Like most creative endeavors, scholars' research papers can vary widely, but, in general, the format includes certain sections: a general introduction; a literature review; a section connecting the present study to the literature; an explicit statement of the purpose, research subjects, apparatus, design, and procedure; presentation of the study results; and discussion of the implications of those results. All these writing tasks can be carried out by a single person, or they can be divided among several people. Innovations arise from two sources: the knowledge available for an innovative activity[13] and the ability of individuals and teams to apply the available knowledge.[14]

Academic publishing is the sub-field of publishing that distributes academic research and scholarship. Most academic work is published in the form of books (monographs) or journal articles. Much academic publishing, though not all, relies on some form of peer review or editorial refereeing to qualify a text for publication. Most established academic disciplines have their own journals and other outlets for publication, though many academic journals are somewhat interdisciplinary and publish work from several distinct fields or sub-fields. The kinds of publications that are accepted as contributions to knowledge or research vary greatly between fields, as do the processes of review and publication.

A research paper submitted to a journal may undergo a series of reviews, edits, and resubmissions before finally being accepted or rejected for publication; this process typically takes several months. Next, there is often a delay of many months (or, in some fields, more than a year) before publication, particularly for the most popular journals, in which the number of accepted articles outstrips the number of pages available. For this reason, many academic authors offer pre-print copies of their papers for free downloading on their personal or institutional Web sites. When investigating how knowledge is combined, it is important to examine all innovations, not just those that are successful, by their very nature, innovations are of uncertain value, and inevitably some will fail.[15] Scientists publish their research findings or review existing results in academic journals to ensure a maximal impact on current and future research. The measure of that impact is the degree to which their work is seen, read, used, built upon, cited, and applied by their fellow researchers.[16]

Research Quality

Evaluating the quality of scientific research is a notoriously difficult problem that has no standard solution.[17] Journal rankings are frequently used as a measure of quality for both journals and authors' research and also can affect researchers' academic standing.[18] Journal quality is frequently also used by faculty and university administrators as a surrogate measure for the quality of faculty members' research output.[19] Citations in journal articles and conference papers connect pairs of related documents. The principle behind citation analysis is that an article cited many times is of greater scientific value than one that is not cited. This principle drives various measures used by governments, academic departments, and individual scholars to help evaluate the impact of scientific research. The ISI Web of Knowledge provides citation-based impact factors to help evaluate journal quality, in addition to its searchable citation database, which allows the researcher to find articles citing and cited by given authors and in given publications.[20]

Citation standards fall into two categories: the formatting of citations in derivative works and the inclusion of identifying bibliographical information in original works.[21] Since journal impact factors are so readily available from online databases, it is tempting to use them to evaluate individual scientists or research groups. Committees have therefore tended to resort to such secondary criteria—crude publication counts, journal prestige, the reputations of authors and institutions, and the estimated importance and relevance of the research field.[22] Diverse knowledge of multiple domains and deep knowledge of a specific domain can both lead to innovations.[23] Prior journal evaluation studies have been based either on objective data, usually derived from journal citation indices, or on academics' perceptions of journal ranking lists for a specific research field.[24] This study uses the Web of Science and Scopus databases to collect data—the number of times a research paper has been cited in all other works included in the database—for measuring research performance.

Hypotheses

We can conclude with certainty that five constructs have the potential to explain the significant variance in the value of knowledge created. These constructs are knowledge diversity, work experience, organizational support, teamwork, and article attributes. A more detailed understanding of this relationship can be gained from the research model schematized in Figure 2. Given the theoretical positions taken for the study and the status of the field, as reviewed above, the following hypotheses were proposed.

Diverse knowledge of multiple domains and deep knowledge of a specific domain can both lead to innovations. A large number of authors represents an important source of knowledge diversity.[25] As a result, an increase in the size of a team increases the team's knowledge diversity and its ability to innovate, as well as increasing the likelihood that creative processes such as considering exceptions, challenging well-worn scripts, and playing with ideas will take place. Thus, a positive relationship was predicted between team size and the variance of the research evaluations.

Figure 2
Research Model

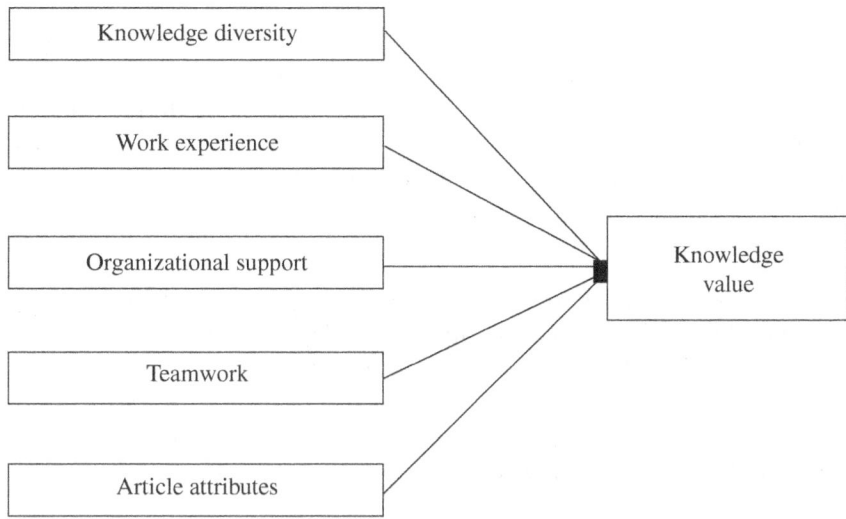

Hypothesis 1: As the number of authors increases, the research team is more likely to generate knowledge whose value is extremely high or extremely low (best or worst knowledge value).

Partnerships are a critical element in developing effective and relevant resources for the next generation of information users.[26] Authors with knowledge in different domains can publish articles in various research areas. Scopus analyzes the domain of the author's published article and generates a subject area to indicate the author's genre. The Scopus research areas include Computer Science, Business, Management and Accounting, Engineering, Decision Sciences, Social Sciences, Mathematics, Environmental Science, Economics, and Econometrics, predicting a positive relationship between the number of genres in which an author has published and the variance of the research evaluations. As the number of genres increases, the potential for knowledge combination also increases. As a result, knowledge combinations within a single individual should produce even greater performance variation. These arguments generate the following hypothesis:

Hypothesis 2: As the authors' knowledge diversity increases, they are more likely to generate research knowledge whose value is extremely high or extremely low (best or worst knowledge value).

Learning by refining existing products and procedures increases mean performance rather than increasing the dispersion of the performance—indeed, procedures that encourage incremental improvements tend to reduce performance dispersion.[27] The publishing experience is a learning process. This study considered the impact of an author's publishing experience on her or his research productivity, generating the following hypotheses:

Hypothesis 3: As authors' total publishing experience increases, they are more likely to generate research knowledge whose value is extremely high or extremely low (best or worst knowledge value).

Hypothesis 4: As authors' average research productivity increases, they are more likely to generate research knowledge whose value is extremely high or extremely low (best or worst knowledge value).

More experienced teams are more likely to develop standard operating procedures, resulting in higher mean performance outcomes.[28] Teams with sufficient experience to have established efficient communication can more easily make use of their members' knowledge diversity.[29] For the same reasons, authors who work with co-authors on collaborative projects should be able to raise the average quality of their research output. These arguments lead to the following prediction:

Hypothesis 5: As co-authors' collaborative publishing experience increases, they generate research knowledge whose value is extremely high or extremely low (best or worst knowledge value).

A research paper will be considered valuable only if it is cited by one or more academics in the same field. A paper's citation number indicates how many other papers cite it; and this is the official method of establishing how many researchers have referred to this paper. Research papers published in high-impact journals will have higher visibility and, ultimately, more citations. Thus, a positive relationship was predicted between journal impact factor and variance in evaluations of research:

Hypothesis 6: A journal with a high impact factor will publish research whose knowledge value is extremely high or extremely low (best or worst knowledge value).

If research results are highly dependent on a specific methodology that needs to be described in the article, then the total number of pages will be one indicator of the value of the article, since a shorter article will not describe the methodology in sufficient detail. The following effect of the total number of article pages was hypothesized:

Hypothesis 7: As the length of a research paper (measured by the number of pages) increases, it is more likely to generate knowledge of higher value.

Investing in work facilities can also increase efficiency. For research work, a technical and administrative support system that relieves authors of routine tasks has the same effect as organizational "slack" devoted to improving the knowledge of innovators.[30] In one study, organization size was significantly related to communication within project teams.[31] Prior research results indicate that the presence of a research center focused on the same area of inquiry, as well as funding received from external sources for research purposes, increases both research productivity and the quality of the resulting articles.[32] As a result of these considerations, it was predicted that

Hypothesis 8: As organizational resources increase, authors generate research knowledge of higher value.

Methods

Data and Sample

To ensure some homogeneity of background, all subjects were selected from the field of management information science. A two-phase data-collection procedure was designed to explore the identification, classification, and application of knowledge value creation. First, the data were collected using Scopus search procedures, locating 160 authors who have published at least two articles in the scholarly journals *Decision Science* and *MIS Quarterly*. A Scopus author search using these author names yielded a data set consisting of 4,525 papers from academic journals and conferences. This article presents a general framework for evaluating the value of knowledge created by individual scientists and research groups. Analysis tools must be used appropriately if useful results are to be obtained. In order to clarify the relative contributions of these variables, a linear regression analysis was performed.

Measures

Dependent variable: Knowledge value. The number of times a paper has been cited is the key driver of knowledge value. A critical appraisal of these indicators reveals a number of weaknesses and suggests refinements that more accurately reflect the impact of the published material. The citation method does provides a better index of the contribution of published work than journal impact factors alone.[33] Although citations-based rankings are believed to be objective, they may suffer from some inherent biases, including self-citation.[34] According to Dunford et al.'s study of *Regional Studies,* based on standard ISI citation scores, the journal's record remains strong. As noted earlier, the dependent variable in the present study was the number of citations of a paper published by the authors selected from the journals *Decision Science* and *MIS Quarterly*.[35] The study also obtained author information for 2006 from the Scopus database. The dependent variable, knowledge value, was measured using data from the Web of Science and Scopus databases. The number of citations to a given article is treated as the indicator of knowledge value, and normalized by using the square root of this number.

Independent variables. To test Hypothesis 1, the number of authors was measured by counting the writers and artists involved in each research paper. To test Hypothesis 2, diversity of background was coded as the number of knowledge domains in which the authors had worked during the year prior to the publication of a research paper. This variable, *domain knowledge experience*, was the number of genres obtained from Scopus. To test Hypotheses 3 and 4, publishing experience and research productivity were examined via the total number of citations and the average number of articles published by each author during the previous year. Testing Hypothesis 5 required calculating the number of coauthors who had previously worked together. To test Hypothesis 6, the impact factor variable (the impact factor of the journal in which the article appeared) was measured. The number of article pages published was measured in order to test Hypothesis 7. To test Hypothesis 8, organizational resources were measured according by ranking universities according to size.

Descriptive Statistics and the Correlation Matrix

The analysis was carried out using the Statistical Package for the Social Sciences (SPSS) software. First, the descriptive statistics were computed; Table 1 provides the basic descriptive statistics and presents the mean score and standard deviation for each variable. Next, reliability as a measure of internal consistency was calculated. As shown in the correlation matrix in Table 2, high correlations were found between number of citations and past average number of citations; past coauthors and past total number of citations; and author subject area and past co-authors. None of the other variables had high correlation coefficients. A preliminary analysis showed that these results were stable when subsets of the variables were omitted from the model. In order to clarify the relative contribution of these variables, a linear regression analysis was performed. Table 3 shows the results of the linear regression analysis.

Results

Prior work on the factors affecting research productivity has focused on such factors as teaching load, consulting activity, size of the faculty, and seniority.[36] In analyzing the data, this study found the number of authors, article length (number of pages), document type, total number of citations, coauthors, and impact factor all have a significant effect on the value of knowledge created. Several findings are of interest; these are shown in Table 4. First, the results of the study support Hypothesis 1, but in one direction only: as the number of authors increases, their research is more likely to generate less valuable knowledge. The findings clearly indicate that a single author is better able to generate valuable knowledge, while articles co-written by many authors tend to produce knowledge of more limited value. These results appear to reject Hypothesis 2: there is no significant evidence that as the knowledge diversity of the authors in-

Table 1
Descriptive Statistics

		Mean	SD
1.	Number of citations	2.5	2.4
2.	Number of authors	2.6	1.3
3.	Single author	0.1	0.3
4.	Article pages	14.2	7.8
5.	Document type	1.7	1.2
6.	Past total number of citations	416.5	295.9
7.	Past coauthors	45.1	38.2
8.	Author subject area	6.8	2.5
9.	Past average number of citations	9.9	7.2
10.	Journal impact factor	0.9	0.6
11.	Affiliation size	20.7	6.6

Table 2
Correlations Matrix *

	1	2	3	4	5	6	7	8	9	10	11
1. Number of citations	1										
2. Number of authors	-0.08	1									
3. Single author	0.04	-0.45	1								
4. Article pages	0.27	0.04	-0.06	1							
5. Document type	-0.25	0.01	0.10	-0.22	1						
6. Past total number of citations	0.13	-0.00	0.05	0.01	0.09	1					
7. Past co-authors	-0.18	0.26	-0.12	-0.11	0.21	0.45	1				
8. Author subject area	-0.13	0.20	-0.14	-0.09	0.18	0.32	0.72	1			
9. Past average number of citations	0.37	-0.11	0.07	0.14	-0.10	0.38	-0.33	-0.23	1		
10. Journal impact factor	0.11	-0.01	-0.01	0.09	-0.18	-0.06	-0.07	-0.09	0.06	1	
11. Affiliation Size	-0.00	-0.03	-0.01	0.03	-0.02	-0.01	-0.09	-0.12	0.00	0.01	1

* Correlation coefficients with a magnitude greater than 0.03 are significant at $p = 0.05$.

Table 3
Results of the Linear Regression Analysis (N = 4525)

	β	t	Significance
Number of authors	-0.032	-2.114	0.035**
Single author	0.028	1.859	0.063*
Article pages	0.188	13.812	0.000***
Document type	-0.176	-12.588	0.000***
Past total number of citations	0.067	3.450	0.001***
Past coauthors	-0.072	-3.011	0.003***
Author subject area	0.027	1.432	0.152
Past average number of citations	0.271	14.932	0.000***
Journal impact factor	0.042	3.101	0.002***
Affiliation size	-0.016	-1.232	0.218

* p > 0.1.
** p > 0.05.
*** p > 0.01.

creases they become more able to produce extremely valuable knowledge. Diversity of background yielded limited improvements in performance variance. The research results support Hypotheses 3 and 4, showing that as their publishing experience and research productivity increase, authors are more likely to generate knowledge of higher value.

The results show that, as authors' publishing experience with their coauthors increases, their research generates knowledge of higher value, which supports Hypothesis 5. A journal with a high impact factor tends to publish articles of higher knowledge value, supporting Hypothesis 6. The results also reveal that journal impact factor appears to be an important variable in determining whether an article has a high knowledge value. As the number of pages in an article increases, the knowledge generated tends to be of higher value, supporting Hypothesis 7. The results of the study does not support Hypothesis 8, however: there is no significant evidence that as the organizational resources available increase, authors' research generates more valuable knowledge. Therefore, a large organization does not increase the likelihood that the knowledge produced will be of high value.

Conclusion

As the value of knowledge created by researchers is perhaps the most important factor in determining salary raises and promotions, this study identifies the factors that drive the knowledge creation of individual

Table 4
Research Results

Hypothesis	Result
1: As the number of authors increases, the research team is more likely to generate knowledge whose value is extremely high or extremely low (best or worst knowledge value).	Supported
2: As the authors' knowledge diversity increases, they are more likely to generate research knowledge whose value is extremely high or extremely low (best or worst knowledge value).	Not supported
3: As authors' total publishing experience increases, they are more likely to generate research knowledge whose value is extremely high or extremely low (best or worst knowledge value).	Supported
4: As authors' average research productivity increases, they are more likely to generate research knowledge whose value is extremely high or extremely low (best or worst knowledge value).	Supported
5: As coauthors' collaborative publishing experience increases, they generate research knowledge whose value is extremely high or extremely low (best or worst knowledge value).	Supported
6: A journal with a high impact factor will publish research whose knowledge value is extremely high or extremely low (best or worst knowledge value).	Supported
7: As the length of a research paper (measured by the number of pages) increases, it is more likely to generate knowledge of higher value.	Supported
8: As organizational resources increase, authors generate research knowledge of higher value.	Not supported

scientists and research groups. We can conclude with certainty that the presence of eight factors affects knowledge creation. The results of the present study suggest that a single author will tend to generate more valuable knowledge; as the number of authors increases, the outcomes of their researches are likely to be less valuable. Many authors do not increase the likelihood of producing extremely valuable knowledge; when the goal is to create valuable knowledge, it is best to find one excellent individual. As authors' publishing experience and research productivity increase, it becomes more likely that their research will generate knowledge of higher value. The results of this study clearly support the notion that as coauthors gain more collaborative publishing experience increases, their research generates knowledge of higher value. Journals with higher impact factors publish articles that contain more valuable knowledge; longer articles also tend to convey more valuable knowledge. There is no evidence, however, that authors who have access to more organization resources generate knowledge of higher value; large organizations do not produce more valuable knowledge.

These findings have four important policy implications for the improvement of research productivity and quality. First, the combination of individual knowledge and deep knowledge plays an important role in publication. Second, better previous research experience and productivity increases the value of the knowledge created by researchers. Third, the study also shows that a well-designed study is more likely than a poorly designed study to yield useful results. Finally, the impact factor of the journal in which an article is published is significantly associated with the quality and knowledge value of the research output.

This article has explored the critical factors in determining the value of knowledge created by individual scientists and research groups. However, the research is subject to a number of limitations. First, the study investigated only authors who have published at least two articles, which means that many excellent research articles were excluded from the sample. Second, the research method has limitations related to the difficulties of generalization to other subject domains that are different from management science. It is hoped that further work will clarify these concerns for different contexts. Despite the encouraging results of this study as to the positive effects of knowledge creation by individual scientists, future research is required to explore citation behaviors on the Internet.

Contributor

Chen-Chi Chang is an Assistant Professor in the Center for General Education of Nanya Institute of Technology and a doctoral candidate in the Department of Information Management, National Central University, Taiwan (ROC). His research interests include digital libraries, knowledge management, virtual communities, and online user behavior. His research has appeared in *Online Information Review*.

Notes

1. Donald W. King and Nancy K. Roderer, "The AIP Journal System: Relationship of Price, Page Changes, Demand, Cost, and Income," *American Institute of Physics Function Planning, Part II, Appendix B* (1981): 1982–7; Carol Tenopir and Donald W. King, "Trends in Scientific Scholarly Journal Publishing in the United States," *Journal of Scholarly Publishing* 28, 3 (April 1997): 135–70.

2. Alva Taylor and Henrich R. Greve, "Superman or the Fantastic Four? Knowledge Combination and Experience in Innovative Teams," *Academy of Management Journal* 49, 4 (August 2006): 723–40.
3. Kate Wittenberg, "Beyond Google: What Next for Publishing?" *Journal of Scholarly Publishing* 38, 1 (October 2006): 31–5.
4. Kenneth A. Borokhovich, Robert J. Bricker, Kelly R. Brunarski, and Betty J. Simkins, "Finance Research Productivity and Influence," *Journal of Finance* 50, 5 (December 1995): 1691–717.
5. Michael John Jones and Roydon Roberts, "International Publishing Patterns: An Investigation of Leading UK and US Accounting and Finance Journals," *Journal of Business Finance and Accounting* 32, 5/6 (June/July 2005): 1107–40.
6. Carl Schweser, "The Doctoral Origins of Contributors to the *Journal of Finance* from 1964 through 1975," *Journal of Finance* 32, 3 (June 1977): 908–10; Robert C. Klemkosky and Donald L. Tuttle, "The Institutional Source and Concentration of Financial Research," *Journal of Finance* 32, 3 (June 1977): 901–7; Albert W. Niemi, Jr., "Institutional Contributions to the Leading Finance Journals, 1975 through 1986: A Note," *Journal of Finance* 42, 5 (December 1987): 1389–97; Jean Louis Heck and Philip L. Cooley, "Most Frequent Contributors in the Finance Literature," *Financial Management* 17, 3 (Autumn 1988): 100–108; Terry L. Zivney and William J. Bertin, "Publish or Perish: What the Competition Is Really Doing," *Journal of Finance* 47, 1 (March 1992): 295–329; Borokhovich et al., "Finance Research"; Kevin A. Borokhovich and Richard Chung, "Financial Research: Evidence from Recent Graduates of Doctoral Programs," *Financial Practice and Education* 10, 1 (Spring/Summer 2000): 85–92; Jones and Roberts, "International Publishing"; Elisabeth Oltheten, Vassilis Theoharakis, and Nickolas G. Travlos, "Faculty Perceptions and Readership Patterns of Finance Journals: A Global View," *Journal of Financial and Quantitative Analysis* 40, 1 (March 2005): 223–39.
7. Stevan Harnad, "The Research–Impact Cycle," *Information Services and Use* 23, 2/3 (2003): 139–42.
8. Stuart J. Barnes, "Assessing the Value of IS Journals," *Communications of the ACM* 48, 1 (January 2005): 110–2.
9. M. Ann McFadyen and Albert A. Cannella, Jr., "Social Capital and Knowledge Creation: Diminishing Returns of the Number and Strength of Exchange Relationships," *Academy of Management Journal* 47, 5 (October 2004): 735–46.
10. *Ibid.*
11. George C. Hadjinicola and Andreas C. Soteriou, "Factors Affecting Research Productivity of Production and Operations Management Groups: An Empirical Study," *Journal of Applied Mathematics and Decision Sciences* 2006, 2 (2006): 1–16.
12. W. Brian Arthur, "Competing Technologies, Increasing Returns, and Lock-In by Historical Events," *Economic Journal* 99, 394 (March 1989): 116–31; J.G. March and H. Simon, *Organizations* (New York: Wiley 1958).
13. Gautam Ahuja, "Collaboration Networks, Structural Holes, and Innovation: A Longitudinal Study," *Administrative Science Quarterly* 45, 3 (September 2000): 425–55; Walter W. Powell, Kenneth W. Koput, and Laurel Smith-Doerr, "Interorganizational Collaborations and the Locus of Innovation: Networks of Learning in Biotechnology," *Administrative Science Quarterly* 41, 1 (March 1996): 116–45.
14. John Seely Brown and Paul Duguid, "Organizational Learning and Communities of Practice: Toward a Unified View of Working, Learning, and Innovation," *Organization Science* 2, 1 (February 1991): 40–57; Mary Tripsas, "Surviving Radical

Technological Change through Dynamic Capability: Evidence from the Typesetter Industry," *Industrial and Corporate Change* 6, 2 (March 1997): 341–77; Eric Von Hippel, *Sources of Innovation* (New York: Oxford University Press 1988).
15. Taylor and Greve, "Superman or the Fantastic Four?"
16. Harnad, "The Research–Impact Cycle."
17. Per O. Seglen, "Why the Impact Factor of Journals Should Not Be Used for Evaluating Research," *British Medical Journal* 314 (February 1997): 498–502.
18. Oltheten et al., "Faculty Perceptions"; Terttu Luukhonen, "Is Scientists' Behaviour Reward-Seeking?" *Scientometrics* 24, 2 (1992): 297–319.
19. John C. Alexander, Jr., and Rodney H. Mabry, "Relative Significance of Journals, Authors, and Articles Cited in Financial Research," *Journal of Finance* 49, 2 (June 1994): 697–712.
20. Mike Thelwall, "Scientific Web Intelligence: Finding Relationships in University Webs," *Communications of the ACM* 48, 7 (2005): 93–6.
21. Peter Jörgensen, "Citations in Hypermedia: Implementation Issues," *Information Technology and Libraries* 24, 4 (December 2005): 186–91.
22. H.F. Hansen and B.H. Jørgensen, *Styring af forskning: kan forskningsindikatorer anvendes?* (Frederiksberg, Denmark: Samfundslitteratur 1995).
23. Taylor and Greve, "Superman or the Fantastic Four?"
24. Hans Baumgartner and Rik Pieters, "The Structural Influence of Marketing Journals: A Citation Analysis of the Discipline and Its Subareas Over Time," *Journal of Marketing* 67, 1 (April 2003): 123–39; G. Tomas M. Hult, William T. Neese, and R. Edward Bashaw, "Faculty Perceptions of Marketing Journals," *Journal of Marketing Education* 19, 1 (Spring 1997): 37–52.
25. Michael A. West and Neil R. Anderson, "Innovation in Top Management Teams," *Journal of Applied Psychology* 81, 6 (December 1996): 680–93.
26. Wittenberg, "Beyond Google."
27. Mary J. Benner and Michael Tushman, "Process Management and Technological Innovation: A Longitudinal Study of the Photography and Paint Industries," *Administrative Science Quarterly* 47, 6 (December 2002): 676–706; James G. March, "Exploration and Exploitation in Organizational Learning," *Organization Science* 2, 1 (February 1991): 71–87.
28. Lucy L. Gilson, John E. Mathieu, Christina E. Shalley, and Thomas M. Ruddy, "Creativity and Standardization: Complementary or Conflicting Drivers of Team Effectiveness?" *Academy of Management Journal* 48, 3 (June 2005): 521–31.
29. David A. Harrison, Kenneth H. Price, and Myrtle P. Bell, "Beyond Relational Demography: Time and the Effects of Surface- and Deep-Level Diversity on Work Group Cohesion," *Academy of Management Journal* 41, 1 (February 1998): 96–107; David A. Harrison, Kenneth H. Price, Joanne H. Gavin, and Anna T. Florey, "Time, Teams, and Task Performance: Changing Effects of Surface- and Deep-Level Diversity on Group Functioning," *Academy of Management Journal* 45, 5 (October 2002): 1029–45.
30. Wesley M. Cohen and Daniel A. Levinthal, "Absorptive Capacity: A New Perspective on Learning and Innovation," *Administrative Science Quarterly* 35, 1 (March 1990): 128–52.
31. Irja Hyväri, "Success of Projects in Different Organizational Conditions," *Project Management Journal* 37, 4 (September 2006): 31–41.
32. Hadjinicola and Soteriou, "Factors Affecting Research Productivity."
33. Paul Davis and Gustav F. Papanek, "Faculty Ratings of Major Economics Departments by Citations," *American Economic Review* 74, 1 (March 1984): 225–30.
34. Alexander and Mabry, "Relative Significance."

35. Michael Dunford, Diane Perrons, Barry Reilly, and Rebecca Bulls, "Citations, Authors and Referees: Regional Studies, 1981–2002," *Regional Studies* 36, 9 (December 2002): 1053–65.
36. Borokhovich et al., "Finance Research Productivity"; John E. Mitchell and Douglas S. Rebne, "Nonlinear Effects of Teaching and Consulting on Academic Research," *Socio-Economic Planning Sciences* 29, 1 (March 1995): 47–57; Terence Hancock, Julia Lane, Russ Ray, and Dennis Glennon, "The Ombudsman: Factors Influencing Academic Research Productivity: A Survey of Management Scientists," *Interfaces* 22, 5 (September/October 1992): 26–38.

Exploring the Willingness of Scholars to Accept Open Access: A Grounded Theory Approach

Ji-Hong Park and Jian Qin

This article aims to explore what factors increase or decrease scholars' willingness to publish and use articles in open-access journals and discusses how these factors are related to one another. Research-oriented publications on the topic of open-access journals have been few, and there is widespread concern about whether scholars will adopt this new form of scholarly communication. The growing number of open-access journals leads scholars to encounter decision-making situations in which they must choose one journal among multiple alternatives, including open access and non-open access. We conducted open-ended and semi-structured in-depth interviews with eight faculty members and six doctoral students at Syracuse University. Based on the interview transcripts, willingness factors and their relationships were identified and refined using the iterative steps of grounded theory approach proposed by Strauss and Corbin in the 1998 edition of their Basics of Qualitative Research: Techniques and Procedures for Developing Grounded Theory. The findings show seven factors (perceived journal reputation, perceived topical relevance, perceived availability, perceived career benefit, perceived cost, perceived content quality, and perceived ease of use) and eight relationships. There were six positive and two negative relationships. The factors and relationships were then compared to the relevant literature to increase internal validity and generalizability of the study. Both theoretical and practical implications of the research are discussed. Theoretically, this study broadens the scope of relevance criteria studies, first identifies the relationship between two important scholarly communication activities, conceptually contributes to the concept of open access, and applies literature comparison methodology in a pure qualitative study to increase internal validity and generalizability. Practically, the findings of this study may be helpful for promoting open-access publishing by encouraging facilitators and discouraging hinderers. The research may also provide an ongoing working framework for evaluating open-access journal systems.

Introduction

During the past ten years, there has been a transition in scholarly communication channels. Among the various channels, emerging open-access journals are a blessing to academia. Open-access (OA) journals are one form of electronic academic communication that presents distinct and different characteristics from restricted-access (RA) electronic journals that are subscription based. On the one hand, OA journals are free to readers and may have an impact-factor advantage,[1] since they have a higher degree of availability than RA journals and can be expected to immediately and significantly extend the dissemination of an author's work. On the other hand, OA journals are not free journals. There are significant costs for the peer-review process and production of a journal, even if that cost may be lower than for traditional paper-based journals.[2] OA journals will survive only if they can raise sufficient funds to cover the costs of publication. One of the currently prominent revenue models (e.g., as used by BioMed Central) is charging authors a "publication fee" instead of charging readers a subscription fee.[3] Further, most OA journals are not highly regarded in their academic fields. Because of their virtual nature, some tend to consider them "not real."

Such advantages and disadvantages for scholars, both as authors and readers, have stirred up much discussion recently.[4] However, most of this discussion is not research oriented, with the exception of some studies comparing OA journals with electronic journals.[5] While the boundary between the two is often blurred, there is widespread concern about whether or not scholars will adopt this new form of scholarly communication. The growing number of OA journals, however, will lead scholars to encounter decision-making situations in which they must choose one journal among multiple alternatives, including those with open and non-open (restricted) access. The increasing number of OA publication outlets does not necessarily suggest, however, that these journals will be accepted by their respective academic communities, and little research has been done to address this concern.

It is important to know what factors determine scholars' decisions to select OA journals as publication venue and as an information source.

The purpose of this article is to explore what factors increase or decrease scholars' willingness to publish and use articles in OA journals and describe the relationships among these factors. The study further explores several conditions under which scholars view their formal scholarly communication activities as a rational response to the complexities in their environment. For instance, traditional criteria for tenure and promotion may discourage untenured faculty members from publishing in unrecognized journal outlets, whereas a perception of faster and wider dissemination may attract tenured faculty to publish more in OA journals. This research thus addresses the following questions:

1. What factors affect scholars' willingness to publish their works in open-access journals?
2. What factors affect scholars' willingness to use open-access journal articles for their potential publications?
3. How do these factors relate to one another?

Definitions and Dimensions

The term "open access" is the name given to Stevan Harnad's free-access model for the publication of peer-reviewed, full-text scholarly articles in digital form free of charge to users.[6] The concept is based on the peculiar nature of academic authorship that academic authors are interested primarily in wide dissemination of their publications and seek no direct financial reward. In contrast, trade authors seek to profit from their work and thus protect it from unauthorized use.[7]

The "open" in "open access" means that access to full-text academic works is available free of charge. C.L. Borgman proposes three essential elements to define the term "access": connectivity, content, and usability.[8] The term "connectivity" refers to a prerequisite physical connection to use computer networks. "Content" is the information residing on those computer networks. The term "usability" refers to ease of use for both computer networks and content in terms of searching, reading, and dissemination. The ease of use of content can be interpreted as free availability of content. The meaning of "open access" includes both access to the content and free availability of that content. It does not mean free connectivity of physical networks, as James Keller distinguishes between access to the network and access to the information the network contains.[9]

From a practical standpoint, Table 1 shows key concepts of OA as they appear in definitions from major OA initiatives: Bethesda;[10] the Budapest Open Access Initiative (BOAI);[11] the Scholarly Publishing and

Table 1
Key Concepts of Open Access

Initiatives	Key concepts in the definition
Bethesda	• All users have free, irrevocable, worldwide, perpetual right of access
	• All users have a license to copy, use, distribute, transmit, and display publicly
	• Deposits the works shortly after publication
	• Provides long-term archiving
	• Author holds copyright
Budapest Open Access Initiative (BOAI)	• Self-archiving (deposit)
	• Peer review
	• Free availability on the public Internet
	• All users can freely read, download, copy, distribute, print, search, or link to the full texts
	• All users can use the texts for any lawful purpose
	• No financial, legal, or technical barriers exist
	• Author holds copyright
Scholarly Publishing and Academic Resources Coalition (SPARC)	• Cost-effective way to disseminate and use information
	• Does not apply to materials for which the author expects to generate revenue
	• Operates within the current legal framework of copyright law
	• Intended to be free for readers, but not free for producers
	• Focuses on academic research
	• Peer review is required
Public Library of Science (PLoS)	• Same as Bethesda definition

Academic Resources Coalition (SPARC);[12] and the Public Library of Science (PLoS).[13] The common key elements in these definitions include that concepts that (1) open access is freely available through the Internet, (2) there is a peer-review process, (3) the author holds copyright, and (4) the content has an academic purpose.

Based on both theoretical and practical viewpoints, for the purposes of this research open access is defined as peer-reviewed academic work created with no expectation of financial revenue and made available online at no cost for the purposes of research to all interested readers who have access to the public Internet. Since authors hold copyright, users can freely read, download, copy, distribute, print, search, or link to the full texts.

Exploring the Willingness of Scholars to Accept Open Access   185

The free availability concept is the main factor distinguishing OA from non-OA journals. Open access differs from traditional subscription-based journals (non-open access) in terms of its financial infrastructure. Under this model, authors and institution or funding agencies are asked to pay fees for dissemination of scientific information, as opposed to the traditional library subscription model. Based on our observations, we have created a matrix to show the distinctions between journal forms and access modes.

Researchers have studied open access from different perspectives. Kling, Spector, and Fortuna studied the transition to OA journals from a social perspective. Their in-depth study investigated how E-Biomed was transformed into PubMed Central. They extracted data from both online and face-to-face forums on this transformation and qualitatively analyzed the data. Kling's group found, among other things, that various social groups shaped these Internet resources, contradicting the assumption that the Internet is a powerful autonomous actor.[14] Lagoze and Van de Sompel describe the technical aspects of the Open Archive Initiative (OAI), including its origin, focus, and standards; the applications of those standards; and future directions. They stress the importance of interoperability, which can be enhanced by metadata harvesting. They believe that interoperability increases the dissemination of scholarly information. They also argue that OAI will become an alternative model to

Table 2
Differences between Open-Access Journals and Electronic Journals

	Open Access (free of charge to readers)	Non–Open Access (subscription based)
Electronic based	• Mostly OA journals • No subscription fee • Publication fee • Authors hold copyright	• Subscription-based electronic journals • Subscription fee is less than for paper-based publication • No publication fee • Publishers hold copyright
Paper based	• Theoretically possible form, but less meaningful than electronic-based • No subscription fee • Publication fee • Authors hold copyright	• Subscription fee • No publication fee • Traditional type of journal publication • Publishers hold copyright

the traditional scholarly publishing paradigm because of the problem of publication delay in the sciences and the "serials crisis."[15] Bjork proposes business models, an academic reward system, and marketing as major obstacles in promoting OA publishing.[16] The academic reward system focuses on the tenure and promotion system in academics, an area that is also relevant to this article.

A number of factors have been identified as inhibitors of electronic journal proliferation, including the availability of computers and computing infrastructures,[17] document formatting,[18] and a strong preference for having a print version of articles.[19] Similarly, Gadd and others focused on how academic authors perceive and how they wish to protect the copyright of self-archiving and freely available e-journals.[20] In another study, the same authors examined how academic authors expect to use OA research papers.[21]

Many of these earlier studies have focused on external factors, either in the social or in the technological context, or on the result of using OA journals (e.g., the statistics of usage behaviors, such as copying, aggregating, displaying, and annotating). Internal factors (e.g., scholars' perceptions of OA journals) have been rarely examined. This study employs the qualitative approach of interviews to explore scholars' motivational factors for publishing and using OA journal articles. More detailed explanations on the methodology used in this study are presented in the next section.

Methodology

The nature of this study is exploratory and empirical, with qualitative data collected from interviews. We designed semi-structured interviews to explore scholars' willingness to publish in and use OA journals, as well as what factors affected their decisions. Based on the findings, we have developed a set of propositions related to scholars' communication activities.

Data Sources and Data Collection

Fourteen university faculty members and doctoral students were purposively selected for the interviews. The rationale for choosing academic subjects was that they are more likely to be explicitly concerned with publishing in and using scholarly journal articles. Their work by nature involves frequent interactions with other scholarly works: scholars identify relevant works, assess the quality of the information, use that information in the research process, and publish their research output in scholarly journals or other outlets. The motivations of faculty and doctoral students would be the most representative of publication issues in the scholarly communication population.

A purposive sampling method was applied. A purposive sample is one selected by the researcher subjectively. We attempted to obtain the sample of scholars that appears to us to be representative of the population (scholars) and tried to ensure that wide range of the sample of scholars is included. The sample of scholars consisted of eight faculty members (three tenured and five tenure track) and six doctoral students from Syracuse University. In the grounded theory method, according to Lincoln and Guba, "a dozen or so interviews, if properly selected, will exhaust most available information; to include as many as twenty will surely reach well beyond the point of redundancy."[22] The mixture of tenured and tenure-track faculty members may provide broader representation. We also tried to recruit participants from diverse backgrounds, and to achieve gender balance, in order to maximize the breadth of the sample. Participants in the final sample have backgrounds in education, information science, information systems, information technologies, library and information science, political economy and public policy, public administration, and telecommunications; six were female and eight male. An open-ended, semi-structured interview took place with each of these scholars between March 26 and April 18, 2004. Before the main interview session, two pilot interviews were conducted with doctoral students at the School of Information Studies, Syracuse University, to test the interview questions. The pilot-test respondents were not included in the main sample to avoid potential interview bias.

Each formal interview lasted about twenty minutes and was loosely structured around four topic areas: (1) general perceptions of OA journals, (2) past experiences involving OA journal articles, (3) future willingness to publish in and use OA journals, and (4) ideas for promoting OA journals. These question areas were targeted to gather data on different aspects of scholars' perceptions of OA journals. At the beginning of each interview, the respondent was asked to describe his or her perceptions of OA journals, followed by a brief explanation of OA journals and their development trends. Respondents were encouraged to talk about their perceptions of open-access journals. After the scholars explained their perceptions, the interviewer asked whether they had experience with OA journals and, if so, asked about the reasons for these activities. Participants were also asked whether they would be willing to pay a publication fee in the future. The last question requested their ideas for promoting

OA journals. The interviews were recorded and transcribed. A content analysis was then conducted using the grounded theory approach.

Data Analysis

The interview transcript was analyzed using the method for theory development suggested by Strauss and Corbin.[23] This method involves a rigorous process of evaluation whereby the data are analyzed iteratively to identify categories, code incidents, and organize the data. Concepts are the key elements of this analysis, since the model is developed from the conceptualization of data. Strauss and Corbin define this methodological approach as follows: "The grounded theory approach is a qualitative research method that uses a systematic set of procedures to develop an inductively derived grounded theory about a phenomenon."[24] The primary objective of the approach is thus to go from general to specific without losing sight of what makes the subject of a study unique.

The grounded theory approach yields propositions empirically grounded in the data. Two factors make grounded theory a valuable tool: (1) it concentrates on concepts and relationships or linkages between concepts, and thus is particularly suitable for creating a framework directly from accumulated data; and (2) it uses the constant comparison method to allow the theory behind actions to emerge, in this case allowing the study to detect factors that appeared to motivate scholars' communication activities.

As the categories began to emerge, the researchers coded the data by comparing categories until theoretical saturation was achieved. Strauss and Corbin indicate that coding "represents the operations by which data are broken down, conceptualized, and put back together in new ways."[25] They suggest three types of coding: open coding, axial coding, and selective coding.[26] In this case, *open coding* involved initial analysis of the data; the names or labels were given at this stage. Initial analysis closely examined the data and the development of initial categories based on the data, thus allowing similar concepts to be compared with one another. This initial process was able to develop conceptual categories and subcategories, the latter often referred to as *properties*.

Axial coding followed open coding. It interconnected each category by regrouping the data. Axial coding identified relationships between open codes for the purpose of developing core categories. Core categories emerged as aggregates of the most closely interrelated codes.

Selective coding raised the level of abstraction and produced core categories around which the data were integrated. It required selection of the core categories that emerged from the axial coding process. All other codes derived from the axial coding process need to be related in some way to the core categories, either directly or indirectly. Notes taken throughout the process were used as fundamental clues for identifying the factors and describing their relationships to each other. These clues were also used to reflect upon and explain meanings ascribed to the codes by the researchers; to identify relationships between the codes; and to clarify, sort, and extend ideas arising from the coding.

Coding

In this study, we are interested in the factors that increase or decrease scholars' willingness to publish in and use OA journals. Open coding was done sentence by sentence initially. Open coding identified several categories of causal factors for OA journal publishing and use. A portion of the axial coding was done informally (linking subcategories to categories) as the codes were generated and refined.

Table 3 presents a few examples from the open coding of the interview transcripts. A few points regarding the process of open coding are worth noting. First, coding is hermeneutic and emergent—that is, coding is essentially an interpretive act on the part of the researchers. Second, a significant number of the codes used tended to be recurrent. For example, Table 3 shows a number of recurring themes, such as *journal reputation* and *topical relevance*. Finally, deciding on a code for some concepts involved combining multiple sentences. For example, categorizing codes into *publishing* and/or *using* required analyzing multiple sentences from the transcripts for comparison and making sense of the categories.

Table 4 shows categorized sample codes that were generated from open coding during the first round of data analysis. The initial categories were *journal reputation, career benefit, content quality, topical relevance, cost, availability,* and *ease of use*. Publishing and using activity were identified as core categories that played an axis role for further coding. Any sentences not related to these core categories were eliminated.

Through constant comparing of codes, category labels continued to be merged, modified, and occasionally eliminated. As the emerging categories stabilized, as shown in Table 4, the initial categories were conceptually rearranged. The goal of axial coding is to establish connections between the categories around the core categories that emerged from the open coding. The researchers attempted to accomplish this goal of axial coding by searching for similarities among the initial categories (see Table 4).

Table 3
Examples of Open Coding

Sample transcripts	Sample codes generated and notes
The decision isn't going with whether it is open-access versus non-open access journals, but it is on what's good, well-read, well-regarded, and the appropriate journal ... it happens to be open access journal, but it wouldn't be a main reason for choosing.	• journal reputation—for publishing and using • relevance of journal topic—for publishing and using
Because the prestige of being published in printed journals is much higher than the prestige of being published in open access journals. Even if they have the same or harsher editorial guidelines, for me, the decision is completely made by the perception of these journals by the people who are making my tenure case.	• journal prestige—for publishing • career benefit—for publishing
The criteria to select to publish is always reputational capital. The thing is that if you publish in high quality your reputational capital goes up; if not, it goes down. It is a matter of how the journal is perceived and who reads it.	• journal perception—for publishing • journal audience—for publishing
If I know authors and as long as a paper is good, I can cite anything ... Information quality or content quality is the main key factor for selecting journal articles. Open or non-open does not matter ...	• paper quality—for using • author reputation—for using • fit with current research—for using
Because the citation is relevant and easy to access ... I mean I sometimes choose my article to be only available in electronic form in my discipline.	• topical relevance—for using • accessibility—for using • ease of use—for using

The axial coding revealed some overlaps between the categories, mainly between *journal reputation* and *career benefit* and between *career benefit* and *content quality*. As shown in Table 4, the code *prestige of journals* in the career benefit category also appeared in the *journal reputation* category; the content quality code *whether the journals are peer reviewed or not* was conceptually connected with the journal reputation code *acceptance rate*. Having compared the categories and identified the

Table 4
Initial Categories in Open Coding

Emerging categories / core categories	Publish	Use
Journal reputation	journal reputation, journal perception, prestige of journals, trust, publicity, desire for priority	journal reputation, author reputation, acceptance rate, well-known, authority
Career benefit	effect on tenure process, recognition, desire for membership, prestige of journals, whether the journals are peer reviewed or not	
Content quality		content quality, whether the journals are peer reviewed or not, goodness, coherence, reliability of content
Topical relevance	journal scope, audience, potential for discussion of work, fit with current research, information need for current research	journal scope, fit with current research, information need for current research
Cost	turnaround time, potential publication cost, acceptance rate	
Availability	desire to disseminate knowledge	accessibility, timeliness
Ease of use		easy to access, availability

relationships among them, the researchers collapsed the categories into a number of broader concepts.

The following list demonstrates the results of axial coding. It shows connections between the categories that emerged from open coding. Note that each pair in the list has a unidirectional relationship; the relationship from right to left may not hold true.

Publishing in OA journals:

- *Journal reputation* positively affects *career benefit*
- *Topical relevance* positively affects *journal reputation*
- *Career benefit* negatively affects *cost*
- *Availability* positively affects *career benefit*

Using OA journals:

- *Content quality* positively affects *journal reputation*
- *Journal reputation* positively affects *content quality*
- *Topical relevance* positively affects *journal reputation*
- *Availability* negatively affects *content quality*
- *Availability* positively affects *ease of use*

After open and axial coding, the researchers developed a selective coding procedure that integrated the results of axial coding. The objective of selective coding is to explicate a story by identifying a core category and linking the other categories around that core category. A storyline is either generated or made explicit. A story is simply a descriptive narrative about the central phenomenon of study, and the storyline is the conceptualization of this story. Selective coding requires the selection of the core category, that is, the central phenomenon that has emerged from the axial coding process. All other core categories derived from the axial coding process must be related in some way to this core category, either directly or indirectly. The role of the core category is well represented by the following analogy: "The core category must be the sun, standing in orderly systematic relationships to its planets."[27]

Figure 1
Identification of core categories

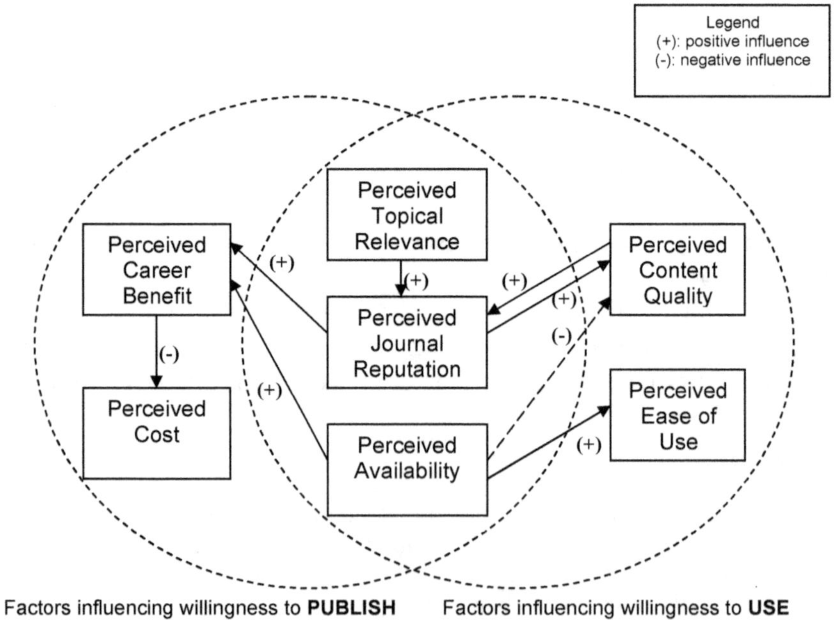

Legend
(+): positive influence
(-): negative influence

Factors influencing willingness to **PUBLISH**   Factors influencing willingness to **USE**

Findings: A Grounded Theory of Scholars' Willingness to Accept Open-Access Journals

This section describes what factors affect scholars' willingness to publish in and use OA journals and how these factors are interrelated. Figure 1 presents these factors and their relationships.

The core categories identified are *publish* and *use*, since these play central roles in integrating the relevant factors within the conceptual boundaries of scholarly communication activities. We will now discuss the factors in relation to the research questions for this study.

Research Question 1: What factors affect scholars' willingness to publish their works in OA journals?

Factor: Perceived Journal Reputation
Statement: Scholars' perception of OA journal reputation positively affects their willingness to publish articles in the OA journal outlet.

The analysis of data relating to journal reputation shows that this factor is linked to topical relevance, content quality, and career benefit, while the latter are linked with other factors. *Journal reputation* can be simply defined as the prestige of a journal as perceived by the members of an academic community. Prestige implies that a journal is well established and highly regarded by the research community. This recognition of the community implies, in turn, that the journal has existed for a certain length of time. The general perception is that OA journals are new, and therefore many uncertainties, such as quality and sustainability, exist. These uncertainties will inevitably affect reputation. The interesting finding here is, however, that OA journals have a strong positive reputation as future scholarly journal outlets.

Factor: Perceived Topical Relevance
Statement: Scholars' perception of topical relevance positively affects their willingness to publish articles in the OA journal outlet.

As journal reputation is formed within academic communities that have common research interests, topical relevance emerged as a key factor. *Topical relevance* is the users' perception of whether or not the topic of a document is related to their academic interests. Scholars have their own academic interests, even those who have a strong interdisciplinary background. This disciplinary academic interest is also supported by the cliché defining the sociology of science (i.e., that an academic community is a social group with a topical interest).[28]

Topical relevance is important in defining a potential audience. Scholars as authors are likely to reach the audience they want. The target audience should be familiar with terminology, theories, and publications in the topic area, which is critical in evaluating the authors' work. This audience, however, is not necessarily restricted to a single academic community. A larger target audience is better than a more limited audience because the key factor for authors is the reward mechanism. Wider dissemination of authors' works provides wider intellectual recognition in return. Such a reward perspective on publication outlets is closely related to the perceived availability of published works and the perceived career benefit to authors.

Factor: Perceived Availability
Statement: Scholars' perception of the availability of OA journal articles positively affects their willingness to publish articles in the OA journal outlet.

OA journals typically have better availability because readers can access their contents freely, without a subscription. Such availability is the result of many scholars' belief that knowledge should be available to interested members of the public and should be accessible when they need it. Better availability and wider dissemination of journals would promote a wider dissemination of knowledge they contain. Tenured scholars also believed that wider dissemination of research publication may have career benefits for authors, such as increased recognition. For untenured scholars, on the other hand, journal reputation rather than availability positively influenced perceptions of career benefit.

Factor: Perceived Career Benefit
Statement: Scholars' perception of career benefit positively affects their willingness to publish articles in the OA journal outlet.

Journals function as more than a communication device and are deeply embedded in the academic reward system. Tenure and promotion decision making is perhaps the most critical and most unpredictable part of the process. Perceptions of whether or not an OA journal outlet provides advantages for tenure and promotion decision making positively affects scholars' publishing intentions.

As mentioned earlier, the belief of career benefit varies depending on the scholars' academic position. It seems that OA journals have a more positive reputation among tenured than among non-tenured faculty. Career benefit, for non-tenured faculty, really depends on the journal's reputation. The more prestigious an OA journal is, the greater the likelihood that a non-tenured scholar will perceive it as bringing more career benefit and thus be more likely to publish in and use that journal.

Factor: Perceived Cost
Statement: Scholars' perception of cost negatively affects their willingness to publish articles in the OA journal outlet.

Perceived cost refers to any financial cost, time, and effort required to publish an article in an OA journal; it includes potential publication fee, acceptance rate, and turnaround time. OA journals have relatively shorter turnaround times, and some demand a publication fee. The publication fee is usually waived or covered by research grants or institutional sponsors. In the current OA context, scholars seem to believe that the costs of publishing in OA journals are relatively low.

Research Question 2: What factors affect scholars' willingness to use OA journal articles for their potential publications?

Factor: Perceived Journal Reputation
Statement: Scholars' perception of OA journal reputation positively affects their willingness to use OA journal articles for their potential publications.

Perceived journal reputation is a key factor not only in the intention to publish in an OA journal but also in deciding to use OA journal articles. Again, scholars tend to use well-established journals as references in their research. Journal reputation is often associated with number of citations: those with a good reputation are cited more often. While the scholars interviewed for this study had reservations about submitting their manuscripts to OA journals, they were less concerned about journal reputation when using OA journals in their research.

Factor: Perceived Topical Relevance
Statement: Scholars' perception of topical relevance positively affects their willingness to use OA journal articles for their potential publications.

Topical relevance is another important factor in the use of OA journal articles. Generally, scholars have no problem with using OA journal articles as long as they are relevant. This also corresponds to our observation of perceived journal reputation: that is, the use of OA journals is based on the content, rather than on whether a journal is OA or restricted.

Factor: Perceived Availability
Statement: Scholars' perception of the availability of OA journal articles positively affects their willingness to use OA journal articles for their potential publications.

OA journals provide virtually unlimited availability to their readers. Scholars believe that this advantage may promote easy acceptance and more frequent use of OA journals.

Although most scholars consider wide availability as the norm in today's digital environment, and take that availability for granted, some have negative attitudes toward these journals, as they do toward anything on the Internet. This negative attitude reflects an issue of trust with respect to journal quality, which is closely linked with its perceived content quality.

Factor: Perceived Content Quality
Statement: Scholars' perception of content quality positively affects their willingness to use OA journal articles for their potential publications.

Content quality refers to the worthiness and pertinence of journal articles. Along with perceived journal reputation and perceived topical relevance, content quality has a strong positive influence on the use of journal articles. According to our interview data, when scholars come across OA journal articles, they screen the content briefly; if the content is perceived as being of a certain quality, they will use the article. In other words, the higher the quality of journal content, the more likely scholars are to read or download the full text, perceiving it as worthy.

Unlike perceived journal reputation, however, perceived content quality was not identified as a deciding factor for publishing in OA journals. Authors seem to recognize a journal not for its content quality but for its reputation; in other words, content quality itself does not directly motivate scholars to publish in OA journals, though they do assume that high content quality indicates high journal reputation and vice versa.

Factor: Perceived Ease of Use
Statement: Scholars' perception of ease of use positively affects their willingness to use OA journal articles for their potential publications.

Along with perceived availability, ease of use has a strong positive effect on the use of OA journal articles. *Ease of use* refers to the degree of convenience experienced when using OA journal articles. It is also closely linked with availability. Scholars often prefer selecting articles that are instantly available at their desktop to going to the library for a copy of a printed journal issue, even though many of them prefer a print version for reading.

Research Question 3: How do the factors relate to one another?

Connections among the determinant factors emerged through axial coding. The researchers' conceptual interpretation revealed the following relationships:

Relationship: Scholars' perception of the topical relevance of OA journals positively affects their perception of journal reputation.

The researchers interpreted the effect of topical relevance on journal reputation as one of the strongest relationships. The data show that whatever cases scholars face in academic contexts, these two factors are tightly intertwined. They assess journal reputation based on the social norms established within their field. This normative belief is also found among scholars involved in interdisciplinary research.

Relationship: Scholars' perception of OA journal reputation positively affects their perception of career benefits.

Scholars' common perception of journal reputation is an important criterion in evaluating their academic performance. The higher the reputation of the journal, the more credibility and visibility scholars will receive for their publications. Publishing in a journal of good reputation can lead to better career evaluation in terms of academic merit and intellectual rewards. This relationship may be true across all access modes, because OA or not is not material to journal reputation.

Relationship: Scholars' perception of career benefit negatively affects their perception of cost of publishing.

Scholars often have considerable intellectual capital tied up in the research articles they publish. This intellectual capital is created through the expenditure of time, money, and effort. As evidence of scholarship, intellectual capital can be translated into visible returns through an academic reward system, such as tenure and promotion. Because of the importance of tenure and promotion, the cost for individuals to succeed in the process is often ignored, which implies a negative relationship between perceived career benefit and perceived cost.

Relationship: Scholars' perception of the availability of OA journals positively affects their perception of career benefit.

Most scholars acknowledge that OA journals have higher user accessibility than traditional subscription-based journals, which is an advantage of OA journals. This belief leads them to choose OA journals strategically for disseminating their works to a wider audience. The more recognition they receive for their work, the more intellectual capital that work will gain. As mentioned above, intellectual capital is perceived as a career benefit. Contradictions arise when we examine the relationship between perceived availability and perceived career benefit. Availability encourages career benefit in terms of wider recognition, but it seems to weaken career benefit through its relationship with journal reputation and content quality. As shown in Figure 1, availability seems to reduce perceived content quality, which is strongly tied to journal reputation. Journal reputation, as a result, affects career benefit. It is also noticeable that tenured professors mostly acknowledge the effect of availability on career benefit; they seem to be more interested than untenured scholars in wider dissemination of their work.

Relationship: Scholars' perception of OA journal reputation positively affects their perception of content quality, and vice versa.

Boundaries are blurring between journal reputation and content quality. Scholars' perceptions of an OA journal prefigure its rank and evaluate its quality as a result. Conversely, the perceived quality of an OA journal article provides enough rationale for the scholars to evaluate the overall reputation of the journal. The scholars in our sample assumed that the quality of all articles in one journal is more or less equal, which overgeneralizes the quality of each article to the journal's reputation. Author reputation may also contribute to journal reputation; our interviewees did not distinguish between the two. Rather, they sought evidence of the renown or reputation of authors published in a given journal authors when evaluating the journal's reputation.

Relationship: Scholars' perception of availability seems to negatively affect their perception of content quality.

Although this relationship was weak compared to others, the analysis revealed that the scholars interviewed have a negative attitude toward freely available research resources. This attitude seems to be based on their general attitude toward the Internet. Some extreme responses indicate that some scholars have little trust in any Internet resource. Most were not aware of the fact that OA journals follow a peer-review process and thus treat OA journal content as if it were just uncontrolled Internet information.

Relationship: Scholars' perception of availability positively affects their perception of ease of use.

Ease of use includes the concept of availability, convenience, and lack of complexity. The perceived availability of OA journal articles makes it easier for scholars to obtain a copy of the full text without having to visit the library.

Discussion

The purpose of this investigation was to explore the factors that increase or decrease scholars' willingness to publish and use articles from OA journals and to describe the relationships between these factors. We identified seven factors (perceived journal reputation, perceived topical relevance, perceived availability, perceived career benefit, perceived cost, perceived content quality, and perceived ease of use) and eight relationships (six positive and two negative). The premise of this research was that scholars face situations in which they must decide which journals to use in their research and where to publish the results of that research.

Comparison with Existing Literature: Theory Validation

According to K.M. Eisenhardt, relevant literature reviews can increase validity in qualitative research. Eisenhardt states that "overall, tying the emergent theory to existing literature enhances the internal validity, generalisability, and theoretical level of the theory building ... because the findings often rest on a very limited number of cases."[29] It is common for researchers to examine relevant literature before they start a research project. However, in studying an emergent phenomenon, researchers can begin collecting data as soon as they have a research situation and review the literature later as it becomes relevant. In short, reviewing and comparing relevant literature can become part of a grounded theorizing procedure. For example, Creswell and Brown have developed a grounded theory that interrelates variables of the effect of the academic department chair on faculty members' scholarly performance. They then compare their findings with results in previous studies.[30] Following this procedure, we discuss our findings in relation to relevant literature.

One of the significant findings of this study was that perceived journal reputation, perceived topical relevance, and perceived availability are common factors affecting scholars' willingness to publish and use OA journals. These factors can be applied to a broader scope of scholarly communication processes than identified in previous studies. For example, Wang and Soergel identify authority, topicality, and availability as user decision-making criteria in selecting documents from DIALOG database search results.[31] Rieh identifies cognitive authority and information quality as user judgment criteria for the Web information resources.[32] The samples from both studies are scholars (eleven faculty members and fourteen graduate students for Wang and Soergel's study; seven faculties and nine doctoral students for Rieh's study).[33] These criteria can be applied only in situations where knowledge transfer happens unidirectionally from the public to the private domain (i.e., where information is sought for individual users' consumption without considering users as authors). This project, on the contrary, studies scholars' perceptions of both publishing in and using OA journals, the former representing knowledge transfer from the private to the public domain while the latter represents transfer from the public to the private domain.

Prior research identifies three common factors—perceived journal reputation, perceived topical relevance, and perceived availability—in using scholarly publications. Our findings correspond to those of several previous studies. The concept of journal reputation can be found in the previously articulated concept of *authority,* which appears in the information science literature and is defined as the recognition of a researcher or an agency in an academic field.[34] Several terms are used in the literature to refer to this concept, for example, "well-known"[35] and "cognitive authority."[36] Patrick Wilson defines cognitive authority as the "influence on one's thoughts that one would consciously recognize as proper."[37] He further clarifies the meaning of "cognitive authority" by stating that it is related to credibility and that credibility has two main components: competence and trustworthiness. Cognitive authority and information quality have been identified as primary factors affecting users' selection of Web documents.[38] Another common factor, topical relevance, is also a well-established construct. It is defined elsewhere as users' perception of whether or not the topic of a document is relevant or related to the topic of their academic interests.[39] Linda Schamber identifies accessibility as a user document selection criterion in a media-rich context.[40] All previous studies have focused on the use of publications in relation to these three factors. In an OA environment, the new publishing model has undoubtedly given more flexibility and power to users as authors in choosing where to publish. While the factors affecting the choice of where to publish remain largely the same as those for non-OA channels, we found a generally positive perception of publishing in OA journals, though some scholars, especially the non-tenured, are still skeptical about the reputation and quality of these journals.

Besides these three common factors that affect both publishing and use, we discovered that whether or not a scholar *publishes in* OA journals is affected by both perceived career benefit and perceived cost and that whether or not a scholar *uses* OA journals is decided by perceived content quality and ease of use. These findings validate past studies of these criteria. For instance, source quality is "the extent to which general standards of quality can be assumed based on the source of a document";[41] accuracy and consistency have been regarded as user relevance judgement criteria.[42] Similar concepts were identified in information system evaluative studies. An example is DeLone and McLean's work, which generalizes twenty-three items, such as importance, accuracy, completeness, and content, as constructs of information quality.[43] Lee and others propose an assessment methodology for information quality using DeLone and McLean's taxonomy.[44] The concepts of "goodness" and "content" that we identified in our empirical data can be seen in these studies. We could not find any evidence, however, that perceived content quality is an important factor affecting willingness to publish.

Another important finding of this research is the relationships between the factors. The relationships shown in Figure 1 suggest that factors affecting publishing and use are interrelated. In an OA context, perceived availability positively affects career benefit because it brings wider recognition. Perceived availability also positively affects perceived ease of use, since the two together indicate convenience and easy accessibility. Perceived availability, however, seems to affect perceived content quality negatively, because scholars tend to perceive high availability as low rarity, resulting in less embedded value. This negative relationship between availability and content quality is supported by an existing study. In 1987, E. Burton Swanson introduced and tested a model of "channel disposition" to explain the selection and use of information.[45] In this model, potential users are hypothesized to select and use information based on a psychological trade-off between costs of access and information quality. This trade-off relationship requires further investigation.

Impact of Social Constructs on Open Scholarly Publishing

There are two main social constructs driving open scholarly publishing. One is the noble idea of disseminating and sharing knowledge freely, both within learned communities and with the public; the other is the demand for faster, wider, and more effective dissemination of research products, including not only papers but also the data sets and graphics generated in the research process. While technological advances made open scholarly publishing possible, these social constructs will determine its success or failure.

The factors identified in this study significantly affect the success and sustainability of open scholarly publishing in different ways. Under the current academic reward system, journal content quality and reputation are tied to career benefit. It is common today to find misunderstanding and distrust of OA journals among scholars. Such attitudes are reflected in the tenure and promotion process, which may give less weight to articles published in an OA journal than to those published in a traditional journal, even though both are refereed. Availability, in an OA context, plays the role of providing social opportunities such as career benefit.

Conclusion

Many factors may influence a scholar's decision to publish in and use OA journals. This study examined scholars' perceptions of the reputation, quality, availability, and relevance of OA journals. The contribution of this research is twofold. On the one hand, the analysis of both publishing and use provides insights into the process of scholarly communication from two directions (i.e., scholars as authors and scholars as users). Our participants' perceptions of publishing in OA journals perhaps have more immediate implications for this new channel of scholarly communication, because scholars' willingness to publish in OA journals is vital to the sustainability of such publications. On the other hand, this study improves our understanding of factors such as quality, reputation, relevance, and career benefit that are of concerns to scholars and make many of them hesitate to choose OA journals as their main publishing venue.

This research is among the first to study scholars as both authors and users of OA journals. Given the lack of research-oriented publications in this field, the factors and relationships we have identified and the methodology used in this study will provide a research framework for future investigations. From an open scholarly publishing standpoint, there are growing concerns about how to promote OA publishing. Foster and

Gibbons stress the importance of content recruitment in an institutional repository, stating that "if you build it, they will come does not yet apply."[46] The concept also applies to OA journals. Without content, open access will not succeed. Identifying and understanding the factors that influence such acceptance would provide criteria for recruiting content from scholars.

We acknowledge that the sample size was relatively small and that not all disciplines were covered in this study. The findings from this research may not be applicable to other academic disciplines, since each academic community has its own idiosyncrasies in communication; for example, physicists may not give much weight to journal reputation because institutional repositories (e.g., arXiv.org) that have no quality-control mechanism are well-established scholarly communication channels in the physics community. The works of physics scholars are symbolized using formulas, as are those in mathematics;[47] readers evaluate the quality of each work despite the lack of a peer-review process. Biomedical scientists, on the other hand, are very sensitive to the quality and reputation of journals. Future research needs to focus either on a single academic discipline or cover multiple disciplines.

Finally, this research took a qualitative approach to study scholars' perceptions and acceptance of OA journals. Many new research questions are raised by this study that we did not have time to explore further, including how scholars interact with peers and the journal(s) as a mini-information system; what impact OA journals have on scholarly communication, both socially and behaviorally; and whether OA journals will become the mainstream of scholarly publishing. Future research can include a quantitative approach, such as questionnaires or surveys, to gain a better understanding of this new digital information frontier.

Contributors

Ji-Hong Park is a doctoral candidate at the School of Information Studies of Syracuse University. His areas of research interest include scholarly communication, evaluation of digital library services, and knowledge management. He holds a MS in Information Resources Management from Syracuse University and a BA in Library and Information Science from Yonsei University, South Korea.

Jian Qin is an associate professor at the School of Information Studies of Syracuse University. She has more than forty publications in the areas of knowledge modelling and organization, metadata, and scholarly communication. She holds a Ph.D. from University of Illinois at Urbana-Champaign, an MLIS from the University of Western Ontario and a BA in Library Science from Wuhan University, China.

Notes

1. Stevan Harnad and Tim Brody, "Comparing the Impact of Open Access (OA) vs. Non-OA Articles in the Same Journals," *D-Lib Magazine* (June 2004), available at *http://www.dlib.org/dlib/june04/harnad/06harnad.html*.
2. Peter Suber, "Open Access to the Scientific Journal Literature," *Journal of Biology* 1, 1 (June 18, 2002): art. 3. available at *http://jbiol.com/content/1/1/3*.
3. *Ibid.*; see also BioMed Central, *http://biomedcentral.com*.
4. Bo-Christer Björk, "Open Access to Scientific Publications: An Analysis of the Barriers to Change?" *Information Research* 9, 2 (January 2004), *http://informationr.net/ir/9-2/paper170.html*; Elizabeth Gadd, Charles Oppenheim, and Steve Probets, "RoMEO Studies 1: The Impact of Copyright Ownership on Author-Self-Archiving," *Journal of Documentation* 59, 3 (May 2003): 243–77.
5. E.g., Steve Hitchcock, Les Carr, Steve Harris, Steve Probets, David Evans, Wendy Hall, and David Brailsford, "Linking Electronic Journals: Lessons from the Open Journal Project," *D-Lib Magazine* 4, 12 (December 1998), available at *http://www.dlib.org/dlib/december98/12hitchcock.html*.
6. Stevan Harnad, "Free at Last: The Future of Peer-Reviewed Journals," *D-Lib Magazine* 5, 12 (December 1999), available at *http://dlib.org/dlib/december99/12harnad.html*; Stevan Harnad, "Implementing Peer Review on the Net: Scientific Quality Control in Scholarly Electronic Journals," in Robin P. Peek and Gregory B. Newby, eds., *Scholarly Publishing: The Electronic Frontier* (Cambridge, MA: MIT Press 1996): 107–17.
7. L. Halliday and C. Oppenheim, "Progress in Documentation: Developments in Digital Journals," *Journal of Documentation* 57, 2 (March 2001): 296–302; Stevan Harnad, "Electronic Scholarly Publication: Quo Vadis?" *Serials Review* 21, 1 (Spring 1995): 70–72.
8. Christine L. Borgman, "Digital Libraries and the Continuum of Scholarly Communication," *Journal of Documentation* 56, 4 (July 2000): 412–30.
9. James Keller, "Public Access Issues: An Introduction," in Brian Kahin and James Keller, eds., *Public Access to the Internet* (Cambridge, MA: MIT Press, 1995): 34–45.
10. Bethesda Principles: Summary of the April 11, 2003, Meeting on Open Access Publishing, BiomedCentral, *http://www.biomedcentral.com/openaccess/bethesda/#definition*.
11. Budapest Open Access Initiative (English), *http://www.soros.org/openaccess/*.
12. Scholarly Publishing and Academic Resources Coalition (SPARC), *http://www.arl.org/sparc/*.
13. Public Library of Science (PLoS), *http://www.publiclibraryofscience.org*.
14. Rob Kling, Lisa B. Spector, and Joanna Fortuna, "The Real Stakes of Virtual Publishing: The Transformation of E-Biomed into PubMed Central," *Journal of the American Society for Information Science and Technology* 55, 2 (January 15, 2004): 127–48.
15. Carl Lagoze and Herbert Van de Sompel, "The Open Archive Initiative: Building a Low-Barrier Interoperability Framework," in Edward A. Fox and Christine L. Borgman, eds., *Proceedings of the Joint Conference on Digital Libraries (JCDL), June 17–23, Roanoke, VA* (Roanoke, VA: ACM/IEEE-CS 2001): 54–62.

16. Björk, "Open Access to Scientific Publications."
17. H. Woodward, F. Rowland, C. McKnight, J. Meadows, and C. Pritchett, "Electronic Journals: Myths and Realities," *Library Management* 18 (1997): 155–62.
18. Don Schauder, "Electronic Publishing of Professional Articles: Attitudes of Academics and Implications for the Scholarly Communication Industry," *Journal of the American Society for Information Science* 45 (1994): 73–100.
19. *Ibid.*
20. Elizabeth Gadd, Charles Oppenheim, and Steve Probets, "RoMEO Studies 2: How Academics Want to Protect Their Open-Access Research Papers," *Journal of Information Science* 29, 5 (September 2003): 333–56; Elizabeth Gadd, Charles Oppenheim, and Steve Probets, "RoMEO Studies 3: How Academics Expect to Use Open-Access Research Papers," *Journal of Librarianship and Information Science* 35, 3 (September 2003): 171–87.
21. Gadd et al., "RoMEO Studies 1."
22. Yvonne S. Lincoln and Egon G. Guba, *Naturalistic Inquiry* (London: Sage Publications 1985), 235.
23. Anselm L. Strauss and Juliet Corbin, *Basics of Qualitative Research: Techniques and Procedures for Developing Grounded Theory*, 2nd ed. (Newbury Park, CA: Sage Publications 1998).
24. *Ibid.*, 24.
25. Anselm L. Strauss and Juliet Corbin, *Basics of Qualitative Research: Techniques and Procedures for Developing Grounded Theory*, 1st ed. (Newbury Park, CA: Sage Publications 1990), 57.
26. Strauss and Corbin, *Basics* 2nd ed.
27. Strauss and Corbin, *Basics* 1st ed, 124.
28. Diana Crane, *Invisible Colleges: Diffusion of Knowledge in Scientific Communities* (Chicago: University of Chicago Press, 1972).
29. Kathleen M. Eisenhardt, "Building Theories from Case Study Research," *Academy of Management Review* 14, 4 (October 1989): 532–50, 545.
30. John W. Creswell and Martha L. Brown, "How Chairpersons Enhance Faculty Research: A Grounded Theory Study," *Review of Higher Education* 16, 1 (Spring 1992): 41–62.
31. Peiling Wang and Dagobert Soergel, "A Cognitive Model of Document Use during a Research Project, Study I: Document Selection," *Journal of the American Society for Information Science and Technology* 49, 2 (January 15, 1998): 115–33.
32. Soo Young Rieh, "Judgment of Information Quality and Cognitive Authority on the Web," *Journal of the American Society for Information Science and Technology* 53, 2 (January 2002): 145–61.
33. *Ibid.*; Wang and Soergel, "Cognitive Model."
34. Wang and Soergel, "Cognitive Model."
35. C. Cool, N.J. Belkin, O. Frieder, and P. Kantor, "Characteristics of Texts Affecting Relevance Judgments." *Proceedings of the 14th National Online Meeting, New York, May 3–5, 1993* (New York: Learned Information 1993): 77–84.
36. J.W. Fritch and R.L. Cromwell, "Evaluating Internet Resources: Identity, Affiliation, and Cognitive Authority in a Networked World," *Journal of the American Society for Information Science and Technology* 52, 6 (March 15, 2001): 499–507.
37. Patrick Wilson, *Second-Hand Knowledge: An Inquiry into Cognitive Authority* (Westport, CT: Greenwood Press, 1983), 15.
38. Rieh, "Judgment of Information Quality."
39. Wang and Soergel, "Cognitive Model."
40. Linda Schamber, "Users' Criteria for Evaluation in a Multimedia Environment." *Proceedings of the 54th ASIS Annual Meeting* 28 (1991): 126–33.

41. Carol L. Barry, "User-Defined Relevance Criteria: An Exploratory Study," *Journal of the American Society for Information Science* 45, 3 (February 1, 1994): 149–59, 155.
42. Schamber, "Users' Criteria."
43. William H. Delone and Ephraim R. McLean, "Information Systems Success: The Quest for the Dependent Variable," *Information Systems Research* 3, 1 (March 1992): 60–95, 85.
44. Yang W. Lee, Diane M. Strong, Beverly K. Kahn, and Richard Y. Wang, "AIMQ: A Methodology for Information Quality Assessment," *Information and Management* 40, 2 (December 2002): 133–46.
45. E. Burton Swanson, "Information Channel Disposition and Use," *Decision Sciences* 18, 1 (Winter, 1987), 131–45.
46. Nancy F. Foster and Susan Gibbons, "Understanding Faculty to Improve Content Recruitment for Institutional Repositories," *D-Lib Magazine* 11, 1 (January 2005), *http://www.dlib.org/dlib/january05/foster/01foster.html*.
47. Karin D. Knorr-Cetina, *Epistemic Cultures: How the Sciences Make Knowledge* (Cambridge, MA: Harvard University Press 1999).

Fair Use in Theory and Practice: Reflections on Its History and the Google Case

Sanford G. Thatcher[1]

Director Sanford G. Thatcher's perspective on copyright reflects the experience of trying to survive in a perilous enterprise that exists with one foot in the commercial marketplace and the other in the academic community, creating a condition of chronic schizophrenia. The press he directs is dedicated to serving the mission of disseminating scholarship but is required (under current conditions, anyway) to rely on income from sales to pay most of its bills. Because university presses operate so close to the margin, this sector of publishing is especially vulnerable to expansive interpretations of "fair use."

Introduction

It is probably the height of folly for someone like me, with no formal legal training, to address a group of attorneys on an area of the law that Justice Story once famously described as "metaphysics." But perhaps it may be seen as appropriate if I tell you that I was trained in philosophy, so am not daunted by metaphysics, and I work in a business that has been described by one of its own eminent practitioners as a type of folly. As a former director of Yale University Press once said, "We publish the smallest editions at the greatest cost, and on these we place the highest prices, and then we try to market them to people who can least afford them. This is madness."[2]

The Concept of Fair Use

There is a lot of confusion about "fair use," as we can see from the many conflicting perspectives that have been brought to bear in public discussion of Google's Library Project so far, but it is easy to understand why such confusion exists. As one of those who witnessed the process of Congressional politics playing itself out in the revision of copyright law that resulted in the 1976 Copyright Act, and one who even had an opportunity to testify before a Senate subcommittee on the issue of "fair use," I agree completely with my esteemed colleague Leon Seltzer, former director of Stanford University Press (and a bona fide lawyer), who said, in his critical assessment of Congress's handiwork, that:

> almost the entire attention of Congress with respect to fair use was devoted to one aspect of the technical problem of photocopying, and the complex issues having in general to do with fair use were focused solely on the resolution of a single case—educational copying of copyrighted works. That is, instead of facing squarely the primary question "What do we mean by fair use?' or the secondary question 'How does the advent of the new technologies affect the conceptualization, and therefore the application, of the fair use doctrine?" Congress dealt with fair use on a tertiary level: "How do we fashion a fair-use statute so as to solve, by means of a compromise, a particular and expressly formulated exemption from copyright, the photocopying reproduction of copyrighted works for educational purposes?"[3]

In Seltzer's estimation, Congress thus sowed the seed for rampant confusion later:

> it has failed to articulate a coherent rationale for copyright, it has failed to define fair use, it has introduced confusions between fair use and exempted use, and it has in the end tossed the fair use question, now thoroughly enmeshed in contradictions, back to the courts.[4]

Among other things, of course, Congress for the first time ever imported the notion of intrinsic use of a work through reproduction into the conceptual ambit of "fair use." As Kenneth Crews explains:

> three subtle, but important, changes in Section 107 emerged during congressional reviews and hearings: fair use was expressly applied to the reproduction of materials; it permitted multiple copies for classroom use; and the nonprofit character of a use became an explicit factor in the fair use equation.[5]

As Crews also points out, "despite its denials, Congress was unquestionably changing the law."[6] Its denials were disingenuous, to say the least, for, as Seltzer notes, "In the special Copyright Revision study on fair use prepared by the Copyright Office for Congress [by Alan Latman in 1958], not a single case cited holds that straightforward reproduction of a copyrighted work for its own sake constitutes fair use."[7] That very issue was thrust upon Congress to resolve, of course, by the suit that STM journal publisher Williams & Wilkins had brought against the National Library of Medicine and the National Institutes of Health, which resulted in an evenly split 4–4 Supreme Court decision in 1975 upholding the 4–3 ruling by the Court of Claims finding photocopying by these government agencies to be "fair use"—which one of the dissenting justices described as "the Dred Scott decision of copyright law."[8] Alan Latman was the plaintiff's attorney, by the way.

This, in brief, is the origin of the conceptual confusion that has plagued "fair use" jurisprudence ever since. "Fair use" was thenceforth deployed to justify two very different kinds of activities. To highlight their differences, let's call them "creative" fair use and "quantitative" fair use. "Creative" fair use embodies the core original meaning of the concept, as it was developed to allow for an author to build upon the work of earlier authors, through comment and criticism, in a "value-added" process that involves reproducing copyrighted work just to the extent needed to fulfil this purpose. "Quantitative" fair use came into play when photocopying began to proliferate in the 1960s and some felt the need to defend the making of multiple copies, in a purely duplicative process that is no more than a form of parasitical publishing, as though it were somehow analogous to the activity of "creative" fair use. It has taken on added significance in the era of digital copying, which makes possible duplication on an even more massive scale and with no degradation of quality from the original work.

The application of the same term to these quite different activities is unfortunate, because it can all too easily mislead people into thinking that the two types of fair use are equally essential to the advancement of scholarship. They are not. "Creative" fair use is indisputably necessary for scholarship to flourish. "Quantitative" fair use merely offers a "free ride" for users who like the convenience of having more copies immediately available and who want to avoid contributing to the costs of original publication. Judge Jon Newman, in writing the majority opinion in the Second Circuit's decision in the landmark *Texaco* case, made this very distinction:

> We would seriously question whether the fair use analysis that has developed with respect to works of authorship alleged to use portions of copyrighted material is precisely applicable to copies produced by mechanical means. The traditional fair use analysis, now codified in section 107, developed in an effort to adjust the competing interests of the authors—the author of the original copyrighted work and the author of the secondary work that "copies" a portion of the original work in the course of producing what is claimed to be a new work. Mechanical "copying" of an entire document, made readily feasible by the advent of xerography ..., is obviously an activity entirely different from creating a work of authorship. Whatever social utility copying of this sort achieves, it is not concerned with creative authorship.[9]

The perspective that university presses take on fair use reflects this duality in the concept as it is currently deployed. Our mission, as an integral part of higher education, is to serve the interests of scholars in producing and disseminating their work. To fulfil this mission, we fully support "creative" fair use (though we probably have not been aggressive enough in exploring its limits, as with the use of film stills, for instance). But we consider "quantitative" fair use in many of the ways it is being deployed today (as in e-reserves) to be severely threatening to our ability to carry out our mission because it undercuts the economic basis of our operation—and we therefore question whether these applications of it can properly be construed as fair use at all. We also question whether the long-term interests of scholarship are not being sacrificed to the short-term advantages gained from a too-aggressive pursuit of "quantitative" fair use. Does it make any sense for universities to subsidize their faculty's and students' use of copyrighted materials by aggressively invoking "quantitative" fair use at the cost of undercutting their own presses, which are assigned the task of publishing much of the most valuable scholarship that emanates from higher education? For university presses, then, the key tension in fair use—indeed, what challenges its very coherence—lies in this contrast between the "creative" and "quantitative" applications of the concept.

Several efforts have been made to restore coherence to fair use. One of the most notable was undertaken by Pierre Leval, a judge on the appeals court of the Second Circuit (where the Google case is being tried). Frustrated by the reversals of his own opinions in two cases involving fair use of unpublished works (*Salinger v. Random House* [1986] and *New Era Publications v. Henry Holt & Co.* [1988]), and admitting that judges like him "have repeatedly adjudicated upon ad hoc perceptions of justice without a permanent framework," Leval sought an understanding of fair use "as a rational, integral part of copyright, whose observance is necessary to achieve the objectives of that law."[10] He located it in the "utilitarian message" found in the 1710 Statute of Anne's reference to "the Encouragement of Learning" as the goal of copyright and reflected in our own Constitution's articulation of the purpose of copyright "to promote the Progress of Science and useful Arts."[11] Thus "copyright law embodies a recognition that creative intellectual activity is vital to the well-being of society," and:

> recognition of the function of fair use as integral to copyright's objectives leads to a coherent and useful set of principles. Briefly stated, the use must be of a character that serves the copyright objective of stimulating productive thought and public instruction without excessively diminishing the incentives for creativity. One must assess each of the issues that arise in considering a fair use defense in the light of the governing purpose of copyright law.[12]

For Leval, this approach led to viewing "transformative" use as the key to any fair-use analysis: whether the use at issue "is of the transformative type that advances knowledge and the progress of the arts or whether it merely repackages, free riding on another's creations.... Factor One is the soul of fair use."[13] This approach accords very well with the view that university presses have of fair use, whereby any "social utility" that pure copying without added value should be clearly subordinate to the primary objective of "creative" use and considered justified only where it does not interfere, in a more than *de minimis* fashion, with the fundamental right of the copyright owner to "reproduce" and "distribute" the work.

Leval had made no attempt to apply his preferred approach to the Supreme Court's ruling in the *Sony* case because, focusing as it did on an intrinsic use, *Sony* did not make sense, in Leval's terms, as vindication of a creative use. Nor, as Lloyd Weinreb points out in his rejoinder to Leval's article, did it make sense in terms of the standard four-factor analysis. As Weinreb observes, "Justice Stevens' arguments in favor of fair use, purportedly applying the four statutory factors, are hopelessly inadequate."[14] But another analysis seeking a principled basis for fair use in the Constitutional language was provided by L. Ray Patterson. Patterson's main argument, which features a distinction between use of a work and use of the copyright in a work and which depends on viewing copyright as a regulatory rather than proprietary concept, made the results in both *Sony Corp. v. Universal Studios* (1984) and *Harper & Row v. Nation Enterprises* (1985) seem perfectly reasonable. In the *Sony* decision, as he explains, the Court:

> portrays copyright as a regulatory concept, utilizes the distinction between use of the copyright and use of the work, treats the fair use doctrine as a fair competitive use doctrine, and implicitly acknowledges that the copyright clause incorporates free speech values. By taping copyrighted programs off-the-air for personal in-home use, the individual makes use of the work, not of the copyright.[15]

Similarly, in *Harper & Row,* "without articulating the point, the Court used the distinction between the use of the copyright and the use of the work. The defendant was a competitor who used the copyright, not the work." In Patterson's opinion, "*Sony* and *Harper & Row* are more sound in their results than in their reasoning. The split decisions in both cases indicate that the results were achieved more by intuition than by an understanding of sound copyright principles."[16] Despite their different ways of applying the Constitutional mandate to an understanding of fair use, then, Leval and Patterson both agree that, as Leval puts it, judicial "decisions are not governed by consistent principles, but seem rather to result from intuitive reactions to individual fact patterns."[17] Small wonder, then, that "earlier decisions provide little basis for predicting later ones" and "reversals and divided courts are commonplace."[18] It is for this reason that Georgia Harper, in her recent paper "Google This," can very justifiably argue that what is at stake in any dispute about fair use is really an assessment of "overall social utility," and that the explanation of a court's decision in terms of the four factors is really so much window-dressing for a decision reached on other grounds.[19]

Patterson, in a later work coauthored with Stanley W. Lindberg, elaborates on his theory distinguishing use of a work from use of a copyright and postulates two types of what he calls "users' rights," of which fair use in his sense of "fair competitive use" is one. The other, dubbed "personal use," is defined as follows:

> An individual's use of a copyrighted work for his or her own private use is a personal use, not subject to fair-use restraints. Such use includes use by copying, provided that the copy is neither for public distribution or sale to others nor a functional substitute for a copyrighted work currently available on the market at a reasonable price.[20]

Although "personal use" is a highly controversial concept, I do have some sympathy for it, for a very simple reason well articulated by Jessica Litman:

> The less workable a law is, the more problematic it is to enforce. The harder it is to explain the law to the people it is supposed to restrict, the harder it will be to explain to the prosecutors, judges, and juries charged with applying it. The more burdensome the law makes it to obey proscriptions, and the more draconian the penalties for failing, the more distasteful it will be to enforce. The more people the law seeks to constrain, the more futile it can be to enforce it only sporadically. Finally, the less the law's choices strike the people it affects as legitimate, the less they will feel as if breaking that law is doing anything wrong. In other words, if a law is bad enough, large numbers of people will fail to comply with it, whether they should or not.[21]

I think she has this exactly right. Moreover, since Congress botched the job of making any coherent sense of fair use in drafting the 1976 act, as Seltzer demonstrates, and since judges ever afterward have made their decisions in an ad hoc manner lacking any consistent set of principles to guide them, as Leval and Patterson allege, we desperately need a theory of fair use that is readily communicable to the multitude of citizens we are asking to abide by copyright law.

Litman herself proposes a solution that she readily admits to be "radical," namely, "stop defining copyright in terms of reproduction" and instead "start by recasting copyright as an exclusive right of commercial exploitation," relying on the commonly understood "distinction between commercial and noncommercial behavior."[22] This seems also to be the underlying rationale for the licenses offered through Larry Lessig's brainchild, Creative Commons, which makes much of this distinction. Alas, the distinction is not so intuitively clear as its proponents seem to think. I can illustrate the problem very simply by reference to our own business. Can a university press, as a non-profit enterprise embedded within an educational institution, take advantage of a Creative Commons licensed work for "non-commercial" uses, even though we sell our publications in the "commercial" marketplace the same way for-profit publishers do—and though we even, occasionally, pay royalties to our authors? Who is to say whether this is a "commercial" or a "non-commercial" use? Similarly, although it may strike Patterson as a "non-competitive" use, and hence not "commercial," the copying done for course packs and e-reserves (which is treated as such by the policy he helped draft for the University of Georgia system, drawing from the ideas in his 1991 book, and which even Crews views as pushing the envelope[23]) surely does supplant the market for the publications of university presses, as our declining sales of paperbacks attest, and so cannot qualify either as "personal use" (on the second prong of his definition) or as "fair use" (because this copying does indeed constitute a "use of the copyright"—i.e., the right to distribute—in his own terms).

While I am not prepared to accept Litman's radical solution, or Patterson's application of his theoretical principles, I do think it should be possible to devise an adequate theory of fair use that (1) gives pride of place to "creative" or "transformative" use as "the soul of fair use" because it best exemplifies the underlying Constitutional rationale for copyright, as Leval argues; (2) nevertheless reserves a residual place for "personal use," as construed by Patterson in terms of its being a use of the work rather than a use of the copyright (or else just as a *de minimis* use, as Leval evidently would prefer to construe it,[24] such as the limited single copying done under the exemption in s. 108(d) for the purpose of "private study, scholarship, or research," which is consonant with the basic Constitutional objective of copyright and which publishers first accepted in the 1935 "Gentlemen's Agreement" with the library community); and (3), by so doing, satisfies the dire need for an explanation of fair use that is readily communicable to and easily understood by the general public (not to mention "prosecutors, judges, and juries"!), as called for by Litman. I know this is a promissory note, and the details of such a theory would need to be worked out from the bare sketch I have provided here. But I am confident that it can be done.

The Google Case

Now, having laid out this background and at least adumbrated a theory of fair use, I can tackle the immediate issue of the alleged fairness of the Google Library Project. Let no one mistake the criticisms I am about to make as any sign of a lack of enthusiasm for the Google Print Program as a whole. On the contrary, Penn State University Press was an early enthusiast of the Print Publisher Program, and we remain so today. Just look at the case study about our Press that Google itself has posted, and you'll understand why.[25] We believe that there is considerable "social utility" in this ambitious undertaking and applaud Google for its vision of making all the world's knowledge readily available to everyone who has access to a computer with an Internet connection. If, as Harper surmises, the judges in this case simply apply a basic cost-benefit analysis to the Library Project and then cloak their assessment in the legal garb of the four factors, they may well find this to be "fair use," because they will accept Google's arguments about its obvious "social utility" at face value—as many commentators in the popular press have already done. But I do not believe the Library Project to be fair use, despite its "social utility," because I don't think it can be defended on any of the theories of fair use I have outlined above.

Forget about the "snippets." They are not the heart of this case, in spite of all the attention they have received in the popular press. Rather, the real crux is the making of two digital copies of each copyrighted work, one of which Google will keep itself, the other of which it will give to the participating library that provided the work to be scanned. I do not see how, in the terms set forth in Leval's article, this copying can in any way be considered "creative" or "transformative." (Judge Leval will have the opportunity to apply his own theory himself if this case gets to the appeals level, where he now resides.) It is, as Judge Newman said, merely "mechanical" in nature and multiplies the number of copies of the work available. Yes, it has "social utility," but so too did Texaco's copying, which Judge Newman (and Judge Leval before him in the district court) nevertheless found not to be fair use. At best, it might be seen as an intermediary form of copying that allows other useful activities to be pursued for the public benefit. In this sense, Google's copying might be construed as facilitating the production of a kind of super-index.[26]

But whatever it is that Google produces, the digital copies themselves are still that, just copies, and they may well serve to supplant the market for the original work, in two ways. First, the digital copy that Google retains is subject to no controls other than those that Google itself chooses to apply; there is no contractual agreement between Google and the copyright owner that imposes any responsibility on Google to ensure its security. Hence a copyright owner has no recourse against Google if the security is breached and the digital copy is stolen, to be used potentially for widespread piracy. Second, and equally important, the digital copy supplied to the library becomes available for whatever uses the library itself may consider "fair," which nowadays may well mean deposit in an e-reserve system that functions as a course pack–producing facility. This happens entirely outside of, and as a complete substitute for, a commercial transaction of the kind that publishers like our press have long undertaken through such companies as netLibrary and ebrary. The library's digital copy directly supplants a sale of an e-book to the library by the publisher or by an agent of the publisher. Moreover, the library's use of its digital copy is constrained by no license with the publisher, which is thus left with no legal recourse for any abuse except to sue for copyright infringement—not an option readily available to a university press, I assure you, and not a real option in any event against a state university library like Michigan's that can claim immunity under the Eleventh Amendment.

In terms of the four factors, (1) the digital copying of books by Google to operate its Library Project for the public good—just like the socially useful copying of journal articles by Texaco's researchers—nevertheless serves the "commercial" aims of the company as a whole and is not "transformative" in any sense akin to what has traditionally been understood "to promote the progress of science"; (2) it catches in its undiscriminating grasp works that cover the spectrum from highly expressive to purely factual; (3) the amount copied is the entire book; and (4) the effect on the market is both potentially (through the possibility of hacking) and actually (through the displacement of sales that could readily be anticipated via normal commercial channels in existence today) harmful to the copyright owner. Even in Patterson's terms, this is a use of the copyright, not a use of the work, and it is competitive with the established market for the copyrighted work in digital form; nor by any stretch of the imagination can this be considered a "personal use" analogous to viewing a taped movie in the privacy of one's own home. And even Litman should have to admit that there is here an "exploitation" of the commercial market where it is the copyright owner's right to conduct a sale, which, multiplied by potentially hundreds of titles (and many thousands for larger publishers) located within the collections of participating libraries, is hardly negligible.

Besides the four factors of fair use proper, what else strikes publishers as "unfair" about the Library Project? Initially, Google did not allow publishers like us who had signed up many titles for the Publisher Program to exclude them from the Library Project, arguing that this would be impractical and inefficient because the copying was being done "by the truckload." So, in spite of a licence already in place, Google asserted the right to make a digital copy of every one of these licensed works, too. Under vigorous protest from us and other publishers, Google later relented and provided a mechanism on its Web site whereby a participating Print publisher could, with one click, exclude all of its licensed titles. But Google originally did this using wording that made it impossible for a press like ours to comply with the procedure: "Under penalty of perjury I certify that I am the copyright holder for these titles." Our marketing director, who manages our account with Google, has no authority himself to so certify; the press, in any event, is not itself the copyright holder, the University is; and some books we only distribute or copublish (for museums, historical societies, etc.) and cannot claim to own at all. Again, at our urging, Google obliged by changing the wording to read as follows: "I certify that I am the owner of these books or authorized by the owner to exclude these books." Google has made much of how "easy" it is (in the words of its general counsel, David Drummond) for publishers to "opt out" any books from the Library Project at any time. But this is no trivial matter for a press the size of ours, or, indeed, for a publisher of any size, in the absence of any knowledge about what the collections of the participating libraries contain, and Google initially refused to provide that information, thus imposing on us the daunting task of researching the rights for every title on our backlist not already licensed through the Publisher Program. Google could have generated a lot more goodwill toward itself and this project if it had been more cooperative in these respects from the outset. Instead, it seemed more intent on waging a publicity campaign in the general media to win public sympathy for its project than on working with publishers to implement the project in a manner that could have served everyone's interests. What, finally, disappointed me the most was the possibility I saw for Google to play a leading role, with the high visibility of the Library Project, in bringing parties together to resolve the thorny issue of "orphan works," which the Copyright Office began investigating before Google announced this initiative. Since so many of the copyrighted works in the participating libraries' collections are likely to fall into this category, Google had a golden opportunity to work with both publishers and user groups toward crafting legislation that Congress can consider to make this vexing problem disappear—to the public benefit of all!

Contributor

Sanford G. Thatcher is Director of Penn State University Press. He is a member of the copyright committees of the Association of American University Presses and Association of American Publishers and serves on the Board of Directors of the Copyright Clearance Center.

Notes

1. This essay was originally prepared for the panel Dark Archives and Celestial Card Catalogues: Google Print and the Future of Fair Use at the National Association of College and University Attorneys' conference on the Wired University: Legal Issues at the Copyright, Computer Law, and Internet Intersection, held in Arlington, VA, on November 10, 2005. A previous version appeared in *AAUP Exchange* (Fall 2005): 1–7.
2. Chester Kerr, Director of Yale University Press, quoted in Gene R. Hawes, *To Advance Knowledge: A Handbook of American University Press Publishing* (New York: American University Press Services 1967), 5.
3. Leon E. Seltzer, *Exemptions and Fair Use in Copyright: The Exclusive Rights Tensions in the 1976 Copyright Act* (Cambridge: Harvard University Press 1978), 21–2. The testimony I presented to the Senate subcommittee is printed in the U.S. Senate Subcommittee on Patents, Trademarks, and Copyrights, *Copyright Law Revision: Hearings on S. 1361 before the Subcommittee on Patents, Trademarks and Copyrights of the Senate Committee on the Judiciary*, 93rd Cong., 1st sess., 1973, 138–40.
4. Seltzer, *ibid*, 16–7.
5. Kenneth D. Crews, *Copyright, Fair Use, and the Challenge for Universities: Promoting the Progress of Higher Education* (Chicago: University of Chicago Press, 1993), 32.
6. *Ibid.*, 33.
7. Seltzer, *Exemptions and Fair Use*, 24. The study to which Seltzer refers is Alan Latman, "Fair Use of Copyrighted Works," in U.S. Senate, *Copyright Law Revision: Studies Prepared for the Subcommittee on Patents, Trademarks, and Copyrights of the Committee on the Judiciary*, 86th Cong., 2nd sess., Study No. 14, March 1958.
8. U.S. Court of Claims Judge Philip Nichols, in his dissenting opinion, as quoted in Paul Goldstein, *Copyright's Highway: The Law and Lore of Copyright from Gutenberg to the Celestial Jukebox* (New York: Hill and Wang, 1994), 110.
9. *American Geophysical Union v. Texaco*, 60 F. 3d 913 (2nd Cir. 1994), 9–10 (writing for the majority).
10. Pierre N. Leval, "Toward a Fair Use Standard," *Harvard Law Review* 103, 5 (March 1990): 1105–36, 1105, 1107.
11. *Ibid.*, 1108.
12. *Ibid.*, 1109, 1110.
13. *Ibid.*, 1116.
14. Lloyd L. Weinreb, "Fair's Fair: A Comment on the Fair Use Doctrine," *Harvard Law Review* 103, 5 (March 1990): 1137–61, 1153–4.
15. L. Ray Patterson, "Free Speech, Copyright and Fair Use," *Vanderbilt Law Review* 40, 1 (January 1987): 1–66, 65.

16. *Ibid.*
17. Leval, "Toward a Fair Use Standard," 1107.
18. *Ibid.*, 1106–7.
19. Georgia Harper, "Google This," available at *http://www.utsystem.edu/ogc/intellectualproperty/googlethis.htm*.
20. L. Ray Patterson and Stanley W. Lindberg, *The Nature of Copyright: The Law of Users' Rights* (Athens: University of Georgia Press, 1991), 194. Ohio State legal historian Michael Les Benedict and I were the prepublication reviewers of the manuscript of this book for the University of Georgia Press.
21. Jessica Litman, *Digital Copyright* (Amherst, NY: Prometheus Books 2001), 195.
22. *Ibid.*, 180.
23. Crews, *Copyright*, 118–9.
24. See Leval, "Toward a Fair Use Standard," 1116, note 52.
25. "Google Print Case Study: Penn State Press Gets More Traffic, Bigger Margins and New Sales with Google Print" (2006), available at *https://books.google.com/partner/pennstate*.
26. The copyright status of an index is an interesting question in itself. Is it an entirely new work, an "original" creation that merely "quotes" from the primary work, or is it rather a "derivative" work that requires permission from the copyright owner to prepare? Or maybe it is a form of "compilation" of data deserving, because of its minimal "originality," of only a "thin" form of copyright protection, if any at all? Is it most like an abstract, and are abstracts "derivative" works? Probably Patterson would say that it is a "use of the work" rather than a "use of the copyright," and thus outside the scope of copyright.

A Cooperative Publishing Model for Sustainable Scholarship

Robert Schroeder and Gretta E. Siegel

Organizing scholarly publishing as a cooperative business has the promise of making journals more affordable and scholarly publishing more sustainable. The authors describe the development of the modern cooperative from its beginnings in England during the Industrial Revolution and highlight the great extent and diversity of business worldwide that is currently done cooperatively. Some of the current initiatives in scholarly publishing (SPARC, PLoS, German Academic Publishing, etc.) are analyzed in light of cooperative business principles, and it is shown that, while these models often partially utilize cooperative business practices, none of them has adopted the cooperative model in totality.

> A cooperative can be defined for practical purposes as a democratic association of persons organized to furnish themselves an economic service under a plan that eliminates entrepreneur profit and that provides for substantial equality in ownership and control.[1]

The current state of scholarly publishing can best be defined as "transitional." For the past two decades we have been moving from print to electronic dissemination formats, from well-defined economic models that, for the most part, served the learned and research communities to wide-ranging models that span the spectrum from elitist to populist to everything in between. The past two years have been particularly interesting to anyone following the "open access" trend, which, in varying ways (still ranging from elitist to populist), is attempting to broaden access to scholarly output while maintaining fiscal solvency, if not profit.

According to Association of Research Libraries (ARL) statistics, from 1986 to 2004 serials expenditures in ARL libraries have increased 273 percent, while the Consumer Price Index went up only 73 percent over the same period.[2] The current problem is that the "circle of gifts" that Anne Okerson so elegantly described in her 1992 article, which she wishfully projected would embrace the digital wave and continue on as a circle, evolved in a way that has developed a weak link, that of egregious price setting and huge profit motives by commercial (and some society) publishers.[3] Will the circle be unbroken? This is a question that can be answered only by the communities of scholars who are ready to take on ownership of the fruits of their labor. This article presents a tested model that, if applied to the current world of electronic scholarly publishing, could answer that question in the affirmative.

Scholarly journal publication has five major facets: product development, production, marketing, distribution, finance, and general administration.[4] Most of these facets are similar in the traditional print journal realm and in the electronic realm, the only differences being that many processes take place more quickly in the digital environment. Product development for a new journal begins conceptually with the recognition of the need for a new publication and the development of a new publication's scope and niche. Next, an editorial board is commissioned and general editors, outside referees, and copy editors are found, all of whom will assure quality control. Articles are solicited from the scholarly community and the editing and vetting process begins. Once the requisite number of acceptable articles for an issue is produced, production commences. The authors' print and graphic components are reformatted to adhere to the design and computer standards of the publication, and the article is included in the journal's online version and, later, in its digital archive. Production may also include the abstracting and indexing of articles for future retrievability. Marketing and promotion of a new journal begins soon after a journal's conception and continues through a publication's run. Electronic distribution and order fulfilment begin as soon as subscription orders arrive.

The last two facets of journal publishing, finance and administration, are not part of the publication cycle per se but may be considered as overhead. The finance department sets the price of subscriptions and deals with accounting, legal, and tax matters. General administration oversees the publishing cycle and manages and coordinates the business operations.

Private businesses and scholarly communities have published scholarly journals for many years, but what would be the benefits of publishing them cooperatively? In order to answer that question, we must first understand what the cooperative business model is and where it comes from. Cooperatives are much more than neighborhood natural food stores or grain elevators. While these are examples of cooperatives, we must understand what they have in common and how they came to exist.

The modern cooperative movement originated during the Industrial Revolution in Britain. The huge transformation of industry and the economy caused upheaval and great hardships among the workers in many occupations. Traditional individual craftsmen were losing their jobs to mechanized factories, while historically common lands were being privatized. In the north of England, by the early 1800s, "life expectancy had dropped over recent decades from 35 years to 21 years,"[5] and the wages of a handloom weaver dropped from thirty shillings per week in 1797 to five shillings and sixpence by 1830.[6] Newly industrialized workers were forced to purchase goods at inflated prices at the company "truck and badger" shops and were going deeper and deeper into debt. Philosophers and social reformers like Robert Owen began to see cooperation as a potential way to free the workers from their poverty. In the early 1800s Owen set up short-lived cooperative ventures in New Lanark and Orbiston in Scotland, and in New Harmony, Indiana. Dr. William King, founder of a cooperative store, published the newspaper *The Cooperator* for two years, beginning in 1827, and gave a voice to the burgeoning cooperative movement.

On August 15, 1844 in Rochdale, England, a group of twenty-eight weavers and other tradesmen came together for what was to be a momentous event. In order to free themselves from their cycle of poverty, and in order to purchase affordable and unadulterated food, they formed the Rochdale Society of Equitable Pioneers. They had raised £28, and with it they rented a storefront and purchased twenty-eight pounds of butter, fifty-six pounds of sugar, 600 pounds of flour, a sack of oatmeal, and some candles. Their cooperative store was not the first of its kind even in Rochdale, but, because of the unique cooperative principles upon which it was founded, it was to be the most enduring and important one.

The original Rochdale Principles, as they have come to be known, were these: "democratic control; one member one vote and equality of the sexes; open membership; pure unadulterated goods; no credit; profits to be divided on the amount of purchase made; a fixed rate of interest on investment; promotion of education; and political and religious neutrality."[7] These principles have been reviewed, revised, and affirmed over time, and the latest version, issued in 1995 by the International Cooperative Alliance, is as follows: voluntary and open membership; democratic member control; member economic participation; autonomy and independence; education, training, and information; cooperation among cooperatives; and concern for community.[8] These principles are at the core of what makes cooperative businesses unique, powerful, and successful. Control of the business is shared equally among the members of a cooperative, membership is voluntary and limited to the producers or consumers of a product or service, the economic benefits of cooperation return to the members equitably, and, because, there is limited return on investment and the profit motive is non-existent, prices remain low.[9]

These unique principles have made cooperative businesses successful worldwide. In Britain in 1864 there were 100,000 members of cooperatives with £2.5 million in sales,[10] and by 1993 there were eight million co-op members doing £7 billion in retail trade.[11] In 1993 in the European Union there were 45,000 worker cooperatives employing 750,000 people,[12] and worldwide there were estimated to be 800 million cooperative members and 100 million people employed in cooperatives.[13]

The cooperative movement has thrived in the United States as well. By 1985 there were 4.78 million members of farmer cooperatives,[14] and in 1987 agricultural cooperatives had $43 billion in sales of food and $14 billion in sales of farm supplies.[15] In 2000 mutual insurance companies accounted for almost 20 percent of the life insurance in force in the United States (over $3 billion),[16] and, according to the *National Credit Union Administration Annual Report 2004*, there were 9,012 credit unions in the United States with $647 billion dollars in total assets.[17] The range of cooperative business is huge. There are consumer co-ops, housing co-ops (including condominiums), credit unions, savings and loan associations, mutual insurance companies, marketing co-ops, utility co-ops, and agricultural co-ops. Some would even include trade associations and unions as cooperative associations.[18] If all these different types of businesses can organize and flourish cooperatively, why not scholarly publishing?

Non-commercial dominance of the scholarly publishing arena has historical precedent. From the beginning of scholarly publishing in 1685 with the publication of the Royal Society of London's *Philosophical Transactions*, and for at least the first two hundred years, scholarly publication, to a great extent, remained in the hands of scholars. In the United States, until 1945, almost all of the technical and scholarly journals were published by professional societies.[19] And while in Europe most of the scholarly publication is done by commercial firms, in 1995 commercial publishers accounted for only 40 percent of scholarly scientific journals in the United States; 43 percent continued to be published by university presses or by professional or learned societies.[20]

To a great extent these non-commercial entities already understand the publishing business and publishing processes. There are many models for successful publication in existence, and the lack of technology or knowledge of the process is not the issue. The community of scholars knows full well that they are both producers and consumers of the output of their research; they just do not, at this time, control its dissemination. What is lacking is the collective will of the scholarly community to create a sustainable structure that will ensure access to fairly priced publications now and in the future. Cooperative university-supported publishing could accomplish this.

The cooperative business model would sustain publishing in a variety of ways. Democratic control and a limited return on investment would assure that prices rise only enough to cover expenses. Universities and their faculty are in a unique position in that we are the primary producers and consumers of scholarly work. It is in our best interest to keep all production and distribution costs down—the return on our investment will primarily come in continued lower prices for our quality scholarly product. Within the scholarly communities at most universities are experts who already perform, or know how to perform, many of the functions of electronic publishing. Faculty already edit, referee, index, and create online repositories for publications. They could work part time in the publishing cooperative alongside paid workers, thus further decreasing the cost of publication. There are many other faculty well-versed in database creation and networking, as well as in marketing, sales, and accounting. For faculty in aligned disciplines—such as those in writing and publishing programs, business administration, and library science—there is a natural fit for engaging in publishing activities and even in the scholarship of publishing. Participating universities' recognition of this scholarship in the faculty evaluation process would greatly facilitate participation by junior faculty members. While faculty in other fields—the sciences, humanities, and social sciences—are establishing and maintaining their intellectual presence in their respective fields of research, there will be some, generally senior, faculty who may choose, and could be encouraged, to take their prior experiences of writing, editing, and peer review a step further to actively engage with other activities in the publishing enterprise.

In these ways, not only could faculty contribute their talents, they could also disseminate new models and ideas of scholarly publishing to others. This task dovetails with the cooperative principle of "education, training, and information." The scholarship of publishing would also allow experts to teach new cooperative members how to start up and maintain their own new publications within the cooperative. This outreach and support aligns with the cooperative principle of "cooperation among cooperatives."

The current state of scholarly publishing is one of flux. The rallying cry over the past few years has been that the publishing models of the past decade or so have created an unsustainable environment. Experiments are being tried and new models tested. The following comments offer a brief look at some of these experiments and models in the context of established cooperative principles that have been successful in other arenas of enterprise and commerce. In Table 1, the far left column lists cooperative principles that seem appropriate to the area of publishing, as well as a few more related "desirable" principles that would help to round out the picture of what an ideal cooperative model for publishing might look like. The rest of the table identifies which of these principles or characteristics are being met by some of the current "en vogue" models. Discussion of these follows.

Table 1
Cooperative/Desirable Principles for Publishing Models

	SPARC	Open Access Model (e.g. PloS; PubMed)	Current Elsevier / Springer type Models	GAP Project
Basic Co-op Principles				
Democratic member control				Partial
Voluntary and open membership	X			X
Member economic participation	X			X
Pure unadulterated goods (Quality Control)	X	X	X	X
Autonomy and independence	X			X
Limited return on Investment (No profit motive)	X	X		X
Benefit proportional to contribution				X
Promotion of education, training and information	X			X
Cooperation among cooperatives				
Concern for community	X	X		X
Other Related Desirable Principles for Publishing Models				
Appropriate and integrated application of diverse expertise				X
Sustainability (or at least the goal of such)	X	X	X	X
High visibility/access	X	X	X	X

* From the original Rochdale Principles or the 1995 International Cooperative Alliance.

SPARC

The Scholarly Publishing and Academic Resources Coalition (SPARC) is an alliance of universities, research libraries, and organizations. Their agenda within the scholarly publishing arena is threefold: (1) "Incubation of competitive alternatives to current high-priced commercial journals and digital aggregations"; (2) "Public advocacy of fundamental changes in the system and the culture of scholarly communication"; and (3) "Education campaigns aimed at enhancing awareness of scholarly communication issues and supporting expanded institutional and scholarly community roles in and control over the scholarly communication."[21] In these efforts, the work of SPARC, while not exactly a co-op model, does acknowledge the cooperative values of care for the community, quality control, education and information, support for the non-profit sector, open membership, sustainability, and high visibility/access.

Open Access

Open access models, such as those put in place by the Public Library of Science (PLoS) or PubMed, are the types supported by SPARC. These differ somewhat in that PLoS is a commercial venture and PubMed is government based, but both share the approach that the results of scholarly research should be made freely available to the public. The definition of "open access," as drafted at the Bethesda Meeting of 2003 and adopted by PLoS, is as follows:

An Open Access Publication is one that meets the following two conditions:

> The author(s) and copyright holder(s) grant(s) to all users a free, irrevocable, worldwide, perpetual right of access to, and a license to copy, use, distribute, transmit and display the work publicly and to make and distribute derivative works, in any digital medium for any responsible purpose, subject to proper attribution of authorship, as well as the right to make small numbers of printed copies for their personal use.

> A complete version of the work and all supplemental materials, including a copy of the permission as stated above, in a suitable standard electronic format is deposited immediately upon initial publication in at least one online repository that is supported by an academic institution, scholarly society, government agency, or other well-established organization that seeks to enable open access, unrestricted distribution, interoperability, and long-term archiving (for the biomedical sciences, PubMed Central is such a repository).[22]

Implicit in this definition is the principle of care for the community, as the purpose of such a definition is to remove access barriers and allow the free flow of information. The requirement for immediate deposit into a digital repository demonstrates the lack of an ongoing profit motive, though of course there are costs to be covered in the initial publication of these works. Most journals that publish "open access" articles are not member-based, so the principles of democratic control, member economic participation, and related other principles do not really apply to this model. An aggregator, such as BioMed Central, that specializes in the publication of open access journals could be in a position to adopt more of these member-oriented principles and possibly approach a true co-op model, should they be interested in exploring this route.

Profit Driven

Recently, premier scientific imprints such as Elsevier, Springer, and Kluwer have responded to market pressures by offering "deals" to offset wholesale cancellations of journal subscriptions. They have offered libraries broader access to lists of titles in exchange for reduced cancellations of existing subscriptions and for transferring all existing subscriptions to electronic access only. There are variations on this theme, and while quality control and high visibility are maintained, and while the sustainability of the publishing companies is improved, there is by no means any kind of commitment to any other cooperative principles.

GAP

As far as we are aware, the model most closely aligned with established cooperative principles to date is that of the German Academic Publishers Project (GAP).[23] GAP's purpose is to set up a cooperative consortium of academic presses, scholarly societies, universities, academic departments, and even individuals. The project's focus is on infrastructure rather than content. The stated goals are cooperation, sustainability, quality control (peer review), online publication (high visibility), and open access. Mostly for tax reasons, GAP has adopted a member-based model (in German, *eingetragener Verein*), with voluntary and mostly open membership (the project reserves the right to deny memberships).[24] While there is democratic involvement on some levels of operation and the benefits are proportional to the contribution made, GAP is not organized as a legal cooperative, which means that ongoing democratic control is not assured. The organization provides training workshops and information on electronic and scholarly publishing, as well as assistance to entities wanting to become members. The structure of the project involves a "back office" (which provides technical services such as document storage, metadata transfer, support for universities wanting to start new presses, and the basic publication mechanisms) and multiple "front offices," which are the members utilizing the "back office." Members are able to contribute expertise on the various aspects of running the "back office," which makes the GAP model much closer to a true cooperative.

* * *

Historically, the society model of publishing came very close to the cooperative model, in that profit was not generally a motive and the academic producer/consumer engaged in all five of the major facets of production and distribution, especially if the society publication was based at an academic institution. When production and distribution became too burdensome, however, many societies turned these aspects over to commercial entities, and the model became much less cooperative. Now that all these processes can be carried out electronically, however, the time is ripe for a more radical paradigm shift than what is offered by many of the "open access" models we are now seeing.

Many of the publishing models discussed above (SPARC, GAP, etc.) came about as a reaction to the economic burden placed on libraries over the past few decades by rising serials costs, and they have demonstrated that there are alternatives to for-profit publishing. The cursory analysis of the trends presented here makes it clear that there are basically two divergent approaches at work. One is the attempt to make for-profit models more sustainable, while the other puts the publication and dissemination of scholarship back into the hands of scholars. It is also clear that the latter approach can be successful only with the participation of many, thus leading to the promise of the more cooperative and democratic ventures being attempted. From the desperation of the Industrial Revolution, the weavers of Rochdale England found a way to supply themselves with the necessities of life. Millions of people have met needs—from electricity to housing, from banking to farming—through the thousands of cooperative societies and ventures that have since prospered. Should the scholarly communities of additional countries adopt the GAP model, or something similar, and from there form a global partnership of a "cooperative of cooperatives," there may be some hope for a truly sustainable model of scholarly publishing.

Contributors

Robert Schroeder is a reference and instruction librarian at Portland State University and the Coordinator of Information Literacy. He has been actively involved in many cooperative ventures for the past thirty years.

Gretta Siegel is the Science Librarian and Coordinator for Scholarly Communication Initiatives and Outreach at Portland State University. She has been wrestling with the economic vagaries of scholarly publishing for most of her more-than-twenty-year career.

Notes

1. Israel Packel, *The Organization and Operation of Cooperatives; Including Consumer, Marketing, Purchasing, and Trade Associations, Labor Unions and Condominiums* (Philadelphia: Joint Committee on Continuing Legal Education of the American Law Institute and the American Bar Association 1970), 2.
2. "Monographs and Serials Costs in ARL Libraries 1986–2004," in *ARL Statistics 2003–04* (Washington, DC: Association of Research Libraries), *http://www.arl.org/stats/arlstat/graphs/2004/monser04.pdf*.
3. Ann Okerson, "The Missing Model: A 'Circle of Gifts,'" *Serials Review* 18, 1/2 (Spring/Summer 1992): 92–6.
4. For the following discussion we have relied on Gillian Page, "The Economics of Traditional Journal Publishing," in Hazel Woodward, ed., *The International Serials Industry* (Aldershot, UK: Gower 1993): 61–87, and Sally Morris, "Who Needs Publishers," *Journal of Information Science* 25, 1 (February 1999): 85–8.
5. Tom Cannon, *The Ultimate Book of Business Breakthroughs: Lessons form the 20 Greatest Business Decisions Ever Made* (Oxford: Capstone 2000), 238.
6. John Barnett, *Plenty and Want: A Social History of Diet in England from 1815 to the Present Day* (London: Scholar Press 1979), 51.
7. Cannon, *Ultimate Book,* 240.
8. International Co-operative Alliance, "What Is a Co-operative?" (International Co-operative Information Centre, January 8, 1996), *www.wisc.edu/uwcc/icic/def-hist/def/what-is.html*.
9. Packel, *Organization and Operation of Cooperatives*, 4–5.
10. John Birchall, *Co-op: The People's Business* (Manchester, UK: Manchester University Press 1994), 65.
11. "150 Years of the Co-op," *New Statesman and Society* (June 17, 1994): iii–iv.
12. *Ibid.*, vii.
13. International Co-operative Alliance, "Dimensions of the International Co-operative Movement" (International Co-operative Information Centre, 1995), *http://www.wisc.edu/uwcc/icic/def-hist/def/dim-int.html*.
14. John A.C. Hetherington, *Mutual and Cooperative Enterprises: An Analysis of Customer-Owned Firms* (Charlottesville: University Press of Virginia 1991), 108.
15. *Ibid.*
16. Institute of Life Insurance, *Life Insurers Fact Book 2001* (New York: Institute of Life Insurance 2001), 3.
17. National Credit Union Administration, *Annual Report of the National Credit Union Administration 2004* (Alexandria, VA: National Credit Union Administration 2004), *http://www.ncua.gov/ReportsAndPlans/annualrpt/2004AR.pdf, 107–8*.
18. Packel, *Organization and Operation of Cooperatives*, 11–23.
19. Carol Tenopir and Donald W. King, *Towards Electronic Journals: Realities for Scientists, Librarians, and Publishers* (Washington, DC: Special Libraries Association 2000), 60.
20. Carol Tenopir and Donald W. King, "Trends in Scientific Scholarly Journal Publishing in the United States," *Journal of Scholarly Publishing* 28, 3 (April 1997): 135–70, 136.

21. Judith Matz and Kaylyn Hipps, eds., "Scholarly Publishing and Academic Resources Coalition," *ARL Program Plan 2002* (Washington, DC: Association of Research Libraries 2002), *http://www.arl.org/arl/pp2002/pp12.html*.
22. "Bethesda Statement on Open Access Publishing," *The SPARC Open Access Newsletter, http://www.earlham.edu/~peters/fos/bethesda.htm* (explanatory footnotes omitted).
23. Kim Braun, "The German Academic Publishers Project—GAP," in Sely Maria de Souza Costa, et al., eds., *From Information to Knowledge: Proceedings of the 7th ICCC/IFIP International Conference on Electronic Publishing held at the Universidade do Minho*, Portugal, 25–28 June 2003, (Minho: Universidade do Minho 2003), *http://elpub.scix.net/cgi-bin/works/Show?0323*.
24. Kim Braun, "GAP—German Academic Publishers: A Network Approach to Scholarly Publishing," *Canadian Journal of Communication* 29, 3/4 (2004): 301–15, 307; Kim Braun, e-mail to author, August 5, 2005.

Selected Bibliography

Abel, Richard and Lyman W. Newlin. *Scholarly Publishing: Books, Journals, Publishers, and Libraries in the Twentieth Century.* New York: Wiley, 2002.

Alexander, Alison, James Owers, Rod Carveth, C. Ann Hollifield, and Albert N. Greco (Eds.), *Media Economics: Theory and Practice.* 3rd ed. Mahwah, NJ: Lawrence Erlbaum Associates, 2004.

Anglada, L. and N. Comellas. "What's Fair? Pricing Models in the Electronic Era," *Library Management 23*, 4(April 2002): 227-233.

Arkenbout, Erwin, Frans Van Duk, and Peter Van Wuck. Copyright in the Information Society: Scenario's and Strategies. *European Journal of Law and Economics* 17(2004): 237-249.

Baker, Nicholas. *The Oxford University Press and the Spread of Learning: 1478-1978.* Oxford: Clarendon Press, 1978.

Baker, Nicholson. *Double Fold: Libraries and the Assault on Paper.* New York: Random House, 2001.

Banner, James M., Jr. "Guidelines for Peer Review of Sponsored Book Manuscripts," The *Journal of Scholarly Publishing* 20, 2(January 1989): 116-122.

Banner, James M., Jr. "Preserving the Integrity of Peer Review," The *Journal of Scholarly Publishing* 19, 2(January 1988): 109-115.

Bartlett, Rebecca Ann and Tom Radko. "Significant University Press Titles for Undergraduates, 2007-2008," *The Journal of Scholarly Publishing* 40, 1(October 2008): 40-65.

Bartlett, Rebecca Ann. "University Presses 2008: A Snapshot in Time," *The Journal of Scholarly Publishing* 40, 1(October 2008): 21-39.

Barzun, Jacques. *On Writing, Editing, and Publishing.* Chicago, IL: University of Chicago Press, 1986.

Baye, Michael R. and John Morgan. "Information Gatekeepers on the Internet and the Competitiveness of Homogeneous Product Markets," *The American Economic Review* 91, 3(June 2001): 454-474.

Becker, William C. The Crisis—One Year Later. *The Journal of Scholarly Publishing* 4(1973): 291-302.

Bell, Bill (Ed.), *Where is Book History?* Toronto: University of Toronto Press, 2002.

Bell, Hazel. "Editors and Copy Editors in Fiction: Taking A Carpet-Sweeper in the Jungle," *The Journal of Scholarly Publishing* 439, 2(January 2008): 156-167.

Bell, Hazel. *Indexers and Indexes in Fact and Fiction*. Toronto: University of Toronto Press, 2002.
Bennett, Scott. "The Boat That Must Stay Afloat: Academic Libraries in Hard Times," The *Journal of Scholarly Publishing* 23, 3(April 1992): 131-137.
Birkets, Sven. *The Gutenberg Elegies: The Fate of Reading in an Electronic Age*. Boston: Faber & Faber, 1994.
Birkets, Sven. "Perseus Unbound," *The Journal of Scholarly Publishing* 24, 3(April 1993): 151-156.
Black, M.H. *Cambridge University Press: 1584-1984*. Cambridge, England: Cambridge University Press, 1984.
Bogart, Dave, ed. 2008. *The Bowker Annual: Library and Book Trade Almanac 2008*. Information Today, Inc., New Providence, NJ.
Bowles, Gloria. "'Feminist Scholarship' and 'Women's Studies': Implications for University Presses," The *The Journal of Scholarly Publishing* 19, 3(April 1988): 163-168.
Brosius, Matt. "The OECD as Publisher," *The Journal of Scholarly Publishing* 22, 1(October 1990): 44-50.
Brynjolfsson, Erik and Michael D. Smith. "Frictionless Commerce? A Comparison of Internet and Conventional Retailers," *Management Science* 46, 4(April 2000): 563-585.
Brynjolfsson, Erik and Michael D. Smith. "The Great Equalizer? Consumer Choice Behavior At Internet Shopbots." Working Paper MIT Sloan School of Management (July 2000b): 1-63.
Brynjolfsson, Erik, Yu Hu, and Michael D. Smith. "Consumer Surplus in the Digital Economy: Estimating the Value of Increased Product Variety at Online Booksellers." *Management Science* 49, 11 (2003): 1580-1597.
Burchfield, Robert. "The Oxford English Dictionary and the State of the Language," The *Journal of Scholarly Publishing* 19, 3(April 1988): 169-178.
Burlingame, Roger. *Of Making Many Books: A Hundred Years of Reading, Writing, and Publishing*. University Park, PA: Pennsylvania State University Press, 1997.
Campbell, Robert. "Document Delivery and the Journal Publisher," The *Journal of Scholarly Publishing* 23, 4(July 1992): 213-222.
Caplette, Michele. *Women in Publishing: A Study of Careers in Organizations*. Ph.D. dissertation, SUNY at Stony Brook, 1981.
Carrigan, Dennis P. "The Emerging National Periodicals System in the United States," *The Journal of Scholarly Publishing* 25, 2(January 1994): 93-102.
Carrigan, Dennis P. "Publish or Perish: The Troubled State of Scholarly Communication," *The Journal of Scholarly Publishing* 22, 3(April 1991): 131-142.
Carrigan, Dennis P. "Research Libraries' Evolving Response to the 'Serials Crisis,'" *The Journal of Scholarly Publishing* 23, 3(April 1992): 138-151.
Cheney, O.H. *Economic Survey of the Book Industry, 1930-1931*. New York: R.R. Bowker, 1960.

Conaway, James. *America's Library: The Story of the Library of Congress, 1800-2000*. New Haven, CT: Yale University Press, 2000.
Coser, Lewis A., Charles Kadushin, and Walter W. Powell. *Books: The Culture and Commerce of Publishing*. Chicago: University of Chicago Press, 1985.
Crane, Gregory. "'Hypermedia' and Scholarly Publishing," The *Journal of Scholarly Publishing* 21, 3(April 1990): 131-156.
Davidson, Cathy N. (Ed.), *Reading in America: Literature and Social History*. Baltimore, MD: Johns Hopkins University Press, 1989.
Derricourt, Robin. *An Author's Guide to Scholarly Publishing*. Princeton: Princeton University Press, 1996.
Dizard, Jr., Wilson P. *Old Media New Media: Mass Communications in the Information Age*. 3rd ed. New York: Longman, 2000.
Dowling, William C. "Saving Scholarly Publishing in the Age of Oprah: The Glastonbury Project." *The Journal of Scholarly Publishing* 28, 3(1997): 8.
Downs, Robert B. *Books That Changed the World*. New York: Macmillan, 1970.
Downs, Robert B. and Ralph E. McCoy. *The First Freedom Today: Critical Issues Relating to Censorship and to Intellectual Freedom*. Chicago: American Library Association, 1984.
Edelman, Hendrik. "Copyright and the Library of the Future," *Book Research Quarterly* 2(Fall 1986): 51-61.
Edelman, Murray J. *The Politics of Misinformation*. Cambridge: Cambridge University Press, 2001.
Edgar, William B. "Toward a Theory of Collection Development: An Activities and Attributes Approach." *Library Collections* 27, 4(2003): 393-423.
Eisenberg, Daniel. "The Electronic Journal," *The Journal of Scholarly Publishing* 29, 1(October 1988): 49-58.
Eisenberg, Daniel. "Problems of the Paperless Book," *The Journal of Scholarly Publishing* 21 (October 1989): 11-26.
Eisenstein, Elizabeth L. The *Printing Press as an Agent of Change,* 2 vols. New York: Cambridge University Press, 1979.
Epstein, Jason. *Book Business: Publishing Past, Present, and Future*. New York: W.W. Norton, 2001.
Epstein, Jason. "The Decline and Rise of Publishing," *New York Review of Books*, 1 March 1990, 8-12.
Ervin, John. Jr. "An Approach to Self-Appraisal by University Presses," The *Journal of Scholarly Publishing* 21, 3(April 1990): 157-170.
Ervin, John., Jr. "The Dimensions of Regional Publishing," The *Journal of Scholarly Publishing* 20, 3(April 1989): 178-191.
Evans, Philip and Thomas S. Wurster. *Blown to Bits: How the New Economics of Information Transforms Strategy*. Boston: Harvard Business School Press, 2000.
Ezell, Margaret J.M. *Social Authorship and the Advent of Print: The Editor's Advice to Writers*. Baltimore, MD: Johns Hopkins University Press, 2000.

Felber, Lynette. "The Book Review: Scholarly and Editorial Responsibility," *The Journal of Scholarly Publishing*, 33, 3(April 2002): 166-172.

Fischel, Daniel L. "Planning for Book Reprints," *The Journal of Scholarly Publishing* 19, 4(July 1988): 195-201.

Flacks, Lewis. "The Evolution of Copyright," *Book Research Quarterly* 2(Summer 1986): 14-24.

Follett, Robert J. R. *The Financial Side of Book Publishing.* Oak Park, IL: Alpine Guild, 1988.

Francois, Patrick and Tanguy van Ypersele. "On the Protection of Cultural Goods," *Journal of International Economics* 56, 2(March 2002): 359-369.

Friedland, Martin L. *The University of Toronto.* Toronto: University of Toronto Press, 2002.

Fruge, August. *A Skeptic among Scholars: August Fruge on University Publishing.* Berkeley, CA: University of California Press, 1993.

Geiser, Elizabeth A., Arnold Dolin, and Gladys S. Topkis (Eds.), *The Business of Book Publishing.* Boulder, CO: Westview Press, 1985.

Germano, William. *Getting it Published: A Guide for Scholars and Anyone Else Serious about Serious Books.* Chicago: University of Chicago Press, 2001.

Germano, William. "Surviving the Review Process," *The Journal of Scholarly Publishing*, 33, 1(October 2001): 53-69.

Gershon, Richard A. "The Transnational Media Corporation: Environmental Scanning and Strategy Formation," *Journal of Media Economics* 13, 2(2000): 81-101.

Gershon, Richard A. *The Transnational Media Corporation: Global Messages and Free Market Competition.* Mahwah, NJ: Lawrence Erlbaum Associates, 1997.

Getz, Malcolm. "Electronic Publishing: An Economic View," *Serials Review* 18, 1-2 (1992): 25-31.

Ghose, Anindya, Michael D. Smith, and Rahul Telang. 2005. "Are Internet Used Product Markets Cannibalizing New Product Sales? An Analysis of Internet Markets for Books." Working paper; Carnegie-Mellon University and Stern School, New York University; SSRN # 584401.

Ghose, Anindya, Michael D. Smith, and Rahul Telang. 2004. "Internet Exchanges for Used Books: An Empirical Analysis for Welfare Implications." Working paper; Carnegie Mellon University.

Gifford, Sharon. "Endogenous Information Costs." Paper available at the Social Science Research Network Electronic Library (February 24, 2001): 1-20. *http://papers.ssrn.com/sol13/papers.cfm?abstract_id=262183*.

Giles, Michael W. "From Gutenberg to Gigabytes: Scholarly Communication in the Age of Cyberspace." *Journal of Politics* 58, 3(1996): 613-626.

Gillerot, Dominique and Marc Minton. "Development of the Internet, Market Structure, and Commercial Practices: The Case of the Publishing Sector," *Communications and Strategies*, 38 (2nd Quarter 2000): 221-239.

Ginsburg, Jane C. "What to Know Before Reissuing Old Titles as E-Books," *Communications of the ACM* 44, 9(September 2001): 25-27.
Glass, Amy Jocelyn. "Price Discrimination and Quality Improvement," *Canadian Journal of Economics* 34, 2(May 2001): 549-569.
Gleason, Paul. "Publishers' and Librarians' Views on Copyright and Photocopying," *The Journal of Scholarly Publishing* 29, 1(October 1988): 13-22.
Graham, Andrew. 2001. "The Assessment: Economics of the Internet." *Oxford Review of Economic Policy* 1, 2(2001): 145-158.
Graham, Gordon and Richard Abel (Eds.), *The Book in the United States Today*. New Brunswick, NJ: Transaction Publishers, 1996.
Graubard, Stephen R. and Paul LeClerc (Eds.), *Books, Bricks, & Bytes*. New Brunswick, NJ: Transaction Publishers, 1998.
Greco, Albert N., Susan B. Neuman, Donna Celano, and Pamela Shue. *Access for All: Closing the Book Gap for Children in Early Education*. Newark, DE: International Reading Association, 2001.
Greco, Albert N. *The Book Publishing Industry*. Mahwah, New Jersey: Erlbaum, 2005.
Greco, Albert N. 2004. "The Changing Market for U.S. Book Exports and Imports." *The Bowker Annual 2004: 49th edition*, ed. Dave Bogart. Medford, NJ: Information Today, Inc.
Greco, Albert N., Clara Rodriguez, and Robert M. Wharton. *The Culture and Commerce of Publishing in the 21st Century*. Stanford, CA: Stanford University Press, 2007.
Greco, Albert N. "Domestic Consumer Expenditures for Consumer Books: 1984-1994," *Publishing Research Quarterly* 14(Fall 1998): 12-28.
Greco, Albert N. 2004. The Economics of Books and Magazines, in *Media Economics: Theory and Practice*, 3rd Edition, eds. Alison Alexander, James Owers, Rod Carveth, C. Ann Hollifield, and Albert N. Greco. Mahwah, NJ. Lawrence Erlbaum Associates; 127-148.
Greco, Albert N. "The General Reader Market for University Press Books in the United States, 1990-1999, with Projections for the Years 2000 Through 2004," *The Journal of Scholarly Publishing* 32, 2(January 2001): 61-85.
Greco, Albert N. "The Impact of Horizontal Mergers and Acquisitions on Corporate Concentration in the U.S. Book Publishing Industry, 1989-1994," *The Journal of Media Economics* 12, 3(Fall 1999): 165-180.
Greco, Albert N. "International Book Title Output: 1990-1999," in *The Bowker Annual 2000*: 45th Edition, Dave Bogart (Ed.), New Providence, NJ: R.R. Bowker, 2000, pp. 528-531.
Greco, Albert N. "Market Concentration in the U.S. Consumer Book Industry: 1995-1996," *The Journal of Cultural Economics* 24, 4(November 2000): 321-336.
Greco, Albert N. "The Market for Consumer Books in the U.S.: 1985-1995," *Publishing Research Quarterly* 13(Spring 1997): 3-40.
Greco, Albert N. "The Market for University Press Books in the United States: 1985-1999, *Learned Publishing* 14, 2(April 2001): 97-105.
Greco, Albert N. "Mergers and Acquisitions in the U.S. Book Publishing Industry: 1960-1989," in *International Book Publishing: An Encyclopedia*,

Philip G. Altbach and Edith S. Hoshino (Eds.), New York: Garland Publishing, Inc., 1995, pp. 229-242.

Greco, Albert N. "Publishing Economics: Mergers and Acquisitions within the Publishing Industry 1980-1989," in *Media Economics: Theory and Practice,* Alison Alexander, James Owers, and Rodney Carveth (Eds.), Hillside, NJ: Lawrence Erlbaum Associates, 1993, 205-224.

Greco, Albert N. "Teaching Publishing: A Global Perspective," in *The Encyclopedia of Library and Information Science,* Allen Kent (Ed.), New York: Marcel Dekker, 1993.

Greco, Albert N. "U.S. Book Returns, 1984-1989," *Publishing Research Quarterly* 8(Fall 1992): 46-61.

Greco, Albert N. "University Presses and the Trade Book Market: Managing in Turbulent Times," *Book Research Quarterly* 3(Winter 1987-1988): 34-53.

Greco, Albert N., Robert Wharton, and Hooman Estelami. "The Changing Market for University Press Books: 1997-2002." *Journal of Scholarly Publishing* 36, 4(July 2005): 187-220.

Greco, Albert N., Walter O'Connor, Sharon Smith, and Robert Wharton. "The Price of University Press Books, 1989-2000." *Journal of Scholarly Publishing* 35, 1(2003): 4-39.

Griffin, Keith. *Studies in Globalization and Economic Transitions.* London: Macmillan, 1996.

Gross, Gerald. *Editors on Editing.* New York: Grove Press, 1993.

Grossman, John. "Researching the Fourteenth Edition of *The Chicago Manual of Style,*" The *Journal of Scholarly Publishing* 25(October 1993): 63-64.

Hackett, Alice Payne and James Henry Burke. *80 Years of Best Sellers, 1895-1975.* New York: R.R. Bowker, 1975.

Haight, Anne Lyon and Chandler B. Grannis. *Banned Books, 387 B.C. to 1978 A.D.,* 4th ed. New York: R.R. Bowker, 1978.

Hall, Max. *Harvard University Press: A History.* Cambridge, MA: Harvard University Press, 1986.

Hansmann, Henry and Reinier Kraakman. "Hands-Tying Contracts: Book Publishing, Venture Capital Financing, and Secured Debt." *Journal of Law, Economic, and Organization* 8, 3(1992): 628-655.

Harnum, Bill. "The Characteristics of the Ideal Acquisition Editor," *The Journal of Scholarly Publishing* 32, 4 (July 2001): 182-188.

Harris, Claudia. "Ranking the Management Journals," *The Journal of Scholarly Publishing* 439, 4(July 2008): 373-409.

Hart, James D. *The Popular Book: A History of America's Literary Taste.* New York: Oxford University Press, 1950.

Hauptman, Robert. "Authorial Ethics: How Writers Abuse Their Calling," *The Journal of Scholarly Publishing* 39, 4(July 2008): 323-353.

Hayes, Robert H. and William J. Abernathy, "Managing Our Way to Economic Decline," *Harvard Business Review* 58 (July-August 1980): 67-77.

Hecker, Thomas E. "The Post-Petroleum Future of Academic Libraries," *The Journal of Scholarly Publishing* 38, 4(July 2007): 183-199.

Hench, John B. "Toward a History of the Book in America," *Publishing Research Quarterly* 10(Fall 1994): 9-21.
Henderson, Bill. *The Art of Literary Publishing: Editors on Their Craft.* Wainscott, NY: Pushcart Press, 1980.
Henriques, Irene and Perry Sadorsky. "Export-Led Growth or Growth-Driven Exports? The Canadian Case," *Canadian Journal of Economics* 29, 3(August 1996): 540-555.
Hinckley, Karen and Barbara Hinckley. *American Best Sellers: A Reader's Guide to Popular Fiction.* Bloomington, IN: Indiana University Press, 1989.
Hoffman, Frank. *Intellectual Freedom and Censorship: An Annotated Bibliography.* Metuchen, NJ: Scarecrow Press, 1989.
Hofstadter, Richard. *Anti-Intellectualism in American Life.* New York: Random House, 1966.
Horowitz, Irving Louis. *Communicating Ideas: The Crisis of Publishing in a Post-Industrial Society.* New Brunswick, NJ: Transaction Publishers, 1992.
Horowitz, Irving Louis and Mary Curtis. "The Impact of Technology on Scholarly Publishing," *The Journal of Scholarly Publishing* 13(April 1982): 211-228.
Hutchinson, Ann M. *Editing Women.* Toronto: University of Toronto Press, 1998.
Jagodzinski, Cecile M. "The University Press in North America," *The Journal of Scholarly Publishing* 40, 1(October 2008): 1-20.
Jeanneret, Marsh. *God and Mammon: Universities as Publishers.* Urbana and Chicago: University of Illinois Press, 1990.
Jeanneret, Marsh. "The Origins of Scholarly Publishing," *The Journal of Scholarly Publishing* 29, 4(July 1989): 197-202.
Jones, Candace. "Creative Industries (Book)," *Administrative Science Quarterly* 46, 3(September 2001): 567-571.
Josey, E.J. and Kenneth D. Shearer. *Politics and the Support of Libraries.* New York: Neal-Schuman Publishers, 1990.
Joyce, Donald Franklin. "Changing Book Publishing Objectives of Secular Black Book Publishers, 1900-1986," *Book Research Quarterly* 2(Fall 1986): 42-50.
Joyce, Donald Franklin. *Gatekeepers of Black Culture: Black-Owned Book Publishing in the United States, 1817-1981.* Westport, CT: Greenwood Press, 1983.
Kahin, Brian and Hal R. Varian. (Eds.), *Internet Publishing and Beyond: The Economics of Digital Information and Intellectual Property.* Cambridge: MIT Press, 2000.
Kaiserlian, Penelope. "Kate Turabian's *Manual:* A Best-Seller for Fifty Years," The *Journal of Scholarly Publishing* 19, 3(April 1988): 136-143.
Katzen, May. "A National Information Network," The *Journal of Scholarly Publishing* 19, 4(July 1988): 210-216.
Kazin, Alfred, Dan Lacy, and Ernest L. Boyer. *The State of the Book World, 1980: Three Talks Sponsored by the Center for the Book in the Library of Congress.* Washington, DC: Library of Congress, 1981.

Keller, Morton and Phyllis Keller. *Making Harvard Modern: The Rise of America's University.* Oxford: Clarendon, 2001.

King, Donald W., Carol Tenopir, and Carol Hansen Montgomery. 2003. "Patterns of Journal Use by Faculty at Three Diverse Universities." *D-Lib Magazine* 9, 10:1.

Kingston, Paul William and Jonathan R. Cole. *The Wages of Writing: Per Word, Per Piece, or Perhaps.* New York: Columbia University Press, 1986.

Kister, Ken. "Encyclopedists Head for Cyberspace," *Library Journal*, November 15, 1998, S3-S6.

Klein, Benjamin, Andres V. Lerner, and Kevin Murphy. "The Economics of Copyright 'Fair Use' in a Networked World," *The American Economic Review* 92, 2(May 2002): 205-208.

Knauer, Joyce. "Scholarly Books in General Bookstores," The *Journal of Scholarly Publishing* 19, 2(January 1988): 79-85.

Knopf, Alfred A. *Publishing Then & Now:* 1912-1964. New York: New York Public Library, 1964.

Kobrak, Fred and Beth Luey (Eds.), *The Structure of International Publishing in the 1990s.* New Brunswick, NJ: Transaction, 1992.

Korda, Michael. *Making the List: A Cultural History of the American Bestseller 1900-1999.* New York: Barnes & Noble Books, 2001.

Koschat, Martin A. and William P. Putsis, Jr. "Who Wants You When You're Old and Poor: Exploring the Economics of Media Pricing," *Journal of Media Economics* 13, 4(2000): 215-232.

Kotha, Suresh, Shivaram Rajgopal, and Mohan Venkatachalam. 2004. "The Role of Online Buying Experience as a Competitive Advantage: Evidence from Third-Party Ratings for E-Commerce Firms." *Journal of Business* 77, 2(2004): S109-S133.

Kotler, Philip. "From Sales Obsession to Marketing Effectiveness," *Harvard Business Review* 55(November-December 1977): 67-75.

Kotler, Philip. "Operations Research in Marketing," *Harvard Business Review* 45(January-February 1967): 30-38.

Kotler, Philip. *Marketing Management,* 13th ed. Upper Saddle River, NJ: Prentice-Hall, 2008.

Kwak, Hyokjin, Richard J. Fox, and George M. Zinkhan. "What Products Can Be Successful Promoted and Sold Via the Internet?" *Journal of Advertising Research* 42, 1(January-February 2002): 23-38.

Laband, David N. "Measuring the Relative Impact of Economics Book Publishers," *Journal of Economic Literature* 28, 2(June 1990): 655-660.

Laband, David and John Hudson. "The Pricing of Economics Books." *Journals of Economic Education* 34, 4(2003): 360.

Labunski, Richard. "The Evolution of Libel Laws: Complexity and Inconsistency," *Book Research Quarterly* 5(Spring 1989): 59-95.

Lacy, Stephen and Walter E. Niebauer, Jr. "Developing and Using Theory for Media Economics," *Journal of Media Economics* 8, 2(1995): 3-13.

Lafollette, Marcel C. *Stealing into Print: Fraud, Plagiarism, and Misconduct in Scientific Publishing.* Berkeley, CA: University of California Press, 1992.

Lal, Rajiy and J. Miguel Villas Boras. "Price Promotions and Trade Deals with Multiproduct Retailers," *Management Science* 44(1998): 935-949.
Lancaster, K. "The Economics of Product Variety: A Survey," *Marketing Science* 9 (Summer 1990): 189-206.
Lanham, Richard D. *The Electronic Word: Democracy, Technology, and the Arts.* Chicago: University of Chicago Press, 1993.
Lanning, Meryl. "Working with Freelancers—and Enjoying It," *The Journal of Scholarly Publishing* 24, 1(October 1992): 52-56.
Lariviere, Martin A. and V. Padmanabhan. "Slotting Allowances and New Product Introduction," *Marketing Sciences* 16, 2(1997): 112-128.
Lee, H.G. "Do Electronic Marketplaces Lower the Price of Goods?" *Communications of the ACM* 41(1997): 73-80.
Leslie, Larry Z. "Manuscript Review: A View From Below," *The Journal of Scholarly Publishing* 29, 2(January 1989): 123-128.
Leslie, Larry Z. "Peering Over the Editor's Shoulder," *The Journal of Scholarly Publishing* 23, 3(April 1992): 185-193.
Levack, Kinley. "Pressing the POD Issue: The MIT Classics Series." *EContent* 26, 7(July 2003): 9.
Levitt, Theodore. "Marketing Myopia," *Harvard Business Review* 53 (September-October 1975): 26-37.
Levy, Leonard W. *Emergence of a Free Speech.* New York: Oxford University Press, 1985.
Li, Tiger and Roger J. Calantone. "The Impact of Market Knowledge Competence on New Product Advantage: Conceptualization and Empirical Examination," *Journal of Marketing* 62, 4(1998): 13-29.
Lichter, S. Robert, Stanley Rothman, and Linda S. Lichter. *The Media Elite: America's New Powerbrokers.* Bethesda, MD: Adler & Adler, 1988.
Lipscombe, Trevor. "The Greatest Story Ever Sold: The Pitfalls of Publishing," The *Journal of Scholarly Publishing* 31, 4(April 2000): 179-188.
Litan, Robert E. and Alice M. Rivlin. *Beyond the Dot.coms: The Economic Promise of the Internet.* Washington, DC: Brookings Institution Press, 2001.
Litan, Robert E. and Alice M. Rivlin. "Projecting the Economic Impact of the Internet," *The American Economic Review* 91, 2(May 2001): 313-317.
Liu, Ziming. "Trends in Transforming Scholarly Communication and Their Implications." *Information Processing & Management* 39, 6(2003): 889.
Long, Elizabeth. "The Book as Mass Commodity: The Audience Perspective," *Book Research Quarterly* 3(Spring 1987): 9-30.
Long, Elizabeth. "The Cultural Meaning of Concentration in Publishing," *Book Research Quarterly* 1(Winter 1985-1986): 3-27.
Lucas, Henry C., Jr. *Strategies for Electronic Commerce and the Internet.* Cambridge: MIT Press, 2002.
Machlup, Fritz and Kenneth Leeson. *Information through the Printed Word,* Vol. 1, *Book Publishing.* New York: Praeger, 1978.
Maggio, Rosalie. *The Nonsexist Word Finder: A Dictionary of Gender-Free Usage.* Boston: Beacon Press, 1989.
Maguire, James H. "Publishing on a Rawhide Shoestring," *The Journal of Scholarly Publishing* 22, 2(January 1991): 78-82.

Manguel, Alberto. *A History of Reading*. New York: Penguin Books, 1997.
Max, D.T. "The End of the Book?" *Atlantic Monthly*, (September 1994), 61-62, 64, 67-68, 70-71.
McCormack, Thomas. *The Fiction Editor: The Novel, and the Novelist*. New York: St. Martin's Press, 1988.
McLuhan, Marshall. *The Gutenberg Galaxy*. Toronto: University of Toronto Press, 1962.
McLuhan, Marshall and Quentin Fiore. *The Medium Is the Message*. New York: Bantam Books, 1967.
McLuhan, Marshall and Eric McLuhan. *The New Science*. Toronto: University of Toronto Press, 1992.
McQuivey, James L. and Megan K. McQuivey. "Is It a Small Publishing World After All: Media Monopolization and the Children's Book Market," *Journal of Media Economics* 11, 4(1998): 35-48.
Meltzer, Françoise. *Hot Property: The Stakes and Claims of Literary Originality*. Chicago: University of Chicago Press, 1994.
Meredith, Lindsay and Dennis Maki. "Product Cannibalization and the Role of Prices," *Applied Economics* 33, 14(2000): 1785-1793.
Meyer, Richard W. "The Library in Scholarly Communication." *Social Science Quarterly* 77, 1(1996): 210-217.
Miles, Jack. "Intellectual Freedom and the University Press," *The Journal of Scholarly Publishing* 15, 4(July 1984): 291-299.
Miller, Arthur R. and Michael H. Davis. *Intellectual Property: Patents, Trademarks, and Copyright*. St. Paul, MN: West Wadsworth, 2000.
Miller-Francisco, Emily. "Managing Electronic Resources in a Time of Shrinking Budgets." *Library Collections* 27, 4(2003): 507-512.
Mizzaro, Stefano. 2003. "Quality Control in Scholarly Publishing: A New Proposal." *Journal of The American Society for Information Science & Technology* 54. 11: 989.
The MLA Ad Hoc Committee on the Future of Scholarly Publishing. 2002. The Future of Scholarly Publishing. *Profession*: 172.
Mlawer, Teresa. "Selling Spanish-Language Books in the United States," *Publishing Research Quarterly* 10(Winter 1994/1995): 50-53.
Mokia, Rosemary Nturnnyuy. "Publishers, United States Foreign Policy, and the Third World," *Publishing Research Quarterly* 11(Summer 1995): 36-51.
Morton, Herbert C. "A New Book on New Words," The *Journal of Scholarly Publishing* 22, 2(January 1991): 122-127.
Morton, Herbert C. *The Story of Webster's Third: Philip Gove's Controversial Dictionary and Its Critics*. New York: Cambridge University Press, 1994.
Motavalli, John. *Bamboozled at the Revolution: How Big Media Lost Billions in the Battle for the Internet*. New York: Viking, 2002.
Mott, Frank L. *Golden Multitudes: The Story of Best Sellers in the United States*. New York: R.R. Bowker, 1947.
Moylan, Michele and Lane Stiles (Eds.), *Reading Books: Essays on the Material Text and Literature in America*. Amherst, MA: University of Massachusetts Press, 1996.

Muray, Heather. *Come, Bright Improvement! The Literary Societies of Nineteenth-Century Ontario*. Toronto: University of Toronto Press, 2002.

Myers, B.R. *A Reader's Manifesto*. Hoboken, NJ: Melville House, 2002.

The National Endowment for the Arts. 2004. "Reading at Risk: A Survey of Literary Reading in America," Research Division Report #46.

Nauman, Matt. "Matching the Librarian and the Book," The *Journal of Scholarly Publishing* 29, 4(July 1989): 233-237.

Negroponte, Nicholas. *Being Digital*. New York: Alfred A. Knopf, 1995.

Neil, S.D. *Dilemmas in the Study of Information: Exploring the Boundaries of Information Science*. Westport, CT: Greenwood Press, 1992.

O'Brien, Geoffrey. *Hardboiled America: The Lurid Years of Paperbacks*. New York: Van Nostrand Reinhold, 1981.

O'Connor, Maeve. *Editing Scientific Books and Journals*. Kent, England: Pitman Medical Publishing Co., 1978.

O'Connor, Maeve. *How to Copyedit Scientific Books*. Philadelphia: ISI Press, 1986.

Oda, Stephanie and Glenn Sanislo. 2007. *The Subtext 2006-2007: Perspective on Book Publishing: Numbers, Issues & Trends*. Darien, CT: Open Book Publishing, Inc.

Okerson, Ann. "Publishing Through the Network: The 1990s Debutante," *The Journal of Scholarly Publishing* 23, 4(April 1992): 170-177.

Olmert, Michael. *The Smithsonian Book of Books*. Washington, DC: Smithsonian Institution Press, 1992.

One Book/Five Ways: The Publishing Procedures of Five University Presses. Chicago: University of Chicago Press, 1994.

Owen, John MacKenzie. "The New Dissemination of Knowledge: Digital Libraries and Institutional Roles in Scholarly Publishing." *Journal of Economic Methodology* 9, 3(2002): 275.

Packard, Ashley. "Copyright or Copy Wrong: An Analysis of University Claims to Faculty Work," *Communication and Law Policy* 7 (Summer 2002): 275-316.

Palmer, Jonathan W. "Electronic Markets and Supply Chains: Emerging Models, Execution, and Performance Measurement." *Electronic Markets* 14, 4(2005): 268-269.

Parsons, Paul. "The Editorial Committee: Controller of the Imprint," *The Journal of Scholarly Publishing* 20, 4(July 1989): 238-244.

Parsons, Paul. "The Evolving Publishing Agendas of University Presses," *The Journal of Scholarly Publishing* 23, 1(October 1991): 45-50.

Parsons, Paul. *Getting Publishing: The Acquisition Process at University Presses*. Knoxville, TN: University of Tennessee Press, 1989.

Pasco, Allan H. "Basic Advice for Novice Authors," *The Journal of Scholarly Publishing* 23, 2(January 1992): 95-105.

Pavliscak, Pamela, Seamus Ross, and Charles Henry. 1997. "Information Technology in Humanities Scholarship: Achievements, Prospects, and Challenges—The United States Focus." American Council of Learned Societies, Occasional Paper 37, 1-2.

Perkins, Maxwell E. *Editor to Author.* John Hall Wheelock (Ed.), New York: Charles Scribner's Sons, 1950.

Perrin, Noel. *Vol. I: Bowdler's Legacy: A History of Expurgated Books in England and America.* Hanover, NH: University Press of New England, 1969.

Picard, Robert. *The Economics and Financing of Media Companies.* New York: Fordham University Press, 2002.

Picard, Robert. *Media Economics: Concepts and Issues.* Newbury Park, CA: Sage, 1989.

Picard, Robert. (Ed.), *Media Firms.* Mahwah, NJ: Lawrence Erlbaum Associates, 2002.

Picard, Robert. "The Rise and Fall of Communication Empires," *Journal of Media Economics*, 9, 4(1996): 23-40.

Piternick, Anne B. "Author Problems in a Collaborative Research Project," *The Journal of Scholarly Publishing* 25, 1(October 1993): 21-37.

Plant, Arnold. "The Economic Aspects of Copyright in Books," *Economica* 1, 2(May 1934): 167-195.

Plotorask, Alexander I. and Paul J. Lerner. *Essentials of Intellectual Property.* New York: John Wiley & Sons, 2002.

Pool, Ithiel de Sola. "The Culture of Electronic Print," *Daedalus* 111(Fall 1982): 17-32.

Pool, Ithiel de Sola. *Technologies of Freedom.* Boston: Harvard University Press, 1983.

Pope, Barbara Kline and P.K. Kannan. "Will They Pay? Measuring Consumer Demand and Price Preference for Electronic Delivery of Books." Working paper; The National Academy Press; 2003:1-34.

Porter, Michael E. *Competitive Strategy: Techniques for Analyzing Industries and Competitors.* New York: Free Press, 1980.

Porter, Michael E. and Scott Stern. "Innovation: Location Matters." *MIT Sloan Management Review* 42, 4(2001): 28-36.

Posner, Richard A. *Public Intellectuals: A Study of Decline.* Cambridge: Harvard University Press, 2001.

Potter, Clarkson N. *Who Does What and Why in Book Publishing.* New York: Birch Lane Press, 1990.

Powell, Walter W. "Adapting to Tight Money and New Opportunities," *The Journal of Scholarly Publishing* 14, 1(October 1982): 9-20.

Powell, Walter W. "From Craft to Corporation: The Impact of Outside Ownership on Book Publishing," in *Individuals in Mass Media Organizations: Creativity and Constraint*, ed. James S. Ettema and D. Charles Whitney. Beverly Hills, CA: Sage, 1982.

Powell, Walter W. *Getting into Print: The Decision-Making Process in Scholarly Publishing.* Chicago, IL: University of Chicago Press, 1985.

Quelch, J. and L. Klein. "The Internet and International Marketing," *Sloan Management Review* 37, 3(1996): 60-75.

Radway, Janice A. "Reading Is Not Eating: Mass-Produced Literature and the Theoretical, Methodological, and Political Consequences of a Metaphor," *Book Research Quarterly* 2(Fall 1986): 7-29.

Radway, Janice A. *Reading the Romance: Women, Patriarchy, and Popular Literature.* Chapel Hill, NC: University of North Carolina Press, 1984.
Raff, Daniel M.G. 2000. "Superstores and the Evolution of Firm Capabilities in American Bookselling." *Strategic Management Journal* 21: 1043-1059.
Reginald, R. and M.R. Burgess. *Cumulative Paperback Index, 1939-1959.* Detroit, MI: Gale, 1973.
Reskin, Barbara F. "Culture, Commerce, and Gender: The Feminization of Book Editing," In *Job Queues, Gender Queues: Explaining Women's Inroads into Male Occupations* Barbara F. Reskin and Patricia A. Roos (Eds.), Philadelphia, PA: Temple University Press, 1990.
Riggar, T.F. and R.E. Matkin. "Breaking Into Academic Print," *The Journal of Scholarly Publishing* 22, 1(October 1990): 17-22.
Robinson, Sara. "Forget E-Books," *Interactive Week*, April 2, 2001, 57-58.
Rose, Mark. *Authors and Owners: The Invention of Copyright.* Cambridge, MA: Harvard University Press, 1993.
Rose, M.L. "Everything Old is New Again: Reinventing the Publishing Model," *Poets & Writers*, 30, 2(May-June 2002): 40-44.
Rosner, Charles. *The Growth of the Book Jacket.* Cambridge, MA: Harvard University Press, 1954.
Rowson, Richard C. "A Formula for Successful Scholarly Publishing," The *Journal of Scholarly Publishing* 25, 2(January 1994): 67-78.
Saal, Rollene. *The New York Public Library Guide to Reading Groups.* New York: Crown Trade Paperbacks, 1995.
Sabine, Gordon and Patricia Sabine. *Books that Made the Difference: What People Told Us.* Harnden, CT: Library Professional Publications, 1983.
Salvaggio, Jerry L. (Ed.), *The Information Society: Economic, Social, and Structural Issues.* Hillsdale, NJ: Lawrence Erlbaum Associates, 1989.
Salvaggio, Jerry L. and Jennings Bryant (Eds.), *Media Use in the Information Age: Emerging Patterns of Adoption and Consumer Use.* Hillsdale, NJ: Lawrence Erlbaum Associates, 1989.
Saxby, Stephen. *The Age of Information.* New York: New York University Press, 1990.
Schafer, Arthur. "The Market-Place and the Community," *The Journal of Scholarly Publishing* 24, 4(July 1993): 253-257.
Schick, Frank L. *The Paperbound Book in America: The History of Paperbacks and Their European Background.* New York: R.R. Bowker, 1958.
Schiffrin, Andre. *The Business of Books: How International Conglomerates Took Over Publishing and Changed the Way We Read.* New York: Verso, 2000.
Schiffrin, Andre. "The Corporatization of Publishing," *The Nation*, June 3, 1996, 29-33.
Schiffrin, Andre. "Payback Time: University Presses as Profit Centers." *The Chronicle of Higher Education*, June 18, 1999: B4.
Schiller, Herbert I. *Culture, Inc.: The Corporate Takeover of Public Expression.* New York: Oxford University Press, 1989.
Schlee, Edward E. "The Value of Information in Efficient Risk-Sharing Arrangements," The *American Economic Review* 91, 3(June 2001): 509-524.

Schreyer, Alice D. *The History of Books: A Guide to Selected Resources in the Library of Congress*. Washington, DC: Library of Congress/ The Center for the Book, 1987.

Scribner, Charles, Jr. *In the Company of Writers: A Life in Publishing*, New York: Charles Scribner's Sons, 1990.

Scribner, Charles, Jr. *In the Web of Ideas: The Education of a Publisher*. New York: Charles Scribner's Sons, 1993.

Sebesta, Sam. "A Renewed View of Children's Literature," in Sam Sebesta and Ken Donelson (Eds.), *Inspiring Literacy: Literature for Children and Young Adults*. New Brunswick, NJ: Transaction Publishers, 1993.

See, Carolyn. *Making a Literary Life*. New York: Random House, 2002.

Seybold, Catherine. "The Beginnings of the University of Chicago Press," *The Journal of Scholarly Publishing* 23, 3 (April 1992): 178-184.

Shape, Leslie T. and Irene Gunther. *Editing Fact and Fiction: A Concise Guide to Book Editing*. New York: Cambridge University Press, 1994.

Shapiro, Carl and Hal R. Varian. *Information Rules: A Strategic Guide to the Network Economy*. Boston: Harvard Business School Press, 1999.

Shatzkin, Leonard. *In Cold Type: Overcoming the Book Crisis*. Boston: Houghton Mifflin, 1982.

Shavell, Steven and Tanquy van Ypersele. "Rewards versus Intellectual Property Rights," *Journal of Law and Economics* 44, 2(2001): 525-547.

Shealy, Daniel. "The Author-Publisher Relationships of Louisa May Alcott," *Book Research Quarterly* 3(Spring 1987): 63-74.

Sheehy, Eugene P. (Ed.), *Guide to Reference Books*. Chicago: American Library Association, 1986.

Sheinin, Rose. "Academic Freedom and Integrity and Ethics in Publishing," *The Journal of Scholarly Publishing* 24, 4(July 1993): 232-248.

Shiller, Robert J. *Irrational Exuberance* (Princeton: Princeton University Press, 2000).

Shipp, John. "Commercial Scholarly Publishing: The Devil Incarnate or Divine Savior?" *History of Economic Review* 32(Summer 2000): 37-45.

Shoemaker, Jack. "A Book is a Very Serious Thing," *The Journal of Scholarly Publishing* 19, 2(January 1988): 91-96.

Siegfried, J.J. and C. Latta. "Competition in the Retail College Textbook Market," *Economics of Education Review* 17(1998): 105-115.

Siler, Jennifer. "From Gutenberg to Gateway: Electronic Publishing at University Presses," *The Journal of Scholarly Publishing*, 32, 1(October 2000): 9-23.

Silverman, Al (Ed.), *The Book of the Month: Sixty Years of Books in American Life*. Boston, MA: Little Brown, 1986.

Silverman, Franklin H. *Authoring Books and Materials for Students, Academics, and Professionals*. New York: Praeger, 1998.

Siwek, Stephen. "Copyright Industries in the U.S. Economy: The 2002 Report." Washington, DC: Economists Incorporated and the International Intellectual Property Alliance, 2002.

Skillin, Marjorie and Robert M. Gay. *Words Into Type*. New York: Prentice-Hall, 1974.

Smith, Anthony. *The Politics of Information: Problems of Policy in Modern Media.* London: Macmillan, 1979.
Smith, Eldred. *The Librarian, the Scholar, and the Future of the Research Library.* Westport, CT: Greenwood Press, 1990.
Smith, Erin T. "Changes in Faculty Reading Behaviors. The Impact of Electronic Journals on the University of Georgia." *The Journal of Academic Librarianship* 29, 3(2003): 162-168.
Smith, Gordon V. and Russell L. Parr. *Valuation of Intellectual Property and Intangible Assets*, 3rd ed. New York: John Wiley & Sons, 2000.
Smith, Michael and Eric Brynjolfsson. "Consumer Decision-Making at an Internet Shopbot: Brand Still Matters," *The Journal of Industrial Economics* XLIX(December 2001): 541-558.
Smith, Michael D. 2002. "The Impact of Shopbots on Electronic Markets." *Journal of The Academy of Marketing Science* 30(4): 442-450.
Smith, Michael D., Joseph Bailey, and Erik Brynjolfsson. 2000. "Understanding Digital Markets: Review and Assessment" in *Understanding the Digital Economy,* eds. Erik Brynjolfsson and Brian Kahin. Cambridge: MIT Press.
Smith, Roger H. *Paperback Parnassus.* Boulder, CO: Westview Press, 1976.
Smolla, Rodney A. *Free Speech in an Open Society.* New York: Knopf, 1992.
Solotaroff, Ted. *A Few Good Voices in My Head: Occasional Pieces on Writing, Editing, and Reading My Contemporaries.* New York: Harper & Row, 1987.
Solotaroff, Ted. "The Literary-Industrial Complex," *New Republic*, June 8, 1987, 28, 30-42, 44-45.
Sorensen, Alan T. "Bestseller Lists and Product Variety: The Case of Book Sales." Working paper; Stanford University; 2004.
Sorensen, Alan T. and Scott J. Rasmussen. "Is Any Publicity Good Publicity? A Note on the Impact of Book Reviews." Working paper; Stanford University; 2004; pp. 1-16.
Spector, Robert. *Amazon.com: Get Big Fast.* New York: Harper Business, 2000.
Squires, Bruce P. "The Ethical Responsibilities of the Editor," The *Journal of Scholarly Publishing* 24, 4(July 1993): 214-218.
Standera, Oldrich. *The Electronic Era of Publishing: An Overview of Concepts and Technologies.* New York: Elsevier, 1987.
Starker, Steven. "Fear of Fiction: The Novel," *Book Research Quarterly* 6(Summer 1990): 44-59.
Steinberg, S.H. *Five Hundred Years of Printing.* New York: Penguin, 1974.
Steinberg, Sybil (Ed.), *Writing for Your Life* #2. Wainscott, NY: Pushcart Press, 1995.
Stern, Madeleine B. *Books and Book People in 19th-Century America.* New York: R.R. Bowker, 1978.
Stiglitz, Joseph. E. "The Contributions of the Economics of Information to Twentieth Century Economics," *Quarterly Journal of Economics* 115, 4(November 2000): 1441-1478.
Stiglitz, Joseph. E. *Globalization and Its Discontents.* New York: W.W. Norton, 2002.

Stiglitz, Joseph. E. "Information and Change in the Paradigm in Economics," *The American Economic Review* 92, 3(June 2002): 460-502.
Stoll, Clifford. *Silicon Snake Oil: Second Thoughts on the Information Highway.* New York: Doubleday, 1995.
Stoughton, Mary. *Substance and Style: Instruction and Practice in Copyediting.* Alexandria, VA: Editorial Experts, 1989.
Strainchamps, Ethel. *Rooms with No View: A Woman's Guide to the Man's World of Publishing.* New York: Harper & Row, 1974.
Strong, William S. *The Copyright Book: A Practical Guide,* 5th ed. Cambridge, MA: MIT Press, 1999.
Strothman, Wendy. "Multiculturalism at One Press: The Beacon Experience," *The Journal of Scholarly Publishing* 24, 3(April 1993): 144-150.
Strothman, Wendy. "On Moving from Campus to Commerce," *The Journal of Scholarly Publishing* 18, 3(April 1987): 157-162.
Sugano, Joel Yutaka and Toshio Kobayashi. "Amazon.com E Commerce Platform: Leveraging Competitiveness through the Virtual Value Chain." Osaka Economic Papers 52, 2(2002): 228-258.
Sutcliffe, Peter. *The Oxford University Press: An Informal History.* London: Oxford University Press, 1978.
Szenberg, Michael and Eric Youngkoo Lee. "The Structure of the American Book Publishing Industry." *Journal of Cultural Economics* 18, 4(1994-1995): 313-322.
Tebbel, John. *Between Covers: The Rise and Transformation of Book Publishing in America.* New York: Oxford University Press, 1987.
Tebbel, John. *A History of Book Publishing in the United States,* Vol. I, *The Creation of an Industry 1630-1865.* New York: R.R. Bowker, 1972.
Tebbel, John. *A History of Book Publishing in the United States,* Vol. 2, *The Expansion of an Industry 1865-1919.* New York: R.R. Bowker, 1975.
Tebbel, John. *A History of Book Publishing in the United States,* Vol. 3, *The Golden Age between Two Wars, 1920-1940.* New York: R.R. Bowker, 1978.
Tebbel, John. *A History of Book Publishing* in *the United States, Vol. 4, The Great Change, 1940-1980.* New York: R.R. Bowker, 1981.
Teute, Fredrika J. "To Publish and Perish: Who Are the Dinosaurs in Scholarly Publishing?" *The Journal of Scholarly Publishing,* 32, 2(January 2001): 102-112.
Thornton, Patricia H. "Institutional Logics and the Historical Contingency of Power in Organizations: Executive Succession in the Higher Education Publishing Industry," *The American Journal of Sociology* 105, 3(November 1999): 801-843.
Thornton, Patricia H. "Personal versus Market Logics of Control: A Historically Contingent Theory of the Risk of Acquisition," *Organization Science* 12, 3(May-June 2001): 294-311.
Timko, David A. "A Study of the Book Reviewing Habits of *The New York Times,* 1950-2000." Unpublished M.S. in L.S. Master's Thesis; University of North Carolina, Chapel Hill; 2001; pp. 1-78.
Tomkins, Jane. *West of Everything: The Inner Life of Westerns.* New York: Oxford University Press, 1992.

Turow, Joseph G. *Getting Books to Children: An Exploration of Publisher-Market Relations.* Chicago: American Library Association, 1979.

U.S. Department of Commerce, Bureau of the Census. *The Statistical Abstract of the United States 2008* (Washington, DC: Government Printing Office, 2008).

United States Department of Commerce, Bureau of the Census. 2004. *2002 Economic Census: Information Industry Series Book Publishing 2002.* Washington, DC: GPO.

Underhill, Paco. *Why We Buy: The Science of Shopping.* New York: Simon & Schuster, 1999.

Varian, Hal. "Buying, Sharing, and Renting Information Goods," *The Journal of Industrial Economics* 48, 4(December 2000): 473-488.

The Veronis Suhler Stevenson Communications Industry Forecast. New York: Veronis Suhler Stevenson, 2008.

Vitz, Paul C. *Censorship: Evidence of Bias in Our Children's Textbooks.* Ann Arbor, MI: Servant Books, 1986.

Vogel, Harold L. *Entertainment Industry Economics: A Guide for Financial Analysis.* New York: Cambridge University Press, 2001.

Waajers, L. "Stratum Continuum of Information: Scholarly Communication and the Role of University Libraries," *New Library World* 103, 4(April 2002): 165-171.

Walters, Ray. *Paperback Talk.* Chicago, IL: Academy Chicago Publishers, 1985.

Waters, Lindsay. "Rescue Tenure from the Tyranny of the Monograph." *The Chronicle of Higher Education*, April 20, 2001: B7.

Way, David. "Publishing in Libraries," *The Journal of Scholarly Publishing* 29, 1(October 1988): 35-38.

Weisberg, Jacob. "Rough Trade: The Sad Decline of American Publishing." *New Republic*, June 17, 1991, 16-18, 21.

Weiss, Michael J. "The Clustering of America: Target Marketing to Book Buyers," *Publishers Weekly*, November 11, 1988, 23-27.

Wertenbroch, Klaus and Bernd Skiera. "Measuring Consumers' Willingness to Pay at the Point of Purchase," *Journal of Marketing Research* XXXIX(May 2002): 228-241.

West, James L. W., III. *American Authors and the Literary Marketplace since 1900.* Philadelphia: University of Pennsylvania Press, 1988.

Weybright, Victor. *The Making of a Publisher: A Life in the 20th-Century Book Revolution.* New York: Reynal, 1967.

Whiteside, Thomas. *The Blockbuster Complex: Conglomerates, Show Business, and Book Publishing.* Middletown, CT: Wesleyan University Press, 1982.

Williams, Joseph M. *Style: Toward Clarity and Grace.* Chicago, IL: University of Chicago Press, 1990.

Willison, Ian R. "Massmediatisation: Export of the American Model," in *Les Mutations du Livre et de L'Edition dans Le Monde du XVIII e Siele A'L'An 2000, Actes du Colloque International, Sherbrooke 2000.* Quebec: *Les Presses de L'Universite Laval, L'Harmattan* 2001.

Wolpert, Samuel and Joyce F. Wolpert. *Economics of Information.* New York: Van Nostrand Reinhold, 1986.
Wood, Leonard A. "Demographics of Mass Market Consumers," *Book Research Quarterly* 3(Spring 1987): 31-39.
Zboray, Ronald J. *A Fictive People: Antebellum Economic Development and the American Reading Public.* Oxford: Oxford University Press, 1992.
Zettelmeyer, Florian, Fiona Scott Morton, and Jorge Silva-Risso. "How the Internet Lowers Prices. Evidence from Matched Survey and Auto Transaction Data." Working paper; National Bureau of Economic Research; 2005; #11515; 1-32.
Zill, Nicholas and Marianne Winglee. "Literature Reading in the United States: Data from National Surveys and Their Policy Implications," *Book Research Quarterly* 5(Spring 1989): 24-58.
Zinkhan, George M. "The Role of Books and Book Reviews in the Knowledge Dissemination Process," *Journal of Marketing* 59(January 1995): 106-108.

Index

academic associations and societies, 13-14, 39-41
academic publishing, *see* scholarly publishing
Adesanoye, F.A, 87
African Centre for Technology Studies (ACTS), 98-99
African Consortium of University Presses (A-CUP), 99-101
African Network of Scientific and Technological Institutions (ANSTI), 97-98, 99
African Publishers Network (APNET), 98-99
African University Press (AUP) publishers, 85-102
Ahmed, Abdel Moneim, 50
Aksne, Ernest, 50-51
Albritton, Rogers, 31-32
Allen, Barbara, 93
Al-Mudimigh, Abdullah, 50
Alonso, Carlos, 39-40
Amazon.com, 65-68
American Association of University Presses, 40-41
American Council of Learned Societies (ACLS), 35, 39-41
American Geophysical Union v. Texaco, Inc., see Texaco case
Amin, Mayur, 18
Archaeological Data Archive Project (ADAP), 151, 157-158
archaeology,
  digital projects, 151-152
  electronic publishing, 149, 153-154
  web portals, 152
Archaeology Data Service (ADS), 150
Art Museum Image Consortium (AMICO), 154
Association of African Universities (AAU), 40, 42, 85, 100-101

Association of American University Presses (AAUP), 83, 97
Association of Research Libraries (ARL), 17, 18, 20
authors,
  copyright ownership, 184
  cost for Open Access (OA), 182-183
  journal article submission process, 11-12, 167
  sharing knowledge, 169-171
awards, 40
Axarloglou, Kostas, 51

Bagdikian, Ben, 52
Bailey, Herbert, 119-120
Bankole, S.B., 87
Barnes, Stuart, 164
Barzun, Jacques, 52
Bernassi, Corrado, 51
Bethesda, 183-184
Bgoya, Walter, 100-101
Book Industry Study Groups, Inc. (BISG), 50, 53
books,
  adoptions, 55
  exports, 60-61
  hardbound, 55-57, 59, 67-73
  importance, 29, 84-85
  needs, 120-123
  paperback, 57-60, 69
booksellers,
  Internet sites, 65-73
  use of modern technology, 52, 61-62
  used book sales, 64-65, 72-74
Borgman, C.L., 183
branding, 45-46, 50
Bryn Mawr College, 150
Brynjolfsson, Erik, 67
Budapest Open Access Initiative (BOAI), 183-184

Budd, John, 15
Butler, Nicholas Murray, 84, 123

Carr, R., 95
cataloguing, 95, 96-97
Center for the Study of Architecture/Archaeology (CSA), 150-151
Chang, Chen-Chi, 163-177
Children's Science Publishing in Africa (CHISCI), 97, 99
Chirco, Alessandra, 51
Clay, Karen, 66-67
college bookstores, 63-64
Colorado Digitization Program, 154-155
Columbia University, 84, 114
Combs, Rod, 51
commercial publishers,
  and academic presses, ix-xi, 43-44, 84-85, 91, 108, 126
  costs, 16-23, 84
  marketing, 60, 75
Consortium of African Scholarly Publishers (CASP), 98
Consortium of University Research Libraries (CURL), 95
consortiums,
  library, 92-97
  publishing, 97-101
consumer price index, 15-16
cooperative movement, 221-224
copy-editing, 113
Copyright Act of 1976, 208, 212
Copyright Office for Congress, 208-209
Coser, Lewis, 52
course packs, 43
Creative Commons, 213
Crews, Kenneth, 208
Cukrowski, Jacek, 50-51

Dalton, Margaret Stieg, 107-127
Darko-Ampem, Kwasi, 83-102
Darnton, Robert, 28-29
databases, 41, 95, 116, 147, 151-152, 155, 157-159, 168, 223
Davidson, Cathy N., 35-46
Derrida, Jacques, 31-32
discounts, 67-73
dissertations, 4, 29, 110, 114
distribution channels, 60-64
Dubin, Jeffrey, 50

e-commerce, 51-52
E-LIS, 158
e-print, 158
editors,
  freelancers, 4, 100
  manuscript evaluation, 11-12, 110-111
  role in scholarly publishing, 14-15, 32-33
Ehrmann, Thomas, 51
Eisenstein, Elizabeth, 27-28
Eiteljorg, Harrison II, 156-157
electronic publishing,
  acceptance, 147-148
  archiving, 23-24
  as a print publishing alternative, 28, 41, 114-117, 149
  challenges and opportunities, 155-159
  circumventing refereed publications, 4
  digital book revenue operations, ix-x, xii
  effect on university presses, viii, 51
  financial cost, 157-159
  journals, 19, 95, 114, 147, 153-155, 157
  licensing rights, 95
  Open Access (OA) journals vs. electronic journals, 185-186
electronic reserve systems (E-RES), 50, 73-74
endowments, 20, 36
Epstein, Jason, 51
Estelami, Hooman, 49-77
Evans, G.E., 94
Extensible Markup Language (XML), 156

"fair use," 207-217
Fernandes, Danny, 67
forced productivity, 1-6
Foskett, D.J., 95
Friedlander, Eli, 28
Fruge, August, 51

galley proofs, 12
Ganu, K.M., 84
German Academic Publishers Project (GAP), 226-227
Ghana Universities Press, 86-87, 99
Gilman, Daniel Coit, 84
Goellner, Jack, 51

Google,
  Library Project, 207-208, 214-217
Grafton, Anthony, 27-28
Greco, Albert N., vii-xiii, 49-77
Greenblatt, Steven, 27
Gutenberg-e, 114

Haank, Derk, 15
Haas, Floria, 51
Harms, Rainer, 51
Harnad, Stevan, 159, 183
Harper, Georgia, 212
Harper, William Rainey, 84
Harper & Row v. Nation Enterprises, 211
Harris, Julianna C., 9-24
Haugland, Ann, 52
Hawes, Gene, 84
Heidegger, Martin, 28
Henderson, Albert, 18
high schools, 61
historians,
  as readers and buyers, 119-123
  finding a publisher, 110-111
  getting published, 112-113
  preservation, 116
  publishability of their work, 117-119
Humphrey, John, 50

information systems, 151, 187
Institute for Scientific Information (ISI), 164, 168
Institute of Museum and Library Services (IMLS), 154
International Coalition of Library Consortia (ICOLC), 92
International Conference on Hypermedia and Interactivity in Museums (ICHIM), 154
Internet,
  bookselling, 50, 61, 65-73
  dissertations posted, 28-29
  electronic journals, 19, 153-159, 182-203, 225-226
  importance to academic libraries, 93-94
  uses in archaeology, 152-156

Jeanneret, Marsh, 51
Joint Academic Network (JANET), 95
Jones, B.G., 85-86

journals,
  advertising, xii-xiii
  African, 87
  analyzing, 171-175, 190-191
  and commercial science publishers, 43-44
  book reviewers, 3
  competitive nature, 10-11
  costs, xii, 10, 15-17, 36, 40
  electronic, 19, 95, 114, 147, 153-155, 157
  overview, vii-viii, xi, 20-23, 167
  Open Access (OA) and Restricted Access (RA), 182-203
  page charges, 13-14
  publication process, 10-12, 220
  ranking, 163-164, 177
  research quality, 167-168
  submissions, xi, 11
  subscriptions, 14-16, 124

Kadushin, Charles, 52
Keller, James, 183
Kenya, 87, 98
King, Donald, 15, 18
knowledge,
  creation, 85-86, 163-166
  dissemination, 17-18, 20-24, 75, 84, 167
  value, 168-177
Kohl, D., 95
Krishnan, Ramayya, 66-67

Latman, Alan, 208-209
Leen, Auke, 51
Lessig, Larry, 213
Leval, Pierre, 210-212, 214
libraries,
  budgets, 9-10, 17, 20, 49, 51, 55, 119, 219-220
  computerized cataloguing, 95
  consortium, 92-97
  digitization of materials, 115-116, 154-155
  electronic access to materials, 92-93, 95
  funding, 96
  institutional rankings, 19-20
  journal subscriptions, xii-xiii, 9-10, 14, 16-20, 44
  lack of physical space, 20-21

reserve system, 73
scholarly journals purchases, xi
Lindberg, Stanley W., 212
Litman, Jessica, 212-213
logocentrism, 31
Lukacs, John, 126

Mabe, Michael, 18
Makotsi, Ruth, 86
manuscript,
  preparing, 75, 109
  publishing process, 110-114
  review, 20-21, 43
  submission, 11-12, 42
marketing, 44-46, 50-52, 61, 75-76, 89, 90-92, 98, 113, 186
McLuhan, Marshall, 27-28
Miller, Cass T., 9-24
monographs, xi, 18-20, 36-37, 49, 90, 108-110, 112-113, 117-125
Moran, Joseph, 52
multimedia, 41, 52, 153-154

National Association of College Stores (NACS), 63
National Association of Independent Schools (NAIS), 61
New Era Publications v. Henry Holt & Co., 210
Newby, Gregory, 51
Nietzsche, Friedrich, 29
Nigeria,
  Ibadan University Press, 88
North East Research Libraries (NERL), 95

OhioLINK, 95-96
Okerson, Ann, 19
Old Siwash, 5-6, 7
Olszewski, Ray, 52
"one-book wonders," 2, 6
online museums, 154-155
online public access catalogs (OPAC), 96-97
Open Access (OA) journals, viii-ix, 182-203, 225-226
Open Archive Initiative (OAI), 185-186
"Orange Series," 98
Organization of American Historians, 108
Oxford University Press, 38

page counts, 13-16, 23
Park, Ji-Hong, 181-203
Patterson, L. Ray, 211-212
Payne, Lizanne, 96
Peek, Robin, 51
peer-review process, 10-13, 20-23, 40, 114-117, 135, 149, 165-167, 182-184, 199, 203, 223, 226
Penn State University Press, 214
Plato, 28, 31
Porter, Michael, 50
Potter, William, 93-94
Powell, Walter, 51, 52
Poynder, Richard, 15
preservation, 115-116, 150-157
prestige, 2, 13-14, 45, 74, 110, 115-116, 190-193
Price, Derek de Solla, 18
Princeton University Press, 119-120
Print Publisher Program, 214
printing-on-demand (POD) publications, 41
Project MUSE, 116
Public Library of Science (PLoS), 183-184, 225
"publish or perish," *see* forced productivity

Qin, Jian, 181-203

Rainbird, Mark, 50
reading, 28, 36-38, 52, 61, 120, 126, 141
remaindering, 6
repositories, 159, 203, 205, 226
Robinson, Michael, 52
royalties, 43, 213

Salinger v. Random House, 210
Savage, William W., Jr., 1-6
Schmitz, Hubert, 50
Scholarly Publishing and Academic Resources Coalition (SPARC), 183-184, 225
scholars,
  and Open-Access journals, 193-199
  archaeology, 148-159
  as a journals consumer, 13-14, 16
  attention to new technologies, 147-148
  collaborating with publishers, 22-23
  culture of silence, 28-33
  historians, 107-127

importance of being published, 13, 131-141
publishing for tenure considerations, 1-5, 21-22, 36, 38, 110-111
recommendations from publishers, 22
views on electronic publishing, 4, 150-155
scholarship,
  dissemination, 76, 84, 86, 121, 126-127, 167, 207-213
  insights, 37-39, 113
  keeping silent, 27-33
  marketability, 126, 197
  preservation, 109, 116
  publishing model, 219-227
scholarly publishing, see also journals and university presses
  cooperative business, 219-227
  costs, 38, 39-46, 75, 113
  crisis, 112-114, 125-127
  electronic access to its materials, 19, 92, 93-95, 182-183
  future, 35-46
  in developing nations, 83-102
  manuscript submissions, 3-4, 110-111
  overview, ix-xiii
  purposes, 84-85, 167
  social constructs, 202-204
  university press directors' opinion, 51
Schroeder, Robert, 219-227
scientific journals, see journals
Scopus, 165
Scrimitore, Marcella, 51
Siegel, Gretta E., 219
Smith, Michael D., 67
Socrates, 28, 31
Sony Corp. v. Universal Studios, 211
South Africa,
  University of Cape Town Press, 88
Steinle, Claus, 50
Story, Joseph, 207
subscriptions,
  cancellations, 16, 226
  electronic journals, 157-158, 182-183, 185
  individual, 16, 119, 157
  institutional, xii-xiii, 9-10, 14, 20, 44
  prices, 15, 23, 44, 49
  serial, 19-20
subsidies, viii, 21, 36, 39-45, 85-86, 96
Swanson, E. Burton, 201

Swedish Agency for Research Cooperation with Developing Countries (SAREC), 98

teaching,
  and research, 2-3, 39, 44, 84, 95
  as punishment, 5
technology, 51-52, 97, 102, 114-115, 119, 153, 158-160, 222-223
Tenopir, Carol, 15, 18-19
tenure, see university professors
Texaco case, 209
textbooks, ix, 55, 63-64, 84, 86, 89-90, 97-98, 122
Thatcher, Sanford G., 207-217
Torrey, Kate, 35
trade publishing, 38-39, 62-64, 85-86, 90, 113-114, 165

universities,
  allocating resources for university presses, vii, 39, 42-43, 87
  archiving information, 21
  expectations, 3-4, 123
  humanities department, 32-33
  institutional branding, 45-46
  promoting their presses, 2, 44, 84, 91
  view of scholars not wanting to write, 30-31
University of Toronto Press, 51
University Press of New England (UPNE), 99
university presses,
  acquisitions, 90
  as third-party distributors, viii
  backlist, 74
  book adoption, 55
  book costs, 36-37, 45
  competition, 41, 49-51, 52, 67
  consortiums, 97-101
  cooperation, 89-91
  declining sales, 109, 112
  distribution channels, 54
  effect on scholarship, 39
  exports, 55, 60-61
  "fair use," 209-213
  funding, 75-76, 87-88
  Internet sales, 67-72
  market, 49-51, 53-60, 117-120
  origins, 83-85
  overview, vii-ix

partnerships, 90, 169-170
prestige, 13, 45, 74, 84, 110, 115-116, 190
work on trade books, 85-86
university professors,
　pressure to publish, 1-5, 14, 30, 36
　research work, 134
　tenure, 1-2, 5, 13-14, 17, 21, 30-32, 36-40, 42-43, 75, 108, 110, 118-119, 122-126, 166, 183, 189, 191-198, 202
Unsworth, John, 41

value chains, 50
vanity publication, 4

Walters, David, 50
Washington Research Library Consortium, 96
Waters, Lindsay, 27-33

Weedon, Alexis, 51
Weinreb, Lloyd, 211
Wharton, Robert M., 49-77
Williams, G.J., 86
Wilson, Patrick, 200
Wittenberg, Kate, 164
Wolff, Eric, 66-67

Xia, Jingfeng, 147-160
XML, *see* Extensible Markup Language

Yankee Book Peddler (YBP), 55

Zairir, Mohamed, 50
Zambia, 86, 88, 97
Zimbabwe,
　University of Zimbabwe publications, 88
Ziv, Nina, 52

For Product Safety Concerns and Information please contact our EU representative GPSR@taylorandfrancis.com
Taylor & Francis Verlag GmbH, Kaufingerstraße 24, 80331 München, Germany

www.ingramcontent.com/pod-product-compliance
Lightning Source LLC
Chambersburg PA
CBHW070557300426
44113CB00010B/1295